A DANGEROUS
ASSIGNMENT

The Stackpole Military History Series

THE AMERICAN CIVIL WAR

Cavalry Raids of the Civil War
Ghost, Thunderbolt, and Wizard
Pickett's Charge
Witness to Gettysburg

WORLD WAR II

Armor Battles of the Waffen-SS, 1943–45
Army of the West
Australian Commandos
The B-24 in China
Backwater War
The Battle of Sicily
Beyond the Beachhead
The Brandenburger Commandos
The Brigade
Bringing the Thunder
Coast Watching in World War II
Colossal Cracks
A Dangerous Assignment
D-Day to Berlin
Dive Bomber!
A Drop Too Many
Eagles of the Third Reich
Exit Rommel
Fist from the Sky
Flying American Combat Aircraft of
    World War II
Forging the Thunderbolt
Fortress France
The German Defeat in the East, 1944–45
German Order of Battle, Vol. 1
German Order of Battle, Vol. 2
German Order of Battle, Vol. 3
The Germans in Normandy
Germany's Panzer Arm in World War II
GI Ingenuity
The Great Ships
Grenadiers
Infantry Aces
Iron Arm
Iron Knights
Kampfgruppe Peiper at the Battle of
    the Bulge
Kursk
Luftwaffe Aces
Massacre at Tobruk
Mechanized Juggernaut or Military
    Anachronism?

Messerschmitts over Sicily
Michael Wittmann, Vol. 1
Michael Wittmann, Vol. 2
Mountain Warriors
The Nazi Rocketeers
On the Canal
Operation Mercury
Packs On!
Panzer Aces
Panzer Aces II
Panzer Commanders of the Western Front
The Panzer Legions
Panzers in Winter
The Path to Blitzkrieg
Retreat to the Reich
Rommel's Desert Commanders
Rommel's Desert War
The Savage Sky
A Soldier in the Cockpit
Soviet Blitzkrieg
Stalin's Keys to Victory
Surviving Bataan and Beyond
T-34 in Action
Tigers in the Mud
The 12th SS, Vol. 1
The 12th SS, Vol. 2
The War against Rommel's Supply Lines
War in the Aegean

THE COLD WAR / VIETNAM

Cyclops in the Jungle
Flying American Combat Aircraft:
    The Cold War
Here There Are Tigers
Land with No Sun
Street without Joy
Through the Valley

WARS OF THE MIDDLE EAST

Never-Ending Conflict

GENERAL MILITARY HISTORY

Carriers in Combat
Desert Battles
Guerrilla Warfare

A DANGEROUS ASSIGNMENT

An Artillery Forward Observer
in World War II

William B. Hanford

STACKPOLE
BOOKS

Copyright © 2008 by William B. Hanford

Published by
STACKPOLE BOOKS
5067 Ritter Road
Mechanicsburg, PA 17055
www.stackpolebooks.com

Cover design by Tracy Patterson

Printed in the United States of America

10 9 8 7 6 5 4 3 2 1

Library of Congress Cataloging-in-Publication Data

Hanford, William B.
  A dangerous assignment : an artillery forward observer in World War II / William B. Hanford.
    p. cm. — (Stackpole military history series)
  Includes index.
  ISBN 978-0-8117-3485-1
1. Hanford, William B. 2. United States. Army. Infantry Division, 103rd. 3. United States. Army—Radiomen—Biography. 4. World War, 1939–1945—Scouts and scouting. 5. World War, 1939–1945—Campaigns—Western Front. 6. World War, 1939–1945—Personal narratives, American. 7. Radio operators—United States—Biography. 8. Soldiers—United States—Biography. I. Title.
  D769.3103rd .H36 2008
  940.54'1273092—dc22
  [B]
                                                          2008004306

Table of Contents

Introduction

We young men in the World War II generation grew up in the twenties and were fascinated with World War I. We saw dozens of movies about it, and most veterans of that war had thick picture books filled with photos of shell-wrecked buildings, huge cannons, three-winged German warplanes, and trenches. But we were most thrilled by photos of a place called no-man's-land.

In the First World War, no-man's-land remained unchanged for months, and the deep shell-holes, barbed wire, and broken-limbed leafless trees faced by men in rat-infested trenches became familiar to us kids. We learned that observers in that war were up in balloons above or behind the trenches, and that pilots brave enough to fly into heavy machine-gun fire from the trenches vied to become a different kind of ace by shooting down large numbers of those balloons, though none of them became famous like Eddie Rickenbacker or the "Red Baron."

In World War II, no-man's-land became the bailiwick of the forward observer. It was usually several miles across, and often the only soldiers dug in were those manning the outpost lines (OPLs). In my experience, the main lines of resistance (MLRs) for both armies were towns or concrete bunkers, more often than foxholes or trenches.

A 105-millimeter howitzer battery had five officers: battery commander, executive officer, intelligence officer, motor officer, and forward observer (FO). All but the executive officer occasionally went to observation posts (OPs), but only the FO went to OPs in no-man's-land, and only the FO went forward with the infantry on an attack into no-man's-land. The FO's duty, when on an attack, was to call for artillery fire when the infantry got pinned down by enemy defenses. The longer a column was pinned down, the greater were the casualties; therefore, competent and brave FOs were a blessing to infantrymen.

Offensives, when planned, were seldom expected to last more than two to three weeks. When the unit—company, battalion, regiment, division, corps, or army—reached its goal or found it too costly to continue the advance without a resupply, it would stop and dig in.

Supporting units, the rear echelon, would then bring up army and corps headquarters, field hospitals, ammunition and fuel dumps, ordnance and motor repair, transportation corps, laundry, and field shower companies, along with many other lesser units, such as lice control. All such supporting personnel were necessary to the war effort. These outfits would locate in a central city, usually within fifty miles of the front, while the infantry spread out in two front lines—an outpost line and a main line of resistance—with artillery battalions two to three miles back.

Between the outpost line and the enemy was no-man's-land. When the war was static, the two sides were either building better defenses or preparing for the next offensive. During this time, the FO was looking for the highest ground from which he could see enemy movement, often in or near his infantry's OPL. If this required going into no-man's-land, he was expected to go there while doing his best to avoid observation by the enemy.

When on the attack, the FO was in his greatest danger (though not to be compared with that of a rifleman), but while his army was in a static position, and when manning an OP, the FO was in more danger than most other soldiers. The prime targets during these times were called targets of opportunity. Even when well hidden, an observer could expect an occasional round of artillery or mortar fire to seek him out. The FO, if he was experienced and clever, could discern the points from which his enemy FO might have good observation, then bring fire on those places. An FO for either army was always a target of opportunity for his counterpart.

The FO section had four soldiers: a lieutenant, sergeant, radioman, and jeep driver. The officer was the observer, and the sergeant was his assistant, capable of taking over in emergencies. The radioman used a field telephone whenever possible, as the small FM radios they carried in those days were not always reliable. Every battery had a wire section that laid-down telephone lines along roadsides for communication to headquarters switchboards. Headquarters then laid down wire on roads near the OPs. These lines were thick, much like civilian wires. The FO carried a spool with a mile of thinner line, barely thicker than kite string, that weighed less than ten pounds. This he spliced to the heavier wire and ran cross-country to his OP.

I learned most of this in combat, because in training, the duties of an FO were not well taught. We didn't even have the thin field wire until we got to Europe. I suspect that the techniques we used in the war were developed in the combat that preceded our arrival. For instance, in Europe we used "forward observer procedure," which consisted of locating our target on a map after we found it by observation, then calling in the coordinates to a headquarters Fire Direction Center, which worked out the trigonometric details, the amount of gunpowder needed, and so on.

In training, however, we had used "battery commander procedure," whereby the observer (usually a captain) worked out the trig functions and other calculations right there on the OP, then gave commands to his phone or radio operator. "Fire mission!" he would say. "Battery adjust. Shell HE. Fuse quick. Charge four. SI right, three zero zero. Elevation one three four two zero."

There were several different shell and fuse types. HE meant high explosive and was the most common shell, and fuse quick was the most common fuse. Fuse delay allowed the shell to penetrate whatever it hit before exploding. Propaganda shells, upon explosion, sent hundreds of "safe conduct" leaflets signed by Eisenhower into the hands of frightened enemy soldiers, inviting them to desert or surrender. In 1944, the Prosit fuse was developed. Using new technology, it would burst the shell about fifteen feet above the ground and was devastating to enemy ground forces.

The "Charge" order referred to the number of bags of gunpowder to be put in the shell case. I think each bag was enough to push the shell a mile. Charge seven was the most, and seven miles was the distance limit of a 105-millimeter howitzer shell.

The SI command indicated the right or left movement needed to point the guns to the target. "Elevation" gave the guns the angle best suited to have the most range and effect. It was also the command to fire.

When my division got overseas, we no longer used battery commander procedure. The French, as part of the defenses they developed after the First World War, had made accurate-to-the-meter maps of every square meter of France, and our Air Force made equally accurate photographic maps of Germany. These maps allowed a forward observer to send the Fire Direction Center only the map coordinates for his target, after which he needed to make relatively few adjustments for pinpoint accuracy. A 105-millimeter shell had a dispersion of seventy-five yards, meaning that two shells fired at the same coordinates ideally would explode no farther apart than thirty-two and a half yards in either direction within a seventy-five-yard circle.

The Fire Direction Center sent the FO's commands to the batteries after they did all the computing. Fire Direction Centers had communication with all of the division's artillery, as well as with the bigger guns—in our case, the Seventh Army and VI Corps.

The author in Ingviller, France, March 1945.

Chapter 1

Belly gunner, paratrooper, combat marine, infantry rifle-man, infantry scout, artillery forward observer—all these assignments had a common connection: danger and adventure.

I was radioman for a forward observer, and though now I'm proud of it, that assignment was not of my choosing. I fell into the job because no one in the signal section of my artillery battery wanted any part of it.

During most of my two years of training in Louisiana and Texas, I went to observation posts to be a communication man for officers adjusting artillery fire on a target. So I was quali-fied, to that extent, but the summer before we went overseas, I was sent to Fort Monmouth, New Jersey, to learn radio repair and thought I had an especially safe duty facing me. It turned out that assignment was given to me by accident, however. The captain was on leave when the first sergeant sent me, unaware that the captain had already penciled me in as FO radioman.

We went overseas in October 1944, four months after D-Day, a time when all America thought the war was nearly over—that Hitler would be toppled and the Germans would soon sue for peace. Just before we entrained for New York and overseas, my battery commander, Capt. Louis C. Pultz, asked me, "Don't you just pray it isn't over before we get there?" I should have kept my mouth shut, but I was angry about the assignment to forward observer, when I was expecting to be promoted to T/4 sergeant in radio repair, so I answered, "I pray it's already over and we haven't found out yet; a thousand guys are dying every day over there." That sassiness made him hate my guts, so when he gave out promotions on the ship, my

1

name was not on the list—not even for the rank of T/5 corporal that my job called for.

My division, the 103rd, landed in Marseilles in October and became a part of the Seventh Army, under Lt. Gen. Alexander Patch. We were sent up the Rhone River to the Vosges Mountains to enter combat beside the 3rd, 36th, and 45th—veteran divisions that had fought in North Africa, Sicily, and Italy.

On November 9, we were bivouacked in a field just north of Epinal, a Vosges Mountain city, and the weather had turned cold. At sunset, black, blue, and red-violet clouds scudded across the southwestern sky, bringing darkness early. In four days, we had traveled more than 500 miles from Marseilles, and temperatures had gone from 60 degrees Fahrenheit to below freezing. You could feel the snow coming. Just to our east, a Long Tom battery fired for two hours straight, the cannoneers silhouetted by the breechblock flashes against the black of the mountains. In the distance, machine guns were firing in short bursts. It must have been Saturday, because the church bells of Epinal clanged, bonged, and chimed continually into the night.

After my sergeant, Ray York, and I got our tents pitched, we stood in the cold and talked. He revealed that he was engaged to two women—one even had his ring—and he would make up his mind about them after the war. He loved them both and didn't want to give up either one. "I know I'm a pig," he said, "but love is strange."

We shared our ambitions, which were a lot alike. If I got my band to New York to play at the New Yorker at the same time he got to the Plaza with his dancing partner, the older of the two girls he had promised his hand to, we were going to look each other up. I don't think either of us really expected such stuff to happen, but talking about it seemed to suit the mood.

"When you went to New York, did you ever get to the Plaza?" he asked.

"No, I always went to the Village or Fifty-Second Street for the jazz."

"Then you never saw Hildegarde?"

"No, I heard her on the radio once and thought she was lousy."

"She's got to be seen in person. She has the greatest shape in America, and . . ."

Listening to Ray talk, I couldn't help comparing him with all the other Texans I knew. Though I didn't think I'd ever like Hildegarde, she appealed to a very sophisticated crowd, and Ray was that and more. No country bumpkin Roy Acuff for him. I made a pledge to myself to make Ray York my best friend for life after the war.

The entire conversation was a million miles removed from the feelings that stirred in me. The church bells and the guns were portents of a war I was prepared to hate. Lieutenant Ruotolo was a step from heaven, being this close to war. Like me, he was unable to distance himself from movie ideas of war, reveling in words like *valor, honor, glory.* I saw myself as too much into the same dreams as Ruotolo and wished I could distance myself from such juvenility.

The sounds of war got to Ray at about the same time, and we both stayed silent, just breathing in the damp chill air of an impending snowstorm, and letting Epinal and its sad cathedral bells toll for a more violent storm to come.

On November 10, we began the motor march up the Vosges Mountain passes in the dark of late afternoon into a winter blizzard. The column moved slowly, and our winter great-coats were not nearly warm enough, so we huddled under shelter halves and blankets. When we passed the Long Tom (155 millimeter) battery, they fired right over our heads. It was so dark in this storm that I wondered how they knew where to fire.

"Lieutenant, do Long Tom batteries have forward observers?" I asked Ruotolo.

"Not as far as I know. I didn't learn much about them in OCS [Officer Candidate School] at Sill, but I did pull the lanyard on one once."

"Then how do they know where to fire?"

"They use maps. Their intelligence officers plot where the enemy is likely to have troops or artillery, and because they have such a large field of fire, they just cover a large area with shell fire. They seldom fire less than ten miles, and they can fire fifteen."

I didn't understand much of it, and I wasn't sure he did either.

I turned my radio on and put my headset over my ears, because I expected we were in danger from the Luftwaffe. Then it came to me . . . how could planes find us in this weather? I felt like such a rookie. The headset came off.

Here I was, going to have the most dangerous job in the field artillery, and I had no idea what made it so dangerous. All I knew was that I was determined to survive, if my assignment to the silliest lieutenant in the 928th Battalion would allow it. I call him silly because he told us shortly after we left Marseilles that he planned to get a Medal of Honor—even if he had to get it posthumously. How dumb!

We came to a mountain trail and met the troops we were relieving as they left a crude forest path. I thought the dusk conditions were clouding my eyesight—the men in those trucks looked like Japanese or Chinese.

"They're Hawaiians, mostly Japs," Ruotolo told us. "The 442nd Combat Regiment—Nisei shock troops. They just pulled a battalion of 3rd Infantry Division out of a scrape. I think they got surrounded on a ridge, or something."

We didn't have time to think about it, because the trucks in our column began struggling to get up the path in snow that was already a couple feet deep over unfrozen mud, and our jeep slipped and slid sideways in deep ruts made by the trucks ahead of us. Men were standing knee-deep in mud, helping their vehicles get up the slushy path by pushing from behind and on the sides. Ray and I got out and helped and became covered with mud.

When we reached an open place in the dense pine forest where we were to spend the night, it seemed hopeless to try digging foxholes or putting down tent pegs. You were glad not to be a cannoneer that night: they had to immediately begin digging in the howitzers. Ray and I just threw our double shelterhalves atop the snow and buried ourselves under the top halves and blankets.

The first sergeant came around later with his flashlight. "Don't you guys want to stay up till midnight?" he said. "We're gonna fire our first rounds of the war to celebrate Armistice Day."

Ray may have stayed up, but I wasn't impressed by the occasion; I wanted my sleep.

By the early hours of Armistice Day, the wind had turned— 90 degrees in direction and 50 degrees in temperature. Before daylight, water began running in under my top shelter half, and my blankets were sopping wet when I got up for breakfast. The cannoneers were already building fires to dry out blankets on tent ropes suspended between trees. By midday, mosquitoes were biting.

Our own guns stopped firing early, but another battery of artillery was directly behind us and firing over our heads. Their guns sounded weird—*pock, pock, pock*. The cannoneers for those guns looked like black guys and the guns had long barrels. "They're the 614th Tank Destroyers . . . Negro troops," Sergeant Pitts told me. "This is not tank country, so they use 'em like howitzers. They're 105s and use the same shells we do."

Their guns had the same carriages as ours, and I wondered how towed cannons like that could be used to stop tanks. (It was another example of how blacks got screwed by the U.S. Army, I later found out.) In twenty-four hours, we had seen both black men and yellow men—separate but equal in the eyes of Uncle Sam. They could fight beside us but not with us. Who thought that up? Some Ku Klux senator, I guessed.

Though the 614th seemed like a separate unit, it was assigned for the rest of the war to the 103rd Division, and its guns used our Fire Direction Centers, when they weren't at crossroads looking for tanks.

That first day in combat was a disappointment. We could hear far-off explosions, like a distant thunderstorm, and there was an incessant crackle of small-arms fire. The strange-to-our-ears, rapid *brrup* of enemy burp guns was audible all day, as was the slower rattle of our machine guns, but this was still not what we had expected. Enlisted men had not been told that our combat team was in reserve—or even that there was such a thing as a combat team. They hadn't told us we were teamed with the 411th Infantry Regiment, or that the 409th and 410th were already fighting and 103rd Division men were already dying.

In two jeeps, Lieutenants Ruotolo and Rebman took us, their crews, to a wooded area near St. Die (pronounced "song dee-aye") where we could look down 300 feet from a steep cliff and see the eastern edge of that city—mostly railroad tracks and roads and a few boxcars. Opposite us was a similar cliff, and we assumed the enemy was over there. We itched to see just one enemy soldier. We had run a phone line up with us, and the officers had permission to call in missions, but our main purpose was just to observe the impending battle expected on the eastern outskirts of the city.

We spent the entire morning behind brush looking down on St. Die and the road leading into it. It was dumb duty; nothing moved. The only war we heard was distant shooting. When our phone rang, we were surprised. Our officers were wanted at a battalion meeting. They debated briefly what to do with us and finally decided we should stay there and observe, for later when the 409th was expected to attack the city.

We learned our first lesson about the danger of complacency. Like a stupid rookie, one of us stood up from the brush and deliberately exposed our OP to the enemy—if one was actually out there, he was thinking. Then—by dumb luck—we went back 100 feet and started a fire to heat our rations and smoke our cigarettes.

The Germans *were* out there! They fired on the spot where we'd been. It took them a couple minutes, but they were deadly accurate with the very first shell.

It was the first enemy shell any of us had heard, and it must have been the smallest mortar they had, because it was like a firecracker—a firecracker that could kill. One of us was wise enough to realize the next shell would be aimed at the smoke from our fire, so we unplugged the phone and were at the bottom of the slope waiting for the officers when they returned.

Ruotolo wanted to go back, but Rebman talked him out of it. "It isn't all that good an OP, and they know we're there, so why risk it?"

We spent the next five days wondering if this was what war was like. The sound of far-off small arms was persistent. Ruotolo took Ray, our jeep driver Rocky, and me to an observation post every day, but we saw nothing until the sixth day, when we went up to the ridge near the Meurth River where—just weeks before—the 442nd Japanese shock troops had been in fierce combat to save the 3rd Division soldiers from encirclement. The 409th Regiment from our division was going to cross the river, and half the officers from all the units of the 103rd were using this ridge for an observation point.

I ran a telephone line up a steep slope and through the woods to that OP, but so many other forward observers were there with their own phones that Ruotolo sent me back and just kept Ray there as another observer.

When I got halfway back, I ran into most of the other guys from the detail section scrounging for stuff, along with guys from other artillery batteries. Every imaginable kind of equipment had been abandoned by both the Germans and the GIs during the battle for this ridge, and now the melting snow was revealing a treasure trove. I saw many cases of K and C rations, GI hand grenades, and Kraut potato-masher grenades, as well as machine guns—both theirs and ours—and even German burp guns. One guy, not from our battery, found a German P38 pistol, setting everybody in search of a Luger. I was never much into guns, but even I got stirred up enough to want to own a Luger. Guys were licking their chops, not only for new weaponry they could add to their supply of arms, but also for souvenirs. At first we were afraid of booby traps, so Nick Longo, Lieutenant Rebman's driver, tied a wire to one of the boxes and lay on his belly and pulled. He got no explosion, so we just picked up whatever we wanted after that.

—   Ray York came back from the OP to tell me a phone line had been broken, and I was asked to find the break and repair it. I found it in minutes and was stripping the insulation when I saw a bevy of officers at the top of the path coming up from the road. Gen. Charles Haffner, the division commander, was with them, and I was unsure whether I would be expected to salute. Every soldier in the division called him "Cheerful Charlie," and he seemed more concerned with saluting than with fighting. Every directive he issued was about saluting. Before I could make up my mind, he saluted me, and I returned it with my gloved hand. "Good morning, soldier," Haffner said. He asked me what my job was and then complimented me for helping the observers up there have good communication. All the toadying majors and lieutenants with him affected a smile at me without letting their eyes meet mine. The general smiled, so they smiled, but they didn't want to look at the lowly object of the smile. Oh, how that attitude would change in the coming weeks!

A few minutes later, I heard a shell whistling overhead and assumed it was ours en route to the Meurth, until it hit high up in the trees. I did flop to the ground, but far too late to avoid shrapnel from that burst, so I was just lucky. I still thought it was a short from our guns until another one hit the path where the general and his party had been minutes before. German troops were on both sides of that ridge. I was still having rookie luck and was still far too complacent.

Ruotolo, when he got back from the OP, armed himself with an M-1 rifle and plenty of ammo for it, and he had Rockwell load cases of rations and rifle-grenades onto the top of our trailer. The trailers of all our battery officers were also loaded to the top and above. On our way back, we passed the first German soldiers we had seen up until then. They were prisoners, in the hands of 614th black soldiers, some of whom had handfuls of watches they'd taken from the Krauts.

The next day, Nick Longo got boards from someplace, and all the jeep drivers made sides to increase the capacity of their trailers. Our jeep had the highest sides in the battery, and

Rocky was happy because he loved the C rations and the little hard candies that came with them. We had ten cases. Nick Longo quickly became the battery scrounger—every outfit in Europe had one.

This experience turned Rocky on. He now could go to work making his jeep a thing of beauty—at least, in his eyes. The entire bunch of us rookies were seeing things we knew nothing about before: the U.S. Army had become creative in France. Stateside, we were lectured about the importance of uniformity; over here, nearly every jeep or truck was a custom job. Girls in skimpy clothes were painted on the sides of nearly every vehicle, including tanks, and the drivers' GI brains thought up sexy names for the girls: Sioux City Sue, Mattress Mattie, Red-Light Lydia, Kraut Killin' Kitten, even cornball-stale My Gal Sal. Many jeeps had elaborate sides built to keep out the cold, and they looked more like station wagons than military autos. The lumberyards around Epinal must have been looted to the ground.

After he saw them on the jeeps of veteran troops, Rocky got busy writing letters to his sister in Flint requesting reflectors. Eventually we had about twenty of them on our jeep, front, side, and rear. Rocky got to name the jeep only in his head, however, as Ruotolo surprisingly nixed his request to let him paint a name on it. Rockwell later told me the name he had come up with. "I want to call her Bessie," he said proudly. I winked at Ray. Original Rocky wasn't.

Chapter 2

After a week of war, the snow had melted, and I was aware that Lieutenant Ruotolo was restless. Ray and I got up one morning to discover the jeep was gone. Lieutenant Wallace told us at the chow truck that Ruotolo was out looking for an OP and was expected back for breakfast soon. The trailer was still there, so we put our tents and bedrolls in and tied the sides down. I decided to tell Ray the battalion officers' nickname for Ruotolo. "Why Tonto?" he asked.

"I guess they think he looks like the Lone Ranger's faithful sidekick. He's red-skinned and stocky, and they think he's a joke."

"Do you think he knows?"

"Nah. It wouldn't change him if he did. Freshman year at Yale made him confident he knows everything, and OCS got him thinking he has the war under his thumb. I like the name Tonto. I call him that to myself all the time."

We heard Rocky's jeep coming into the battery area, the engine grinding as he tried to get through the deep ruts and waterholes left by the melting snow and added to by the constant coming and going of two-and-a-half-ton trucks bringing in ammunition. The engineers had been here for three whole days cutting down saplings they'd laid over the mud in an attempt to make the trail more manageable, but the skinny trees were quickly pressed below the surface by the next vehicle to run over them, and the trucks' and jeeps' exhaust pipes continued to burble under the yellow soup.

Somehow Rocky got through, and Ruotolo jumped out and ran to the kitchen truck. Rocky didn't follow, because the kitchen truck had nothing he cared to eat. He went to the trailer, got out a can of meat and beans, and opened it with the turnkey. Then he went back to the driver's seat and ate with his palsied, mud-caked hands, using a tiny spoon he'd found somewhere that he now kept in his shoe. All of us were having problems with diarrhea, and how Rocky, with his terrible sanitary habits, could keep from spending each day squatting and grunting over a slit trench was beyond Ray and me.

Ruotolo wasn't gone long; he wanted to get to do his "war thing" too badly to delay any more than necessary. He was still chewing his breakfast when he got back.

When we reached the asphalt road, Rocky put the accelerator to the floor and left a rooster-tail of mud flying behind us. The tires protested with squeals as we rounded corners, and Ray and I looked at each other with raised eyebrows. He was usually a fast driver, but this was different—he was in a race with something.

We came to a small village with many people and their animals on the road, but Rocky did not slow an iota, and Ruotolo sat impassively. Wasn't he going to say something? Ducks, chickens, and geese flew wildly, cackling and honking. Dogs, used to sleeping in the center of the street, dashed for doorways. Old peasant women, missed by inches, were spun around by the jeep's vacuum. I thought we were going to hit something any second.

At first I left it up to the lieutenant to say something, but when Rocky tried vehicular homicide continually and Ruotolo still said nothing, I spoke up. "Rocky! Slow the hell down. You'll hit something driving like this."

"Why don't they get out of the road then?" he said. Ruotolo turned and glared at me.

Couple of great ones, those two! Ray and I shook our heads. Nothing we could do.

We entered a larger village with a wider main street and houses set farther back, and we began seeing military signs indicating that infantry company command posts (CPs) were in the houses. Here Rocky turned left onto a two-lane road. A barn looked like it was sitting dead center about half a mile ahead. As we closed the distance rapidly, a soldier stepped into the road and held up his hand. He had an MP armband and sergeant's stripes. Rocky nearly ran him down.

The MP jumped from the road as we skidded to a halt. When Rocky finally stopped, he had left a long black stripe behind us and produced the foul smell of burning rubber. Though the quick stop nearly put Ruotolo through the windshield, he ignored it, simply stepping from the jeep and returning the stunned salute of the MP sergeant. "Oh, it's you, sir," the sergeant said.

Ruotolo only grunted. "Sergeant York, you and Hanford get the small telephone reel from the trailer, and don't forget the phone." He turned to Rocky. "Corporal Rockwell, you can leave the jeep here with the sergeant and help us at the OP."

Rocky was eyeing two large shell holes in the cultivated field less than twenty feet away. "I'd rather not, sir," he said. "I'd like to stay with our jeep . . . in case you need me to take you somewheres."

"You sure, Rockwell?"

"Yes, sir, I'm sure."

"Well, okay. You'll wait here for us then, okay?"

"I'd rather not, sir. I can wait back in that there town . . . near the edge, where I can see you guys, if you need me."

Given consent, Rockwell threw the jeep in reverse and backed into a rapid jackknife turn, squealed the tires again, and raced back into the town.

Ray looked at the shell holes that scared Rocky. "They been here very long, Sergeant?"

"They was here when I come this morning. Wait'll you see the ones up on that ridge. They're from 88s. That's why you can't go no further."

Ruotolo glared at the sergeant. "Okay, men, we got work to do." He started up the road. We could now see that the road didn't end at the barn. It curved around and continued between the barn and a farmhouse across the road.

"Sir!" the MP said. "Sir . . . Sir, I ain't s'posed to let you go up this road. You went around behind the farmhouse this morning. That's the safe way."

"I know, Sergeant, but I may just have been lucky not to step on an antipersonnel mine."

I looked at Ray, shrugged my shoulders, and sighed. Ruotolo ignored me.

We walked until we could see a small red-roofed village in the valley below—about fifty houses and a church topped by a spire. The battalion wire section had laid a line beside the road well past the top. To our left was the shell-scarred field the MP had told us about. "Looks like something from the Argonne in World War I," Ray said.

The field had holes like Swiss cheese and was crossed by a narrow footpath leading to a thick woods about seventy yards away.

"Here's where we leave you, Hanford," the lieutenant said. "You splice into that line, and Sergeant York and I will dash over into the trees and wait for you."

The line we had was rubber-covered telephone wire, the thickness of kite string, and the reel—with half a mile of wire—was light, so I pulled off about ten yards and stepped on it so that Ray could start reeling it off. They took off running in a crouch, and I got down on hands and knees and crept forward to where the road did an S-curve parallel with the village. I was in a trench about four feet lower than the ground around me, concealing me from that church spire. I thought that belfry was too good a place for an enemy forward observer to pass up and there was probably one up there—the one who had called for the fire that made all the shell holes in that field. While kneeling, I began to crimp the larger wire with my pliers and peel off insulation, well aware I would be visible to the town if I stood up.

That kneeling posture saved my life.

A shell hit on the bluff less than ten feet away— *SsseeeOOOOm!*—shell and warning screech arriving together. An 88!

I was thrown on my face onto the asphalt. My torso began shaking instantly. My teeth chattered. My brain numbed. I had no idea what to do next.

Right then, all I wanted was . . . *not to die.*

SsssOOm! Another one! Farther away. The next one will be on the road, and then . . . They know I'm here, and they'll keep shelling until I'm dead.

I heard distant sirens. Were they sounding a call to the cannoneers over there in the enemy gun battery, like the claxons on a ship? I got a quick answer—something plopped on the pavement two feet away. It looked like orange peel . . . until I saw the screw threading. *Shrapnel!* The sirens were shrapnel spinning back to earth, many seconds after the bursts.

I relaxed. I wanted to pick up the shrapnel for a souvenir, until I saw the orange color turning to red. "It's cooling," I thought. "That shrapnel is red-hot, and the edges are sharp. Pick it up and you'll get cut and burned." Using my brain slowed the shivering.

I tried to resume the splice. There was a voice from the woods. *Ruotolo!* Damned fool wants me to put my head up to show him I'm all right.

I rolled onto my back and yelled, "I'm okay! I'm all right!"

The shouting continued, so I crawled to the edge of my parapet.

"Hanford, come quick. We need you!"

Ray! Ray's been hit! I just knew it!

I put my pliers in my jacket pocket, ran up the slope, and zigzagged around and across the shell holes so that enemy snipers in the town would have a poor target.

My legs tied in knots before I got to the woods. The last ten yards I ran slow motion. I saw Ray lying there and thought he was dead. Ruotolo knelt over him, his face white, his lower lip purple.

"He's in shock," Ruotolo said. "He needs first aid."

Ray's eyes were unmoving, popped out of the lids. His mouth was moving, but no words came out, and he was gagging and gasping—all of it in silence. There was a hole the size of a baseball below his heart, the color of liver. A few drops of blood were on nearby leaves, but bleeding was not Ray's problem—at least, not on the outside.

I felt like a dolt, unable to think . . . and my legs weren't helping. I tottered around like a drunk.

I wanted the lieutenant to take charge, but instantly I knew he couldn't, so I began taking off my pistol belt to get to my first-aid packet, with no idea whether it would do any good. The first-aid can had a key like a sardine can, and I saw Ruotolo turning his at the same time.

"It's too small," I said, when I had the triangle bandage unfurled.

"Tie it to mine," Ruotolo said

The bandages did no good at all; we couldn't get Ray's body lifted. Then, suddenly, he struggled to his knees and strained out, "I got to . . . I got to . . ."

We begged him, "No, Ray! No Ray! Lie down; don't try to get up."

Ray groaned, then lurched forward onto his face, turned over, and lay still. His mouth stopped moving, but his eyes stayed open. I thought he died right there, but then I remembered my first-aid instruction: Never give up. Keep trying.

"He's in shock, sir. Here, put your jacket on top of mine. We got to keep him warm. He's not bleeding, so a bandage is useless."

We dusted sulfa powder from my kit around the wound, grunting our distrust of the good it was doing. He just lay there now.

"I hate to ask you this, Hanford," Ruotolo said, "but . . ."

"I know . . . I'll run call for a doctor. He needs plasma and a doctor. I'll go." I grabbed the telephone case from the ground and ran in place while I tried to think of what I was forgetting. It didn't come, so I ran out to the path and found my second wind.

When I reached the place behind the barn where the MP had been, he was gone. Damn! I took the phone case from my shoulder and immediately realized I had no pliers to peel insulation from the phone line. I was an idiot!

I hated to go back to where I had probably left them near my splice. It was dangerous, and Ruotolo would see me muddling up. I picked up the wire and tried to chew the insulation apart. Couldn't make a dent. There was plenty of gravel next to the road, so I found some bigger pieces, put one under the wire, and pounded on top with another. I got a blue fingernail and a blood blister, but the stones were too small. Where the hell was that MP when I could use him? I looked up toward the barn where the MP had been sitting until we showed up.

A rock! He sat on a boulder! This ground must be rocky! I ran to the cultivated field, jumped into a shell hole and kicked. Two apple-size rocks hit my toe.

Ten seconds later I had the insulation shredded, and I bit into it and tore enough away to bare the copper wire. I'd have felt proud of myself if I didn't know Ray's life was ebbing away while I was doing all this flubbing around.

I put my fingers on the telephone terminals, turned the crank, and got a shock. Good! I rang the phone with the wires on the terminals and waited for a few seconds, then rang again with the handset up to my ear. "Farm dog how . . . over," a voice said.

"Farm dog baker. Do you know where the line you just connected goes to? Over."

"Farm dog how. Say again . . . over."

"Goddam it, forget this crap. Who's there that can get me a doctor for a wounded man at this OP? This is an emergency! Over."

Major Hawkins came on the line a few seconds later. He knew where I was and said he'd have a medic there as soon as possible.

So now all I had to do was wait. I was sure it was too late, that there was nothing I could do for Ray now. I sat on the pavement with my steel helmet in my lap and my head in my hands.

Then it came to me . . . Why hadn't I just run back into the town? Half a mile. There had to be medical people less than three minutes away.

Good God! Where was Rocky? He was supposed to wait for us at the edge of the town. If he was there, he had to have seen me struggling with the wire. I scanned the houses and trees in the town. No Rocky!

How did I get myself in this mess? Jerk for a lieutenant and a jeep driver from Dogpatch, scared of his shadow.

A jeep came down the road twenty minutes later, and a skinny sergeant with a red cross on his helmet jumped out. "Where's the wounded man?" he asked.

"We need an ambulance and a doctor, not a jeep."

"This *is* an ambulance, and we're medical technicians."

The other medic, a PFC, went to the back of the jeep and got a litter.

I led them up the road and across the dangerous path without thinking. Halfway to the woods, I could see that Ray was dead. His arms were crossed over his chest, and his eyes were closed.

"Sergeant York is dead, Hanford," Ruotolo said. "I tried to give him last rites. He was a Catholic, you know."

"When did he die?" I asked.

"Right after you left. I'd have come after you, but I needed to do something about the body."

"Sir, we can't do nothing about getting him out of here," the medical sergeant said. "That ain't our job, sir."

Before the lieutenant could answer, a drawn-out scream sent us to the ground. It was a mortar shell that landed fifty yards or so away. "Jee . . . sus," the tall medic said. He started to get up, and I pulled him down. The branches and the leaves all around us were crackling. I held him down for a full minute. I was learning.

A second mortar whistled closer, and I didn't have to keep them down this time. "I think the Krauts over there saw us," I said.

When the medics had brushed themselves off, the sergeant said, "Is that path the only way out of here?"

"You aren't leaving without Sergeant York's body," Ruotolo said.

"But sir, that ain't . . ."

The lieutenant interrupted. "It may not have *been* your job," he said, "but it damn sure is now. I'm ordering you to take him back to burial detail."

The sergeant sighed and shot a distressed look at his partner. "Yessir, we'll do it, but it ain't our job." He turned to me. "Is there another way out of here?"

I told him about the ravine and the way around the farmhouse, and he thanked me.

"I told you, Hanford, that way may be mined," Ruotolo said.

I said, "That's up to those guys, sir. They got to carry a heavy body, and they can't move fast enough to avoid a shelling." I turned to the sergeant. "You can go that way and risk a mine or across the path and chance a shell. Up to you."

"We'll go through the ravine. Come on, Leiber, let's get the body on this stretcher."

Going down the steep incline, they had trouble with the litter, but they were around the farmhouse in minutes. I didn't look at the lieutenant; I was too full of guilt at my own failure in my first emergency of the war. And I was sure both of us would soon die too.

We sat on the ground for a few minutes, resting and thinking. "I'm truly sorry, Hanford," Ruotolo said. "You and Ray were very close, and . . ."

"Yes, sir. He was a great person."

We sat there on the ground talking about Ray, remembering whatever we could about him, because he was too important to just get up and forget. Ruotolo knew about Ray's two fiancées, because he censored all our mail. I sensed he disapproved of that side of Ray and wanted me to disapprove too, but I refused. I said that Ray was such a gentleman that too many girls were bound to be attracted to him. "Even with glasses, he was handsome, and he had such class," I said. "And he was too kind to reject girls who came after him too desperately."

I was surprised when I realized what a short time I had actually known him. When he was battery clerk, he lived in another barracks, so I got to see a lot of him for only about the last four months. We went to Dallas on pass just twice, yet I felt closer to him than most of my high school and college pals.

I locked onto my thoughts so completely that I lost Ruotolo for a time.

"What's this guy doing?" Ruotolo was saying when I woke up.

A bicyclist was coming up the slope from the enemy-held town. What the hell was a civilian doing in no-man's-land? "Hey, *arrêtez . . . arrêtez!*" I yelled, French for "stop."

The skinny man kept coming until he reached our path, then he got off and began pushing the bike up the path toward us. "*Arrêtez-là!*" Ruotolo shouted. "Don't come in here!" The guy kept coming.

Mortar shells had been falling here only minutes ago, and here was a Frenchman who thought nothing could happen to him while he pushed a bike through fifty shell holes. We gave up; the peasant with the trouser clips laid down his bike and walked right up to us with a smile. "*Bonjour, messieurs.*" His eyes were on Ray's field pack and field glasses lying on my jacket. "*Votre camarade, il est blessé?*" he asked. I knew the words from the pamphlet: Your comrade is wounded?

"*Pas blessé,*" I said. "*Mort. Notre camarade est mort par artillerie allemand.*" Dead by German artillery, I thought I was saying.

"*Mais alors! Le pauvre!*" he said, never taking his eyes off Ray's stuff.

"Get rid of him, if you can," Ruotolo said.

I got my jacket off Ray's pack, reached into one of the large pockets, and took out a box of K rations and two of the small packs of cigarettes that came in C rations. When I handed them to the Frenchman, he beamed. "*Ah, merci, m'sieur. Merci bien. Merci bien.*"

I took his arm and gently turned him around, reached down, picked up his bike, and handed the handlebars to him. "*Bonjour, m'sieur,*" I said. "*Au revoir.*"

He walked back down the path hesitantly, looking back a couple of times. Trying to appear more grateful, I thought. I watched him carefully to be sure he wasn't going to turn around and go right back into the enemy-held village, but he turned to the right at the road and waved *au-revoir* one more time. I'd let the guards at the entrance to the village back there deal with him.

"I didn't like that guy," I said. "I hate vultures preying on the dead." I was putting my jacket back on as I spoke. That jacket was heavy from something. My hand hit my pliers as I reached into the side pocket. I looked at the blue fingernails and the blisters and swore softly, so Ruotolo wouldn't hear.

After I went back to the place where I'd left the wires and my field pack, I finished the splice, then went back behind the barn and repaired that wire, and I felt a little better about myself. Ruotolo then led me down through the woods to the spot he had chosen for our OP.

Good Lord! It was less than 100 feet from the houses in the village—a village occupied by the enemy. Added to that, there was hardly any view of the hill from which 88s had been firing on us. And a two-foot-high bush was all we had for cover! If he hadn't been here earlier, I'd have expected him to immediately take us back up the hill to find a better place. But he *had* been here before. The very bravado that got him called Tonto by the battalion officers was what led him to such stupidity.

If I were going to save myself from this silly lieutenant, I had to dig—the deeper, the better. I was lucky: the earth there was quite soft. In half an hour, I had a three-foot-deep foxhole.

When it comes to foxholes, lieutenants are expected to dig their own. But while I dug, Ruotolo spent the time sweeping his binoculars over the few inches of hill visible past the houses of the village. He had me stop digging once so that he could fire a checkpoint registration.

All the time I was digging, I thought about Ray. Would the brass hats at battalion realize they were responsible for his death? Hadn't they gone ahead and talked him into volunteering in Ruotolo's section—which, even with a competent officer was the most dangerous section in artillery—even though they thought the lieutenant was a clown?

"Would you like to use this hole, sir?" I asked. "I can dig another."

"Thanks, but I prefer not to use one. I won't let my enemy make me go into a hole. It's a matter of principle."

I went back into the woods to smoke. I felt sorry for Ruotolo. He was still playing war the way he must have as a child. His sergeant was dead from his mistake, and he was daring his enemy to kill him, busily making it easier. Ray believed Ruotolo would grow up once he saw real combat, and he refused to think of him as Tonto. I decided never to think of him by any other name. When I came back from smoking, a man in wooden shoes was coming across the small strip between our OP and the town. We were too close to the enemy to yell at the guy, but I asked Tonto, "Should we shoot him?"

"He's a civilian. You can't shoot a civilian because he's stupid."

"*Bonjour, messieurs,*" the Frenchman said, stepping behind the bushes, holding out his hand for shaking. I thought he looked a lot like the guy with the bicycle.

We had no illusions about why he was there, so after we said our bon jours, we weren't surprised when he held out a packet of Gauloises. "*Voulez-vous des cigarettes françaises pour un souvenir, peut-être?*" Offering the crummy smokes as souvenirs—all they were good for.

I dug into jacket pockets where I put my small packs of K-ration cigarettes: Fleetwoods, Wings, Chelseas, off brands I never intended to smoke—anything to get rid of this guy.

From his expression, I could tell he knew these weren't the best, but he had no choice, so he thanked me.

Tonto held him back and began to scratch a drawing in the dirt with a stick. It was a crude drawing of a church. He pointed at the steeple. *"Artillerie allemande officier, il est là?"*

The civilian grinned. *"Ah oui, il est là. Il est là!"*

Tonto was excited. "He says the Krauts have an OP in the church belfry. Give him a pack of regular cigarettes. You got any Camels or Luckys?"

Frenchie knew the difference. American cigarettes were what he wanted, and Fleetwoods were okay, but not what he really was after. He smiled broadly over two packs of Camels and thanked us repeatedly before scurrying back to his house across the field.

Tonto called for a fire mission immediately, but before I could connect with Fire Direction, we heard the whistle of an incoming shell. It landed twenty feet behind us in the woods, and I got well down in my hole. My forward observer lieutenant had to lie elevated by the dirt I had dug for my hole, but he lucked out. About ten more shells, small mortars, rained down on us over the next five minutes. Tonto didn't look scared, but I was trembling hard. Any smart officer would have moved us away from there quickly, but Tonto had things to prove to himself and the world, so I had to stay and sweat out his lack of smarts.

We called for fire on the church repeatedly for the next fifteen minutes, but I didn't see anything hit it—just clouds of red dust rising from village roofs. Just the same, Tonto sent a message of success to Fire Direction: "Cease fire, mission accomplished." What the hell, they'd never know, he probably figured. His radioman was a PFC, so he'd never tell.

It was three in the afternoon. "I want to go back to headquarters," Tonto said, "to tell them about Ray . . . and our day. Pack up your phone."

Rocky saw us quickly this time. Our jeep was speeding down the road toward us before we got to the barn. His eyes showed he knew—those and his tear-stained cheeks. I could no more have bawled him out for not coming to our aid than I could have slapped him.

"I seen Ray layin' on the litter when them Red Cross guys brought him out," he said. "I loved Ray. He was my best friend. I could tell him everything."

Tonto gave Rocky a hug. It never occurred to him that Rocky could have helped get a medic if he had been alert like he promised he'd be.

Chapter 3

The brass chose an auberge on a mountainside for their headquarters. Rocky and I waited outside for nearly an hour while Tonto was in there telling them his story. The parking lot was big, and the restaurant inside was perfect for our lieutenant colonel and his two majors to receive forward observers and battery intelligence officers when they came back from OPs. I wondered what happened to the French owners that made this place available. Our agreement with the French government allowed the residents to stay in any place we chose for billeting: did that include places of business?

The auberge had a terrific view, and the Vosges were beautiful. They reminded me of the Green Mountains of Vermont, where my mother took my sister and me when we were kids. I wished I could enjoy them, but they would forever be associated with Ray's death, and I stood there admiring them and hating them.

When Tonto came back, I could see he was suppressing a smile. "They were all broken up about Ray," he said. "You know they knew him better than any other Battery B man. They're having a service for him tonight, and you're invited, both of you."

Back at the battery, when our jeep burbled in, guys came running from the guns. Only Lieutenant Wallace, the executive officer, stayed with his howitzers.

I didn't know how to act. I sensed I was a hero, but I felt like an impostor. I had mixed feelings about my performance up there. And I hated that they were more excited than depressed by what was in fact a tragedy—an avoidable tragedy.

The first death was something to write home about, and they were feeling proud. Before today, they thought our division was so little respected that we'd been sent to a soft front, and we'd have to lie to the folks back home when the war was over.

I told them what happened honestly, but without the facts that would make any of us—Tonto, Rocky, or me—look bad. With each word, I felt less and less good about myself and what I was saying. They had already made me a hero, their first hero, and my status in this battery would forever be changed. But I knew I should not be having anything good come out of this day.

At the kitchen truck, I got the royal treatment. Mess Sergeant Johnson, who fawned over the officers and was always rude to me—or anyone else with less than three stripes—suddenly knew my name for the first time. "Hanford, I wish I had something better to serve you tonight, but all we have is corned beef hash. How about I fry you up an egg to go with it?"

"Where'd you get an egg?"

"Nick Longo gave me a couple. Payment for frying up two for him this morning."

"Good old Nick. Okay, hash and egg'll taste good."

Frank Lawrence, who had been the third guy along with Ray and me on our passes to Dallas—and who was my next best friend after Ray, came to see me while I ate. "I'm taking Ray's place now," he said. "The captain just told me."

"Good." I said. "I suggested you to Tonto on the way back."

"You call Ruotolo Tonto?"

"Yeah. Battalion called him that back in Texas."

"I'll go along with that," he said. Then he thought awhile and said, "But let's keep it private. Okay?"

We set out for headquarters just before dark, which in November was barely after five o'clock in France. Lawrence was coming at the insistence of Tonto. Rocky was unhappy, and not just about Ray's death; Tonto told him he had to come inside for the service because he was part of the section.

Once we arrived at the auberge, Tonto had to order Rocky inside. I had no idea what to expect from the battalion officers. I was sure none of them knew any of our names, except for Ruotolo, and I expected they would just shake the enlisted men's hands and send Rocky and me back to the battery, then return Tonto later in one of their jeeps.

The restaurant was large and semiluxurious, with two floors and a mezzanine. The work floor for the officers was the top one. All the work tables, maps, and so forth were moved out of the way for this occasion.

Lieutenant Colonel Caesar, the battalion commander, rushed forward to greet us. He did know all our names, and he gave Frank Lawrence just as warm a welcome as he gave Rocky and me. Frank, Tonto, and I got hugged, but Rockwell backed away, and Caesar didn't pursue him.

"Men," the colonel said, "you can't know how sorry I am about what happened this day. We, here at headquarters loved Ray York. He was such a gentle man. We wanted him to get a battlefield commission and be here with us. You must be devastated."

Major Hawkins was next to hug us, and he turned to me afterward. "Hanford, how long did it take for those medics to get there?" he asked.

"Oh, not long, sir. Thank you. I didn't know how to describe where we were on the phone. Thank you for knowing." I was afraid he'd bawl me out for cussing his phone operator, but he just took my arm and guided me to the drink table.

A fifth of liquor per month ration was given all officers, and the headquarters officers must have been given even more. Their first ration had just arrived that morning, so the table had gin, rum, scotch, bourbon, and mixed-blend whiskeys—about thirty bottles, all of them donated to the service, which was rapidly becoming a wake. Orange and lemon Kool-Aid and water were the only chasers, but they even had ice.

Rockwell hung back near the door, so Tonto had to go reason with him. "Rocky! Come in and have a drink. You're welcome here, c'mon away from the door."

"I don't drink nothin', sir."

"Well, they have Kool-Aid. You can have a Kool-Aid with ice, can't you?"

"Well, okay. They got orange?"

Once Rocky got his Kool-Aid, in minutes he slipped out the door to wait for us in the jeep.

Lieutenant Rebman got Frank Lawrence and me to come up to the mezzanine to a table where he was sitting. Rebman was Battery B's reconnaissance officer, and we liked each other. Back in Marseilles, I found out Rebman was a Cornell man, and then we discovered that we were both jazz buffs and our fathers were Cornell classmates in the class of 1913. We seldom got to see much of each other, but when we did, we had a game we'd play. One of us would see the other and yell something like, "Yardbird Parker," and the other one would yell back, "Johnny Hodges." That way we were agreeing on our tastes in alto sax men. Chuck Howard, who was Rebman's radioman, was sort of jealous, being out of touch as he was with jazz and the hold it had on guys like Rebman and me.

When we were settled in our seats, the wake began. Colonel Caeser, when he had the room's attention, introduced the Catholic chaplain, who led the assemblage in prayer. I learned for the first time that Ray's full name was Luther Raymond York. I thought it was strange that a Catholic family would name their firstborn Luther.

When the chaplain was through, he turned the floor back to the battalion commander.

"I don't know if everyone here was familiar with Sergeant York," Colonel Caesar said, "but those of us at headquarters and in Battery B feel Ray's loss as a deep-felt tragedy. He was at headquarters daily as clerk typist for six months from the time in February when he came to us from specialized training, and it was our influence that turned Ray into an FO sergeant . . ."

The colonel's praises of Ray took about ten minutes, during which time most of the officers in the room were drinking. When the colonel finally finished, he told the room: "Now get on with your visiting; I doubt we ever have such a room as this for a gathering of the battalion the rest of the war." By that time, the somber mood had all but left, and the room soon got noisy.

I began telling everything to Rebman and Lawrence, leaving out Ruotolo's blame and my bumbling. I was frequently interrupted by officers coming to shake my hand and offer their condolences.

When Captain Pultz arrived, he was nervous. "Hanford," he began, "Lieutenant Ruotolo tells me you were very brave up there today. I'm pleased. I want all my men to be brave. Keep it up. Keep it up." After he shook my hand, he almost fell on the steps. "What's between you and the captain?" Rebman asked.

"Yeah," Frank said. "He seemed pretty unhappy having to shake your hand."

I told them about the brief talk we had after I got back from Monmouth, how he said he prayed for the war to last until we could get there.

"And you called him on it?" Rebman said. "Big mistake. Officer talk—he was only saying what most of the officers in the division were saying then. Be careful what you say, for God's sake." He winked.

I soon felt all talked out, and the three of us just drank and sat silently for a while.

As the booze began kicking in, the officers' conversations got louder. The mood of the room floated up to us from the tables below in snatches. I kept hearing words like "Jerry," "Fritz," "Boche," "Hun." World War I was reappearing. Playing "world war" as kids was being remembered, and they were unable to hide how much they'd been disappointed with the war up until today.

I was seeing how what started out as a funeral service was becoming a celebration. If not one other man were to get killed before the enemy sued for peace—which they'd been expecting since midsummer when Paris fell—they'd seen real war. Ray's death had "blooded" them.

As my own sips of scotch and water took hold, I found myself concentrating on the joy of my survival and forgetting the day's tragedy. The booze, and being in the company of officers who were treating me as an equal, had me numb to the real significance of the day.

I should have sensed that all officers in that company did not welcome Frank's and my presence among them. When Colonel Caesar and Major Hawkins were hugging us at the door, I noticed Major Thompson glaring at us. Thompson was battalion executive officer, the second of the three field-grade brass-hats that made up battalion headquarters. He was a blond, handsome, dapper guy with a military mustache, the very picture of a field-grade officer. A southerner, possibly with a military school upbringing, he hadn't a bad reputation with enlisted men that I knew about, but when I saw him coming up the three steps to our level, I knew immediately from his scowl that he was not coming to shake my hand.

Thompson swayed as he put his hand on Rebman's shoulder. "Eve-nin', Rebman," he said. "May I sugges' yuh move t' 'nother table. I don' 'prove a off'cers drin . . . drinkin' with . . . with 'listed men, Loo-tent."

"I beg your pardon, Major," Rebman said, "but these men are here at the invitation of Colonel Caesar."

"I KNOW THAT, LOO-TENT!" Thompson shook Rebman's shoulder. "Does 'at mean yuh gotta drin . . . drin . . . drink withum?"

"I'm afraid you've had too much to drink, Major." Rebman said. He remained seated.

"Goddamn it, Rebman, I don' need you to tell me when I have too . . . too . . . too mucha drink, goddamn it! Not in fronta plain-ass PFCs, damn it!" His voice was now audible to the entire room.

The place became quiet like a bar just before a fight. I half wished Rebman would get to his feet and deck Thompson. But Rebman knew better, and he saw the colonel coming to his rescue.

"Come on, Tompy," the colonel said, putting his arms around the major's shoulders. "I think all of us have had our fill." He turned to us. "I want you men to stay here for a few minutes. Come on, Joe, let's get you a big cup of coffee."

Some talking resumed, but most of the officers, understanding that this incident had ended things, got to their feet.

A short time later, Colonel Caesar returned. "I want you to forget what just happened," he said. "Liquor often causes people to say the wrong thing. You are a hero to me, Hanford, and for heroes, rank means nothing. I'll have you drink with me anytime." He gave me a hug and then gently eased me toward the door.

In the jeep, halfway back to the battery area, Tonto said, "I won't be going back to the OP with you tomorrow, Hanford. They've assigned me to go up in the liaison plane as aerial observer . . . just for tomorrow. Lieutenant Rebman will be going this time, and you'll get a chance to be with your friend, and my new sergeant, Frank Lawrence."

"We aren't going to abandon that OP?"

"No. Why should we?"

"I thought that was apparent. Because the krauts know we're there."

"They knew we were there today. That doesn't mean they'll know it tomorrow."

Chapter 4

Back in my pup tent after the wake, I was groggy from the whiskey, yet unable to sleep. I wavered all over the place emotionally, finally settling on my new fear that what happened tonight at headquarters encouraged Tonto on his path to getting us all killed. They made a hero of the blundering lieutenant for getting his sergeant killed, because they had only his word how it happened. Facing reality made no difference in Tonto. The headquarters officers once called him Tonto behind his back, but tonight, I heard someone call him Tondo to his face. They had to change only one letter, and they changed a buffoon into a superhero.

I got around to blaming myself for Ray's death. After that MP stopped us, I could have said, "I won't go that way, sir! That MP was put there to stop us." Ruotolo would have backed off, I was certain. Then he was still feeling like a rookie officer. That was yesterday when he was Tonto. From today on, I'd be dealing with superhero Tondo.

I decided I had to recognize it: there was nothing I could do to stop it; I was going to die in this war . . . and soon.

I finally fell asleep but woke up frequently. The last time, light filtered through the tent fabric—dawn! The first sergeant would be around soon. When I was fully awake, I remembered throwing up during the night. Lots of guilt goes with seeing a man killed who could just as well have been you. And besides that guilt, I was plenty hungover.

On the way to the observation post with Rebman and Lawrence—this time with Longo as our driver—I told those guys what a lousy OP we were going to. Rebman said, "If you want us to look for another, we'd have to get Battalion's okay. Right now Ruotolo's their fair-haired boy."

But we'd barely gotten there before Rebman said, "This is not a classic example of where to locate an observation post."

"That's what I thought," I said. "Shouldn't you try to get up higher?"

"You should look for the highest ground you can find. This ain't it."

"Why don't we go back there behind the barn?" Frank asked.

"Because Ruotolo chose this spot. Now where is the other foxhole?"

Rebman was a good officer, and good officers don't openly criticize other officers, but he did a lot of head-shaking. With Frank and Nick, who wasn't like Rocky and had come along, we dug three more deep foxholes, and by noon we'd fired a checkpoint registration and all of us settled down in the holes. Nothing was happening, either in the town or in the tiny patch of the hill that was visible.

Frank and I went fifty yards back into the woods to smoke, and when we returned, there was Frenchie coming across the field from the last house in town.

It was the same old routine. He was there to beg cigarettes, and he brought out his Gauloises and Gitanes and offered them as souvenirs again.

We gave him some Old Golds, but didn't ask for him to okay a target. After he disappeared into his house, Rebman said, "I'll bet that guy's a wise-ass Kraut who likes American cigarettes. Would a guy who lived here pick his church for you to shoot at like you say he did yesterday?"

"Proof of what guys won't risk to get American cigarettes," Longo said. "Look at lucky us . . . we get 'em free."

With Frenchie out of range, the expected soon happened: a mortar shell whistled a warning and burst just behind us. We got our heads well down in our holes, and nobody got hit. It was the first shelling for everyone but me, and the others were scared, but they did nothing to disgrace themselves.

The shelling lasted a half hour that seemed much longer. When we didn't hear another shell coming for five minutes or more, Rebman said, "It's time to get out of here. There's nothing to fire on, and it's just a matter of time before a tree burst happens right above one of us or they mount a machine gun in a window over there and wipe us out. I don't know what they've been waiting for."

Nick Longo drove as fast as Rocky, but he slowed down in the towns. We went back to the auberge for Rebman to report our move, and he was in and out in less than a minute. Major Hawkins was at a meeting at Division Artillery, and Major Thompson was temporary Fire Direction head and had a new idea he was trying—a forward Fire Direction Center located in no-man's-land in a hunting shack up in the woods we had just left.

On the way there, I asked Rebman, "What the hell is a forward Fire Direction Center?"

"I don't know. He wants to be ahead of the infantry like Ruotolo, I guess."

"An observation post ahead of the infantry makes sense," Frank Lawrence said. "But Fire Direction . . . ?"

We left Longo and the jeep back near the barn this time. Rebman, Lawrence, and I crossed the plowed field and went on into the woods. The shack was less than 100 yards deep, a log hut with two rooms. Thompson had his switchboard in one room and his desk—a large log—in the other. This location for Fire Direction seemed outright stupid. Why not go as far back as a couple miles? It would be safer and just as effective. What was wrong with being safer? Thompson just wanted to showboat.

Lawrence and I stayed in the room with the switchboard, and Rebman went in to see the major. We could hear everything being said in there.

"Well, Rebman, what brings you to my humble abode?" Thompson said.

"It is pretty humble at that." The two of them chuckled over this dumb exchange, before Rebman said, "We need to change our OP, Joe."

"Why? What's wrong with that one?"

"I could write a book."

"Gimme the first chapter."

"Well . . . it's too low. There's no observation, the houses of that town block the view. York was killed by an 88, Hanford tells me, and I suspect it was direct fire from a tank. If we want to see where that tank might be located, we have to see the entire hill."

"Ruotolo seems to think it's a good OP."

"I disagree. We are only fifty yards from the houses of a town occupied by the enemy. They could kill us in seconds or capture us easily."

"But they don't know you're there, so keep under cover."

"Oh, they know we're there all right. They fired about twenty mortar shells at us already today, and a civilian . . ."

Thompson interrupted: "Ah ha, I think I see what's behind this. You got a little shell fire, and you want to run. Hell, Rebman, this is war. Shelling is part of war. If you run every time you get shelled . . . Why don't we go back up there, so I can see for myself what it is that has you men scared."

This time I interrupted. There was no door between the rooms, so I just went to the doorway and said, "Have you been under a shelling yet, Major?" My voice trembled from an anger I was unable to hide.

"Lieutenant Rebman," Thompson shouted, "what is this man doing here, and who gave him permission to address me?"

Rebman turned to say something to shush me, but I was too angry to stop. "Sir," I said, "if the major wants to go to that OP, I want to go with him. I need to see this. We can guarantee him a shelling. Ask him if I can come along."

"Get that man out of this building, Lieutenant. If you can . . ." The major was now as red-faced as I was.

I turned and went out the door. Lawrence followed. "Gee, did you ever get us in trouble?" he said.

"I couldn't help it."

Frank patted me on the shoulder. "You think he's going to go up there?"

"I hope so," I said. But I didn't really want to ever see that stupid OP again.

Rebman came out of the door minutes later, saying nothing, just pushing Frank and me along. When we were out of hearing distance of the shack, he stopped. "Bill, you called that guy's bluff. He no more wants to get shelled than he wants to become your best buddy. We have permission to go find a new OP."

We spent the rest of the day on the other side of the barn on a hill about half a mile from Ruotolo's OP. We could see about two miles of that hill and all of the town, and we had good cover. The enemy no longer knew where we were. I liked it that he called me Bill.

The next day, Ruotolo became Tonto again. He insisted we go back to the lousy place for which he got Ray killed. It was a matter of pride. I could tell he was ticked off that Rebman had taken us to another spot.

That day he got further evidence that his place stunk: we got shelled for a solid hour. But he insisted he had fired on several very important targets, though Frank looked through field glasses at every bush or tree Tonto called for fire on and saw only shell bursts.

After we got back to headquarters, Ruotolo was in there an hour telling them his invented yarns. I knew that Rebman, who was a competent officer, was being viewed as a failure and was doomed to be a permanent first lieutenant, while Tonto had become Tondo, the fair-haired boy, on the way up.

On our fourth day there, the mess with Tonto's silly OP in the valley still wasn't over. Battalion's illusion of this OP as brilliant had apparently spread within the division. That Tonto-inspired myth brought Col. Donovan P. Yeuell, the 411th Infantry's commanding officer, into no-man's-land to see us. He came with an entourage of two lieutenants. A crowd this close to the enemy had me nervous.

I'd heard about Yeuell but had never seen him before. I recognized his type from his showy gear—an aluminum portable stool that he carried like a riding crop or cane, alternately patting his pigskin-gloved hand with it or leaning on it between steps. Yeuell was the sort of officer for whom the war was a stage upon which he could play the role so many generals and field-grade officers had already typecast. The close-cropped hair, the trim mustache, and the glossy riding boots were the required costume. It was a role I saw as part prissy, part brute. It scared me.

After we arrived in the Vosges, Yeuell made a speech to his officers, in which he told them he had come to this very same place in World War I, only to have the war end before he could see action. He promised them that half of them would be dead before this war was over.

I was hopeful that he was professional enough to drop his pose long enough to tell Ruotolo what a lousy OP this was. Instead, he opened his stool and sat, with binoculars trained on the rooftops of the village, humming softly to himself. I don't remember him saying anything to either his entourage or Ruotolo. He suddenly stood up, brushed aside the few bushes that were all we had for cover, and stepped out into the open to scan the hill with his binoculars and thereby let the enemy FO in the church tower see him. Here's a target, Krauts—an officer you can shoot at.

Yeuell had a fine sense of timing—he was out of there at least five minutes before an hour's intense artillery shelling began. The only good thing to come out of it was that Tonto took us out of there at noon, the earliest yet.

That night, the enemy moved back about five miles, and we had to find a new OP. This one was atop a hill and in heavy woods, a legitimate selection by Tonto—what a surprise. Other than the safety of this observation post, the only thing I remember about the place was the route we took getting there. We came into a town named St. Louis, through which a river flowed, and to cross the river, we drove through what looked like a garage onto a bridge. I have no idea why our route took us this way, but I assume the regular bridge was destroyed and this bridge was one the Krauts didn't know about. I can't even find the town on a map, so I have no idea what river we crossed.

That day, the artillery also moved five miles—at first. The quartering party that found this new position saw a dead body near where they positioned the guns, but they didn't inspect it. After all four guns were placed, the spades were dug in, and men were busy digging foxholes, someone took a look at the body. It was Ray York! The medics who removed him from the woods where he died dumped the body in this spot and pushed his carbine into the ground next to his head, with his dog tags fastened to the trigger housing.

Captain Pultz was furious. He called headquarters and demanded that someone find out who those medics were and have them court-martialed. Meanwhile, he did not want any of his men to see the body, so he pulled out on the road and had the trucks wait there while the quartering party sought a new gun position. The entire 928th Battalion was upset by the incident, but I doubt those medics were ever in real trouble; what they did was SOP (standard operating procedure). Medics and the graves registration unit do not work as a team.

The battery moved twice that day and again the next, and we left forever that death trap Ruotolo had to pretend he liked. The signal section slept for the night in a hayloft. I woke up about midnight from a dream of being on a toilet seat, and I found I had soiled my long johns and trousers with foul-smelling diarrhea. I slid down the loft and went through the courtyard to a privy in the shed adjoining the barn and farmhouse. I threw my long johns in the hole and walked bare-assed back to our jeep to get fresh underwear. Soon I began throwing up, losing it from both ends at the same time, so I looked for and found Cajun Joe, the medic, who gave me paregoric.

After soiling another suit of long johns, I got more paregoric and some other stuff from Joe. Cajun didn't tell me paregoric contains opium, so I wasn't prepared for the hallucinations I began having. Amoebic shapes swam between my eyes and the barn beams, and I never felt sicker, nor more abnormal.

By morning, I was feeling better but was weak as a kitten. First Sergeant Pitts had the supply sergeant give me fresh long johns and trousers and told me to stay in the hayloft and get better while the battery moved to a new position. I slept all day.

About five that evening, Rocky showed up to get me. After we got under way, he said, "Guess what happened today. The first sergeant sent Olson up in your place."

"Olson? Why Olson?"

"Pitts says he hasn't done anything to deserve sergeant stripes."

"How did it work out?"

"He screwed up. Lieutenant Ruotolo had to send him back to repair the phone line, and some machine guns had fired near the OP before that, so Olson was scared and didn't come back, and he didn't even fix the line. He was hiding in a shed back in the town. Captain Pultz ripped his stripes off and made him a cannoneer. He was bawling, said he didn't know how to fix a phone line."

I should have felt some kind of satisfaction, but I didn't. Olson was an unpleasant guy who kept apart from everybody, and he told me *he* should have been sent to Fort Monmouth and made radio sergeant, because his old man was a radio ham. He said that because he grew up around radio, he knew everything about it. In a classroom situation, when he turned his back and refused to listen to instruction, one of us asked him to explain ionosphere, and he said we made that word up to trick him, that there was no such thing. Ionosphere happens to be central to radio theory. His behavior was reported to the first sergeant. Captain Pultz, knowing that, still went ahead and gave him stripes. But what good did it do me for the captain to be wrong? He would never admit it, even to himself.

Back in the battery, the guys who had been in that class-room back in Texas congratulated me over Olson's busting, but I didn't feel any better.

At midday, the battery moved again, this time to a tiny bend-in-the-road village with only ten or twenty houses. They didn't uncouple the howitzers, because we were too far from the front for howitzers to be of use. Out entire combat team was in reserve temporarily.

This was our first occasion to sleep in houses, something, that in training we weren't told could happen. In France, American soldiers could simply walk up to a house and request quartering. Our army, or the French government, I'm not sure which, paid them so much per soldier, but the civilians had no choice—they had to accept us.

Ruotolo was with the rest of the battery knocking on doors, when I saw this little old man in wooden shoes coming toward us from the opposite end of the village. He was smiling from ear to ear. "*Vous desirez une chambre, messieurs?*" he asked.

"How could we ever we turn this guy down?" Frank said.

"*Oui, m'sieur,*" I told the little man, and immediately Frank and I began following him back to his house. I yelled back at Ruotolo that we had a house and to bring Rocky.

We were met at the door by the old guy's wife, a tiny white-haired woman who exuded joy. She kissed both of us on the cheek and nearly pulled us into the house. Frank and I were surprised how well prepared they were for us. When Rocky and Ruotolo got there, she tried the kissing routine all over, but they both backed away. Rocky refused to come into the house.

There was a round table in the center of the all-purpose kitchen-living-dining-room, and all sorts of delicacies were spread out: homemade bread, jars of jam, cookies, wine, tea, and *krapfen*, fried dough buns.

Frank and I, unable to express ourselves in French, kissed Mama again. She took our heads in her hands and planted kisses on our foreheads. Tonto went back to the jeep to get his bedroll and missed the kissing, intentionally perhaps.

Papa led us to a window and showed where a shell had landed less than twenty feet from the house. It was one of ours, but he didn't hate us for it, he told me with sign language. He was strutting in sock feet, as he showed us a shadow-box frame with medals he earned in *La Grande Guerre*. A framed photo of him as a young French Army *poilu* was there also.

Mama insisted she show us our rooms before we ate. She seemed to know Ruotolo was our officer, because she put him in a downstairs room. Frank and I tried to dissuade Mama and

Papa from giving up their room to us, but Mama was determined that we have the room we were sure was theirs. A thick homemade comforter was on the bed. Both Frank and I patted it for Mama.

She went outside to try again to persuade Rocky to come in, but that only made him unhappy, so she took out a tray of cookies, bread, and jam. Rocky, flexible as Gibraltar, was going to stay out and sleep in the jeep, no matter what. He did say, "Mercy, mercy," which was as close to French as he'd learned.

We sat at the table and began putting things on our plates, and then Tonto did the unforgivable: he put his pistol on the table next to his plate!

"What the *hell* did you do that for, sir?" I said.

"Let them know we won't put up with any shenanigans."

"Like what?"

"Like *anything*. We don't know anything about *these people*."

I was red-faced. If he couldn't see *who* and *what* these people were . . . *my God!* I had no answer. Mama was near tears. I don't know when I felt so weak and hopeless. Had I just one bar on my shoulder, I'd have gotten to my feet, taken his pistol, jammed it back in his holster, and slapped his face. Frank was just as distraught, I could tell.

Even as things were, I should have got to my feet and gone over to Mama and kissed her cheek again; I wonder if that would have told Tonto anything he could understand.

But I would forever remember . . . I did nothing.

I'm sure the jam was delicious, but I didn't taste it, nor did I taste the tea, the wine, or anything else. Shame took away my sense of taste . . . and my hearing, and my touch, and my eyesight. I felt only one emotion—hate. I hated that lout, Donn "Tonto" Ruotolo. I hated the war. I hated the uncouth army. But mostly, I hated myself for not going in the air corps like my college buddies, who, by so doing, got commissions and wisely avoided the sort of thing I had just been forced to undergo.

The comforter was warm in the bed Frank and I shared, but we slept poorly, so intense was our rage.

The next morning, I kissed Mama and hugged Papa in front of slobbish Tonto and rude Rockwell. I think Mama by instinct knew that Frank and I were better humans than our officer. But Lieutenant Ruotolo left those beautiful people with an image of Americans as slobs like himself. Fat lot of good it did to be on the right side in the goddamn war, I thought.

Chapter 5

My rage was tempered when Ruotolo was sent up in the liaison plane again and Frank and I went forward with Rebman once more, this time with Rocky driving.

We came into the small city of St. Martin, where all sorts of vehicles milled around. This was a juncture of almost the entire Seventh Army. We saw the bumper markings of Seventh Army, and VI Army Corps for the first time. There were no signs of combat, but we heard nearby artillery and machine guns, as well as the grinding of engines and the clattering of half-tracks. MPs were directing traffic. Shoulder patches of Seventh Army or VI Corps usually meant the soldiers were from the rearmost rear echelon, so the sounds of nearby combat made the whole scene eerie, but we were still rookies, so we hadn't learned much yet.

Minutes after entering St. Martin, we saw strange signs: *Hermann Goering Strasse* and *Adolf Hitler Platz*. Rebman had been briefed and was prepared for this. This was Alsace, he explained, a French palatinate the Germans reclaimed after they defeated the French in 1939. "They'll be pulling down those signs soon," he said, "but right now we got to climb that steep slope to make an OP." The slope he pointed to was a nearly vertical hill that rose 400 or 500 feet above the city, to its northwest. Rocky drove us to the foot of the hill, and Rebman told him to go back to the battery and return for us before evening chow.

We unloaded the radio, as there was no way we could have run telephone wire up that steep slope.

We had only canvas straps to carry the radio and battery pack, so climbing straight up like that had us sweating and swearing, and I soon could feel blisters starting on both my thighs.

Six peasants were cultivating terraces on the hill. As we got near them, we expected some sort of greeting, but they either ignored or scowled at us. From those hostile glares, I was beginning to think we might actually be in Germany.

Rebman pointed out the unusual animals pulling the plows. At first we thought they were oxen, until we saw udders filled with milk. The peasants controlled them entirely with verbal signals. I heard one of them get his cow to turn by going, brrrruup.

We reached the top of the hill in half an hour and sat down to rest. Rebman had helped carry the radio, something you could bet Tonto never would have done—nor would any other officer I had yet encountered. The hilltop was flat and forested with young trees, none more than ten feet tall. We moved toward the eastern slope, back toward the city, to see if a good OP was there. Smoke came from that direction, as did the sounds of gunfire and artillery. We passed a number of narrow trenches where there were empty tins—tins with Spanish printing. "Corned beef from Argentina," Frank read. I picked up a sardine can from Norway.

I became aware of a smell I seemed to remember: German cigarettes. "How long can the smell of cigarettes linger in the open air?" I asked Rebman.

"Is that what that smell is?" Rebman said. "Smells like gunpowder to me."

I told him about the Frenchman back in Valence who gave me the German Waldorf Astorias. "I tried one," I said. "That's the smell."

"Has this hill been cleared by our infantry?" Frank asked.

"Good question," Rebman said. "I don't know. Waldorf Astorias . . . hmm . . . recently smoked . . . Makes you wonder."

"Shouldn't we get the hell off here?" I asked him.

We went clear to the edge of the hill overlooking St. Martin before I turned on the radio. Back in Texas and Louisiana, the 609 radios seldom worked, so I was pleased when Fire Direction answered my call.

Fire Direction had no idea whether the hill was cleared, so they said to get out of there. We could see a tank battle that looked like it was ten miles away to the east.

It took no time at all to get down. We almost slid all the way, passing the terraces and the peasants cultivating with cows nearly unnoticed.

Lieutenant Rebman decided we had to find quartering for the night before we did anything else. He led us down the first short street abutting the hill, walked up to the door of the second house, and knocked. A frumpy woman in a dust cap answered, looking frightened by us.

Rebman tried his college French, and the woman replied in German that she spoke no French. "Either of you guys got the 'When you meet the Germans' pamphlet?" he asked.

Neither of us had one handy, so Rebman tried again in French. We all thought the old gal understood French more than a little and was just being difficult. She finally backed off and let us in, not once coming close to a smile. As soon as we were in the door, she disappeared upstairs. We set all our stuff down and sat down in the chairs and couch that were in the kitchen. Minutes later, she rushed through wearing an overcoat and hustled out the door without saying a word. At that time we were puzzled, but later, when we learned the hard way about the politics of Alsace in 1944, we realized she was probably a German national who settled there for the Fatherland. Had we known that then, we'd have been even more scared than we were later that day.

Just for something to do, Rebman took us back to the town center with the Nazi street signs. It turned out to be a good thing, because a truck column came into town, and we saw they were from Battery B. The guys on the trucks all waved at us, and pretty soon Rocky came along and pulled out. Rebman told him to go along with the battery, so we'd know where they were going, and to come back for us about dinnertime. "We have a house to stay in, so if they're going to be sleeping in tents, we'll stay here tonight," he said.

The column was barely out of sight when we heard the ear-splitting screech of many incoming shells. We slammed ourselves to the hard brick pavement. The explosions shook us, though they were two or three city blocks away. It wasn't like anything we'd ever heard before. Several MPs were directing traffic nearby, and when we were on our feet, one of them told us what we just heard: "Screaming meemies. They're Nebel-werfers . . . big rockets. The Krauts fire them from a huge rack, sometimes as many as forty at a time. We saw a lot of them in Italy. Scary!"

This place strained our courage; it felt like we were in Germany and were surrounded by the enemy. Alsace was definitely unlike the France we'd been seeing. In combat barely more than two weeks, the whole time in reserve, and already we'd experienced almost everything—or so we thought.

The three of us walked around the block At the corner of Hermann Goering Strasse and Rudolph Hesse, we heard what sounded like a Tommy Dorsey record coming from a GI radio in a half-track several soldiers were leaning against, smoking. We got into a conversation with those guys immediately.

"How can you get civilian broadcasts on a GI radio?" Reb-man asked.

"It's AM radio. We can get anything."

They were tuned into the Armed Forces Network. They explained that AM radio, with its long-distance reception, was necessary for antiaircraft batteries, because they had to get alerts from as far as 100 miles away.

We stood there talking with those guys for an hour. They'd been in North Africa and Italy. They told us they didn't like this place any more than we did. "It's too close to the infantry for us. AA is rear-echelon duty, because planes don't attack doughboys much: it's too close to their own troops. This general you got don't got good sense, bringing us up this close."

We also learned that the rear echelon caught more fire in Anzio than the front line. "First place in the war where the quartermasters had more casualties than the infantry," they said.

When we got ready to leave, the ack-ack men agreed to bring their radio over to our billet after chow. We'd get a chance to listen to Berlin Sally and Lord Haw-Haw.

We kept expecting Rocky, and when he didn't come at five or six, we decided to walk down the road in the direction the battery went and see if we could find them. Less than half a mile down the road, Rebman stopped and held out his hands. "Hold it men, there's a dead body up there."

The body was in the dead center of the road and was not easy to identify because it had no helmet. Darkness didn't let us get a good look, and we had no flashlight, so we stayed back. If it was a Kraut, we reasoned, maybe the GIs who shot him wouldn't take the time to identify us before they shot again. And if it was a dead GI, then the Krauts who shot him were probably still around.

Rebman decided we didn't want to go any farther. Back at the house, we threw a few more bricks of charcoal into the stove to heat the kitchen, then cooked a couple cans of C rations on our portable Coleman stove. Rocky never showed up—not surprising if he happened to see the dead guy on the road.

The whole day had us feeling plenty foolish. St. Martin was an enigma. Was it French or German? Had the infantry actually cleared it yet?

Shortly after dark, our new friends from the antiaircraft artillery showed up with their radio. We got the armed forces station and listened to a prerecorded Jimmy Durante monologue called "I'm Durante da Patron of da Arts." After a few songs by Sinatra with Dorsey, the ack-ack guys got Radio Berlin. The propaganda was so heavy, I had to wonder if the Germans were silly enough to think we'd believe this stupid stuff. Berlin Sally read letters she said were written by American prisoners of war and told us, "Write to the parents of these men and pass on their messages. PFC Walter Healey of Des

Moines, Iowa, writes: 'Dear Mom, The folks here in Germany have been just wonderful to me. I was shot in the right leg, but I'm healing just fine. The doctors here are so kind, and I adore the nurses and their attention . . .'"

Rebman said, "There's where they gave away what crap they're trying to push. No GI in this army would ever use the word *adore.*"

Sally was followed by a band, Bruno and His Flying Tigers, which attempted to play "St. Louis Blues." It was a 1926 stock arrangement and couldn't have been cornier. "Apparently the only kind of jazz Hitler allows is bad jazz," Rebman said.

Lord Haw-Haw was just as silly as Sally had been. He called Roosevelt "Frankie Rosenfeld," saying, "That's his real name, you know, and you are here risking your lives to aid the Wall Street Jewish conspiracy to rule the world . . ."

One of the ack-ack guys stepped out front, when we told him the toilet here was a privy in the back yard. He couldn't have any more than unbuttoned his fly before he jumped back in and slammed the door. "Blow out that lantern! There's a patrol of Krauts outside the door!"

I ran to get my carbine that I'd leaned against the wall, then sank back into a corner pointing it at the door.

Someone asked, "You sure it wasn't a GI?"

"Goddamn sure! I seen enough of them bastards in Italy to know the difference in the helmets. I was two feet away from that guy, and there's at least ten of 'em."

At this point, the door began slowly creaking open, sounding like the squeak we grew up hearing on the "Hermit's Cave" radio show. I felt porcupine quills growing on my spine. Several seconds went by before I remembered to put a round in the chamber and push off the safety.

"Shut the goddamn door before they throw a grenade in here!" somebody yelled.

Another guy ran and slammed the door shut with his foot, but in the dark I didn't know who our hero was.

I could actually hear my own heart thumping. We all became silent, trying to hear our enemy lurking outside ready to spring on us. The silence was broken by one of the ack-ack men shouting, "Henry, go to the back door! They may try to get in that way."

We did not wait more than a few minutes, all of us scared brainless, before Rebman said, "I'm going out to have a look. Who wants to come along?"

We all went, our weapons at the ready. There were stair-wells all along the street, and we used the flashlight of one of the AA guys to search them. After we were certain the Kraut patrol had gone away, we went back inside.

Those veterans of Anzio and Salerno were as scared as us rookies, and they decided to stay all night with us. We went upstairs, only to find a single bed. Altogether, there were seven of us. We worked things out by putting two guys on guard at the front door and one guy at the back, leaving four of us to sleep crosswise on the bed, two hours at a time. Even Rebman pulled two hours on guard. It wasn't the most restful sleep any of us ever had, but we were now used to being uncomfortable at night in the army.

In the morning, Rocky came back, and we said good-bye to our friends from the antiaircraft battery. They all agreed that Rebman was the nicest officer they'd ever met, and one of them had been in the army five years. That proved to Frank and me what we already knew.

Chapter 6

The dead body in the road was a German. He'd been shot in the neck and bled a gallon onto the road. Rebman had Rocky stop next to the body, and we all got out and inspected it. Rocky admitted he'd stopped when he saw it, and that was why he had not come for us when we expected him. The Kraut's helmet was in the ditch. We left it for someone who might want a souvenir.

The battery was only another half mile away, and we were met there by Ruotolo. Lieutenant Rebman left us to be with his own crew.

We got breakfast from the chow truck—fat limp hotcakes, thick nasty syrup, greasy thick bacon, and lousy coffee.

Captain Pultz was forward with a quartering party and would be gone at least an hour, so Cajun Joe the medic came over to our jeep and asked if we wanted to go see some dead Krauts. Frank and I went, just out of curiosity.

The dead Germans were next to a bluff on a side road a few hundred yards from the battery bivouac. Five of them lay around a truck turned on its side and riddled with bullets.

"All the guys in the battery have already seen it," Joe said. "Look at this one—musta been the driver. Ever see a human brain before?"

The brain lay a foot from the body.

"Yuck! Looks like a spoiled cabbage," Frank said.

I had to look away to keep from throwing up.

We figured out that a .50-caliber machine gun must have been on the bluff, and the gunners opened fire at point-blank range when the truck came around the curve. Because the bodies all were several feet from the truck, we guessed they managed to get out after the truck ran up the bank and turned over. The gunners simply cut them to ribbons.

The dead all had their eyes open and, except for the yellow color, looked almost alive. The one whose brain lay on the pavement, besides having no top on his skull, had a finger missing.

"I took his ring finger off with my scalpel," Joe said.

"Why?" I asked.

"Needed to. To get his ring. I got seven of 'em already. After the war, I'll cash 'em in and get me a car." Cajun Joe was a nice guy otherwise, but war was a crummy business, and the Articles of War took a beating from both sides.

Back in the bivouac area, we saw the quartering party return. The captain jumped out of his jeep and went immediately to the truck where the first sergeant was sitting. Soon men came running from other trucks, and we knew something was wrong. Ruotolo got out of our jeep and went to the gathering of sergeants and officers. When he came back, he said, "Lieutenant Allison just got killed by a civilian sniper while he was standing next to one of the houses where we're going to stay."

Lieutenant Allison was a stranger to me. He came to the battery while I was in radio school, and I don't think I ever spoke to him. "Mike Allison just got back to the battery yesterday," Ruotolo said.

"Where was he?" Frank asked.

"In the hospital. He got yellow jaundice from some fruit he ate in Marseilles."

He was our motor officer, and I never missed him all that time. I actually had to look at the group picture we had taken in Texas, to see who he was. I was told he was an especially nice guy, a lot like Rebman. Two and a half weeks in combat, and already two very nice guys were dead.

The battery pulled out on the road, grim faces staring out of every vehicle. Going up to that town and finding that sniper was on everyone's mind.

The road led us back into mountains once more, and we passed through one more small settlement before we began going downhill. At a U-turn where the passage was steep—perilous enough to have road-marking soldiers waving trucks to slow down—we saw five dead German soldiers lying helmetless beside the road. We later found out that service battery road markers had gunned them down. The dead Germans had been deserting the Kraut army, and all had safe-conduct passes up their sleeves, evidence of their intentions to surrender. But service battery was very "rear echelon," and those guys had never heard the sound of war from less than ten miles. They probably thought they were heroes.

We were jittery coming into Barr. Because of Allison's murder, we expected the city to be full of Nazis. The houses the quartering party had found for us were on a street forking back in the direction we came from. One large three-story house was right at the center of the fork. It was as big as a small inn.

Our house for the night was on an escarpment rising 300 feet above vineyards stretching for miles. Cannoneers immediately started to dig in next to that cliff. I never found out which house Allison was standing near when he got shot, but I had barely put my bedroll in the front door of the one we were assigned to when I heard a volley of shots.

The sniper was at it again.

Back outside, I saw men everywhere were crouching behind trees and looking down the street. Past the fork was a line of three-story apartment houses on the side of the road next to the escarpment. Each had an iron-grill veranda on the top two levels. The other side of the road had no houses, only a lath-and-tar-paper shack that I took to be a henhouse.

The captain crouched behind a truck to organize a search, with our three officers squatting next to him. "The shots came from one of those apartments," he said. "Rebman, you get about ten volunteers and begin a search. Keep close to the buildings. Don't let the sniper get a shot at you from one of those balconies."

I joined a three-man squad with Rebman and Chuck Howard. Frank Lawrence was put in charge of another two guys. We dropped off a search party at each of the first three

apartment houses, and our group headed for the fourth building. The shooting had stopped momentarily.

When we got near the building we were going to search,
Howard called our attention to the second-floor veranda. A
pretty woman stood there looking down at us. I really couldn't
see a lot of her, but from what I did see, she looked quite different from the plain hausfrau types we'd been seeing all over
France. Was she actually wearing lipstick?

"Let's search the second floor, Kenny," Chuck said. He was
calling Lieutenant Rebman by his first name, and I didn't
think I liked it.

"Let's be serious," Rebman said. "We're looking for a
sniper."

But when we entered the building, somehow he led us
straight to the second floor. The lieutenant looked a little
sheepish as he knocked on the door.

A frumpy old frau in apron and dust cap came to the door.
She could have been the twin of the unfriendly woman back in
St. Martin, except she had a smile on her face. "*Ja ja, was willst
du?*" she said.

"Do you speak any English?" Rebman asked.

"*Nein. Ich spreche Alsacienne. Ein Augenblick, mein Herr.*" She
turned and called, "*Madame, bitte. Amerikanische Soldaten.*"

Madame wasted no time coming to the door. You could see
she knew we were coming, and had sent the maid to the door
as a matter of form.

She was sensational close up—much more so than we had
expected. Here was a female wearing makeup, a silk dress, silk
hose, and high heels, a girl like none of us had seen since leaving New York, and maybe not even then. This was a one-in-a-
million-looking female.

"May I help you, gentlemen?" she asked in nearly perfect
English, dropping the *h*s Frenchlike. Her liquid black eyes
bowled me over. She had perfect teeth, and her smile was
poised and easy. Then there was the glossy, straight, short
black hair and the sort of great legs that tiny women some-

times have. In seconds, three men were smitten . . . by her looks alone.

As for the lady, her gaze fastened on the lieutenant. I stole a glance at him and saw he was swaying and shuffling his feet. "You speak English?" he said, like he had something stuck in his throat.

"Yes, but not good. I have not the practice, I think. I live on Long Island, it is six years since." (I'm trying to remember the pattern of her speech and accent.)

"We need to search your apartment, madame. Just routine; no offense intended."

"Ah! The gunman. You think he is here, this assassin?"

"We are searching all apartments, sorry. May we come in?"

"But of course. I will show you. No assassin here." She turned to the maid and said something in German. "Lisle will get you a pot of tea while you search. I know Americans like better the coffee, but, *mais alors*, we have no coffee."

"I'm sure we appreciate your hospitality, but I'm afraid we haven't time to stop. Thank you very much." He turned and said, "Hanford, you search that way, and Howard, you go to the right, I'll go to the terrace."

Here was an apartment living room larger than most of the houses we had seen up till then, so I knew these people had money. Wealth was something we hadn't seen before in France.

I was back from my search in a few seconds. "Hey, guys, you got to see this bathroom."

They came when they were through with their search. The tub had gold floral trim and a floral-trim charcoal heater, with gold knobs on the faucets. "What I wouldn't give to take a bath in that," I said.

"But you must come and take the bath . . . if you have the time, of course." The pretty lady was standing beside Rebman. "When you finish the search, perhaps?" She was still looking only at Rebman.

"I'm sorry, madame, but we have a war . . ."

"Of course. I was hoping . . . but, *eh bien*! You are in Barr tonight, perhaps?"

She really wanted to see Rebman again, and—as much as I liked the lieutenant—I felt a pang of jealousy, and I swear I heard Howard panting.

On the stairs as we were leaving, Howard said, "She's got a baby, a little girl. I saw her in the back room."

We had barely reached the street when Lawrence whistled at us. "Get behind the trees. The sniper's over there in the henhouse." He pointed at that tar-papered shack across the road. A thin gray wisp of gunsmoke was drifting above it.

The lieutenant pulled back the slide on his pistol, and Howard and I slammed rounds into our carbines and took aim at the henhouse. "Hold your fire until I count to three, then all fire at the window," Rebman said.

Before he could begin to count, we saw four civilians coming up the road wearing FFI (French Forces of the Interior, the French Resistance) armbands and carrying Thompson submachine guns. "Hold it," Rebman said. "Let's let those guys have a go at it."

One of them opened fire on the shed when they were still fifty yards away. Splinters and bits of tarpaper flew from the door. One of them kept up steady submachine-gun fire while another one advanced to the door. That one kicked in the door and fired a burst inside. There was some yelling from inside, and a man came to the door with his hands on top of his head. The sniper was now an FFI prisoner. One of the Frenchmen did a search of the shed to be sure there was no confederate.

The sniper seemed tranquil as they marched him down the hill. The FFI men were strutting like drum majors.

The house at the center of the fork had a dozen guys standing around in front. They had been an audience to the shooting, and they greeted us like conquering heroes. A fat red-faced Alsatian, the owner of the house, was there shaking hands as though he also enjoyed the show.

Tonto was antsy. He had a mission with an infantry company down the hill in the city center. This was to be our first time as artillery observers forward with a company on an attack.

Rockwell drove crazily, squealing tires both in starting and taking curves. Being in a place where civilians were sometimes snipers had him strung as tight as a banjo. It was half a mile into Barr center, and we flew there. Once more Tonto did nothing to slow down his scared-witless driver.

We drew up, brakes screeching, at the major intersection of Barr. It was like Times Square—trucks, half-tracks, tanks, and jeeps galore, everyone trying to read the many signs put up on several posts by infantry companies representing several regiments of the 103rd Division and dozens of units from Seventh Army or VI Corps. Tonto said he was looking for George Company of the 411th, and somewhere in that cluster of signs their location had to be posted. The problem became the MP directing traffic, who kept yelling at us to move along. "We want to find George Company of the 411th," the lieutenant said.

"I don't know them," said the MP, "but there's lots of infantry that went that way." He pointed to the left, and Rockwell quit racing the engine, threw the jeep in gear, squealed the tires again, and headed the way the MP pointed. In seconds we were going full speed down a street as narrow as an alley. The buildings to our left were right at the foot of the escarpment, and within a few blocks, we saw infantrymen sidling along two-foot-wide sidewalks with their backs up against buildings. They were doughboys expecting to exchange fire with the enemy. Signs to indicate that any units could be in this commercial part of town were absent. Any fool could tell this was not a place for a company headquarters, but Tonto just sat there looking straight ahead as our jeep gained speed.

Yelling to be heard, I said, "I think this is the wrong way, Lieutenant. This street hasn't been cleared yet." He remained rigid, and Rocky applied more foot to the pedal.

A shell whistled over and crashed against the escarpment. Rockwell now went psychotic. We were speeding so fast, I doubted we could stop if the entire German Army should suddenly appear. I slapped Rocky as hard as I could on his steel helmet. "Stop the goddamn jeep, Rocky!" I said. I slapped again. "Stop the jeep. Stop the jeep!"

He stopped as erratically as he'd driven, and the jeep skidded and slid nearly out of control. He almost killed us driving, and he almost killed us stopping. Tonto turned and glared at me. I ignored him. "Now turn around, Rocky," I said.

Rockwell was a near genius at maneuvering a jeep with a trailer behind, and he now showed his skill. He raced into an alley, threw the jeep in reverse, and zoomed back, without buckling the trailer. Another shell whistled over, and the jeep once more tore at breakneck speed back toward the main intersection. This time Tonto spoke up. "Slow down, Rocky. I need to read those signs this time."

Rocky pulled up at the intersection with the MPs and was able—just barely—to stop next to the same MP, who was so in love with his authority that he ranted and raved some more. But the signs were there to be read, and this time Tonto read them.

"Okay, Rocky," he said, "George Company is to the right. Thank you, Sergeant." The MP didn't bother to return Tonto's salute.

Rocky drove fast and faster again, and still Tonto said nothing. After a forty-five- degree curve, we were on a road dead straight for miles. The houses to our right were built into a twelve-foot-high berm, and to our left were no buildings at all, just a park or something. I think I saw swings and slides. A couple miles down the road, two tanks were parked in the center of the road, and the distance between us was closing fast. I had my fingers clenched so tight they pained.

"Lieutenant, I think I saw G Company on one of the signs," Lawrence said.

Tonto ignored him. The tanks seemed to have him mesmerized.

I thought there was a good chance Rocky would ram into the tanks, or have to swerve into the field to avoid them, going as fast as he was, so I used the flat of my hand against his helmet again. He took nearly half a mile to stop, and we were in front of the tank on the left before he braked so hard all of us lurched forward.

They were U.S. Army Shermans, and the tank next to us had a hole the diameter of an 88 shell right next to the gun muzzle.

Smoke curled from it!

"Lieutenant," I said, "these tanks have just been hit. There may be an antitank gun pointed at us right this minute."

I bailed out of the jeep, right over Rocky's head. Lawrence went over Tonto the same way. Rocky got out, lay on the pavement, then slid under the jeep.

Tonto sat there impassive for several seconds. When he did decide to get out, he was slow, deliberate, and silent, showing us he was afraid of nothing in his own perverse way.

While Frank and I went up on the grass in front of one of the houses so we could hit the ground where it was soft, the lieutenant untied the ropes on the trailer's tarp and pulled out the M-1 rifle that we found on the ridge where the nisei regiment had abandoned so much equipment. When he was sure the rifle was loaded, he finally spoke: "I think I'll look around up here aways." He began sauntering along the sidewalk toward our suspected antitank position, carrying the rifle like a country boy out rabbit hunting. I felt that if I could get my hands around his neck, I'd throttle him.

A shell coming from the direction of the vineyards sent its warning scream and put Lawrence and me on our bellies. It landed a couple hundred yards past us in the field. We knew it was intended for us. An adjustment would follow, and we hoped the next one would land behind us, not up our backs.

Damned lieutenant horsing around here!

Now Rockwell decided to add to the problem. Coming out from under the jeep, he said, "I'm getting out of here. If you guys want to come with me, get in quick."

"You can't go driving off and leave the lieutenant," Frank said.

"I'm goin'," Rocky said. "You comin'?"

Before either of us could answer, he threw the jeep in reverse and took off in one of his patented high-speed reverses, fishtailing and swerving all over the road, and was nearly out of sight in seconds. That seemed to wake Tonto up. He began to come back.

When he got near, he said, "What got into Rocky?"

"You didn't hear that shell come over?" I said.

We found Rocky in a garage built into the berm next to the house that was the George Company's command post. I don't remember Tonto even scolding him. Rocky's timorousness was simply accepted.

Our arrival, after a fifteen-minute walk, had us five minutes late from starting with G Company on its attack across the big vineyard. We went over the berm and saw the infantrymen already pinned down in among the rows. By crawling on our bellies, we caught up to the captain of G Company and, to our surprise, found Captain Pultz with him. Mortar shells were already falling near the rear of the column. I tried to look at Pultz's face to see if he showed fear, but with all of us lying prone, I was unable to tell. Some machine guns chattering up there were pinning us all down.

Though I was anything but a veteran, I already had learned that the enemy never kept firing heavy stuff for long. I lay there listening to the infantry captain and Captain Pultz talk about bringing artillery fire down on those machine guns. They seemed indecisive.

Finally, Pultz suggested that he and Ruotolo go back to the berm where they could observe better before they called in the big guns. We crawled some of the way and got up and ran in short dashes the rest of the way. Several mortar shells exploded near us as we ran, but none of us were hit.

Captain Pultz, who was an expert at gunnery, conducted fire for half an hour with me on the radio, and then G Company, for reasons unknown to me, came back out of the vineyard under cover of the smoke shells we provided. Our job was done for the day.

As our jeep climbed the road up the escarpment, I thought about the pretty girl with the bathtub and wondered if we would spend the night in Barr, and where I could get a bath—or was that privilege only for Rebman? Suddenly a light went on: What the hell was she doing, wearing high heels and silk hose while just hanging around in her apartment? Was she expecting guests? The question alerted me: *This gal was up to something.*

Half the battery met our jeep when we got back. They were all excited. The man in the house at the center of the fork had been marched down the hill to the schoolhouse to be shot, after he dropped his role as genial welcoming host and went up to his attic and began sniping. Luckily he hit no one, but the FFI already knew he was a Gestapo agent, and they shot the locks off the unlocked front door and pushed him off to the schoolhouse execution yard. A few minutes later, Frau Genial-host was up in the attic sniping, and the FFI came back and got her. The men of Battery B finally felt like they were in the war.

Lieutenant Rebman saw me at chow. "Bill, I have a favor to ask," he said. "I've been down the hill to the apartment and seen the lady. The invitation is still there for the bathtub, but Battalion is going to have a wake for Allison back in that town near where the dead krauts were, and I have to go. I should be back around ten, so . . . what I want you to do, is go have a bath, and keep her entertained until I get back. Can you do that?"

Frank Lawrence was a true friend and didn't try to horn in, and lucky for me, Chuck Howard had connected with a teen frump across the road from our billet. I got to go to the apartment of the woman all alone. I knew I was only playing Capt. John Smith to Rebman's John Alden, but any chance to just look at that girl some more had me swallowing hard.

She met me at the door, still in silk hose, but this time she wore a dress with a modest bit of decolletage. The entire room smelled of perfume. Though none of this was for me, I was almost faint from the effect. "Ah, Bill, is it? The lieutenant tell me you will be coming. Please come in."

I set my towel and soap down near the door and stumbled awkwardly to the couch she gestured to. There was a portrait of her on the wall, and I knew something more about her from seeing that. It was a quality portrait, like a John Singer-Sargent, expensive—the kind of art only millionaires usually have. I wondered how an art major like me could have missed seeing that before and then fallen on his face over a bathtub. Priorities of war, I guessed.

Sitting uneasily on the edge of the couch, I said, "Your husband, he's in the French Army?"

"Ah, no, Bill. He is in Strasbourg," she said. "But let me get you the cognac, or if you prefer, a glass of wine." Her accent charmed me. She called Strasbourg "Stras-boo" and me "Beel."

"No, thank you. But I might like something after I bathe."

"Yes. When do you think your officer will be here?"

"He said ten o'clock." I was already out of conversation, so I groped. "Were you born here in Barr, madame?"

"Please, call me Chantelle. I am born in Paree. My family name is Chauvin. I am marry to Georg Schumann. He is Alsatian. It is since the war we are marry. He make the barrel for the wine. Now, you wish to take the bath?"

She ran the tub for me and chattered all the while, as though I was the one she wanted to charm. I didn't mind at all. "I have make the water hot for an hour," she said. "Have a good bath."

The water was a foot and a half deep, and I soaked scrunched down in it for ten minutes or so. My hands were all wrinkled up when I was through, but the water was the color of pottery clay. I ran the water out and sloshed more water around to get out the dirty grime, so I wouldn't be embarrassed when she saw her fancy tub.

She surprised me by rapping on the door. "Bill, would you like me to dry your back? I have more towels."

Wow! What was the right thing to say? I was such a skinny guy, I hated to have a beautiful woman see me naked. On the other hand, the gesture was so sexy, I longed to say yes, so that's what I said.

By the time she came into the bathroom with me, I was beginning to show my excitement, so I pulled my wet towel around myself.

"Keep your back turned," she said. "I promise not to look." She rubbed vigorously, and I thought I heard a giggle, but I kept myself under control. My behavior was not something I intended to tell the guys later. My imagination and lack of experience wouldn't permit me to think of what I could do in case she wanted me to take advantages, and I hated it.

She left me to finish drying myself, and she succeeded in convincing me she had intended no hanky-panky, but I was wishing she had.

Once more seated in her living room, it occurred to me that we seemed to be all alone here. When she brought me the glass of cognac, she had read my mind. "I wish to be alone with Kenny, your officer," she said, "so Lisle, my maid, has taken my baby to spend the night with her sister."

I was jealous of Rebman again. The implications were clear. I was not used to females being so open about things, especially with strangers.

"You and your lieutenant are good friends, I think," she said. "Are officers and soldiers like this in your army—good friends like this?"

"No, but Lieutenant Rebman is not an ordinary officer."

"Ah! This I see. Also I think, *peut-être*, you are not the ordinary soldier."

This flattery had me puffed up like a pigeon. I thought then that Chantelle Chauvin was the most exciting woman I had ever met.

During the next hour, Chantelle taught me about cognac. I asked why such a small amount was served in such a large glass, so she showed me things about snifter glasses. I learned to roll the liquid around and let some of it evaporate on the sides of the glass, then smell deeply to increase pleasure . . . and intoxication. She taught me to say "feen" (spelled *fine*) when asking for the best cognac. "Champagne fine is the best, Bill. And Armagnac is good too, but it comes from a different region."

Sitting across from her, when I wasn't feasting on the sight of her fabulous legs, her lip-rouged mouth, and those liquid black eyes, I kept wondering what it would be like to kiss her. That lucky Kenny Rebman.

The two hours passed too soon. A rap on the door announced the arrival of Rebman. When I sighed, Chantelle giggled. She'd enjoyed charming me, and I sensed she'd often used her talent for charming men before—and from that experience, she must have been able to read my every thought.

I gathered my soap and towel and met Rebman at the door. He had a bottle with him—his whiskey ration. Coals to Newcastle . . . "You are in luck, sir," I said.

"I know. I can hardly wait to get in that tub." He winked. "Look, amigo, I think they're going to march order in the morning, so come and get me, even if it's at four or five."

Back at the billet Tonto had chosen for us, I discovered we were mere feet away from number-one gun, which was right next to the window of the kitchen where I was to sleep. The guns fired all night, but I slept through it. They had been firing charge two when I went to sleep, and by morning, they had upped the charge to seven and blown in the kitchen windows. I woke up covered with glass.

The first sergeant woke us at five o'clock. "March order, you guys. Get your butts in gear and you'll have time for a hot breakfast. Anyone know where Lieutenant Rebman's at?"

"I'll get him," I said.

The sergeant gave me a sly smile. "I just bet you will. How was that bathtub?"

Rebman was too much of a gentleman to give me any information on what happened at the apartment, but he did say he wished she would divorce her husband. Later he told me, "I know it makes me some kind of fool, but I actually fell head-over-heels for her. I'll probably spend years forgetting her, but that's the best I can do. Damn war."

On the motor march that day, I began to suspect that Chantelle wasn't totally what she seemed. She was all dolled up and waiting for us, perhaps looking for any handsome American officer with whom to cuckold her husband. Her husband conveniently got himself behind the German lines, and the community in Barr where they lived had quite a few German nationals—birds of a feather, perhaps? I never discussed my thoughts with Rebman. The woman was so gifted with charm and good looks that even to cast a suspicion that his night of love was just a sordid one-nighter with the wife (or paramour?) of an Alsatian Nazi would weaken our friendship.

Chapter 7

The quartering party that returned to Barr was emotional again. They brought a story of another quartering party in the battalion, where a sergeant jumped into a foxhole when some shells came in and got blown up by a booby trap. "Never use Kraut fox holes," the captain said.

There were many red alerts that day, so Ingraham, our battery's antiaircraft gunner, was told to be ready.

We stopped for the night near a small barn at the center of a hayfield. Who owned the barn was a mystery. There was hay inside, but no farmhouse was in sight. We had spent most of the day traveling and now were near Colmar, where, according to *Stars and Stripes*, our Seventh Army teammates, the First French Army, had its hands full.

An antiaircraft battery moved in across the road, so Frank and I went over there to see if the ack-ack men we met in St. Martin were among them. These men had never been to Italy, and though they wore Seventh Army patches like our friends, they were a unit permanently attached to the 103rd Division. Our friends were not there.

Frank and I went to the far end of the field and pitched a tent. A week of staying in a house or barn several nights, made sleeping on the ground again seem like a giant setback. In truth, though during training we never expected such a thing, once given this small luxury for a few nights, we were ticked off at having to endure anything less.

At six the next morning, the first sergeant traveled all the way across that field to wake us. In northern France at that time of the year, it was two hours before daylight. At noon we were still sitting there, though our trucks had been lined up for six hours—typical of the army.

The Signal Section had taken over the barn, and I used the wire truck's side-view mirror for shaving, with my steel helmet as a wash basin. I had just begun when I heard the call to chow. I cursed, because I didn't want to leave while my water was still hot. I saw the men going past, rattling their mess kits, lining up at the chow truck only a few yards past the barn door.

A racket outside the barn sounded like giant tanks coming down the road, so I started toward the door to see them. Tracer bullets bouncing on the pavement stopped me.

Planes flying only ten feet off the ground flashed past, and I caught sight of the iron cross on the sides. Me 109s! Two of them!

I dove for the ground and crawled toward the truck to get under. Someone beat me there, and I panicked, certain that more planes would strafe the barn. A rash of shouting came from out on the road, and I was sure there must be dead and dying everywhere. I wanted to remain away until someone else took care of the dirty work I knew was out there, but I got up and went out just the same.

Guys ran in every direction, yelling, "Medic! Medic!"

Trying to find wounded, looking in circles, I saw only running men. The captain was in the middle. "Get clear of the road!" he shouted. "those planes will be back any second."

I ran to our trailer and removed the tarp—I wanted that M-1. We had been taught to shoot small arms at planes; a single bullet could bring down a Messerschmitt, our training films told us.

Joe the medic soon found the only wounded man in the battery—Byron Krump, the tallest and gentlest cannoneer, the guy I always played catch with. Joe took a good look at the wound on Krump's right forearm. "That's my pitchin' ahm," Krump said. "You think I can still throw, Joe?"

"Shee," Joe said, "that ain't nothin' but a scratch. You got a piece of bullet in there, a fragrunt. You hardly bleedin'. We got to get ever'body off this road soon's I wrap this."

But Cajun Joe's work was not over when Krump's arm was wrapped. Arvid Johnson, the mess sergeant, claimed he had a bullet crease on his right arm. Joe dismissed him. "Hell, Sarge," Joe said, "you sure that ain't a burn from the stove?"

Johnson swore he hadn't touched the stove, but Cajun didn't have time for Band-Aid wounds. "Medic! Medic!" was being called across the road in the antiaircraft battery. One of the ack-ack men had been hit in the knee. It was serious.

Joe gave him a shot of morphine and bound the leg tightly. A jeep from the battalion medics arrived and took Krump and the ack-ack man away. Cajun said, "'At ole boy gonna lose that leg. He took a .40-caliber bullet right through the kneecap."

We heard planes diving and guns chattering from a few miles away to the north. A Messerschmitt, visible on the horizon, flew through puffs of antiaircraft fire, before a second plane appeared.

Only one of those enemy planes flew off from that strafing. We watched unbelieving as one of the planes nosed over and dove to the ground, followed by a flash and a huge plume of rising black smoke. A German pilot, less than five miles away, was burning to a cinder and I should have felt good about it but couldn't. I wasn't going to let anything about this war feel good—that pilot might have been a nice guy who hated Hitler . . . Just the same, I would have liked to have been the guy who shot him down.

Arvid Johnson was exonerated—a bullet was found in the bean pot, probably the same bullet that creased his arm as he jumped down from the truck. It really didn't matter to Cajun; he'd have put the mess sergeant in for a Purple Heart anyway.

When an hour passed and the planes did not reappear, the men began walking around through the truck column and doing an assessment of damage. We were amazed at how lucky we'd been. At least fifty guys were already in the chow line when the planes swooped in without warning, yet only Krump and the ack-ack guy got hit—unless you counted Arvid. Besides the bullet in the bean pot, the planes flattened all four tires on the maintenance truck. Had they hit just one of the gasoline cans in that truck, the whole column would have been set afire.

Our one full-time .50-caliber machine gunner, Ingraham, had fired at the planes, but a single bullet was all that left his gun before it jammed. It turned out that Ingraham's belt had been packed backward at the factory in Flint, Michigan. Either it was an act of sabotage or the officer in charge of inspection at that factory was inept. Ingraham's wasn't the only machine gun in the battery; four other trucks had .50s mounted on them— all with belts packed correctly—but they were unmanned at the time.

The most damage done by the strafing was in morale. Every one of us was jittery the remainder of the day. We had received the march order at six that morning, but we were still just sitting there at three that afternoon. Battery B had been an easy target for a strafing all day.

The weather began getting cold as we moved back into the rolling foothills of the Vosges, but all vehicles had the tops down, with all eyes fastened on the sky. Winter had stayed away since that first night in November, but now the air felt like approaching snow.

The column turned into taller hills just after dark, and we ran with only blackout lights because we thought we were still close to the front, though we had heard no small-arms or artillery fire all day.

After an hour of darkness, the truck ahead of us stopped and the driver came back. "I've lost the column, Lieutenant," he told Ruotolo. "they must have turned away and I missed them."

Ruotolo got out and, with Sergeant Camden, went up to a house in a square of homes enclosed by fences, as in many French villages. All of them had closed blinds over the windows. The French residents of the house let them in, and then a whole truckload of men went in behind them. Before Lawrence or I could get there, they closed the door; they wanted no more inside, so we stayed in the jeep.

A low-flying plane droned above us, and we thought it might be "Bedcheck Charlie," our nightly visitor, on his surveillance flight, but the engine didn't sound right. It most certainly wasn't one of ours—the piston beats were too slow. Rocky, Frank, and I were alarmed when the plane moved away and then returned and continued to circle. The ack-ack guys, who'd been in Italy, had told us about antipersonnel bombs the Luftwaffe dropped near Anzio that scattered small grenades, and we wanted no part of them.

At first we tried to get into the house where the lieutenant and sergeant were, but only Rockwell was successful. After trying most of the other houses in the village without success, Frank and I went to a church we'd seen when the moon was still out, but we found it was locked. We circled it, trying to find the back entrance or the priest's house, but we found no place to get in, and the plane continued circling above us. My heartbeats must have reached 200 a minute.

"If he drops an antipersonnel bomb," Frank said, "we got to get somewhere away from the street."

"But where?" As I spoke, there was a loud pop, and a flare lit the sky. "He's lighting the place up," I said. "Let's put the church between us and the motor column."

We ran around the church and into a nearby woods, just as the plane seemed to move away. We waited in the woods for several minutes until the engine noises faded.

The next day, we learned what it was. The plane was a lost RAF bomber seeking bearings, and the flare must have worked.

We located the battery in a tiny village up in the hills. The guys in the Signal Section were sleeping in a barn and were excited by the news they had for us: just before dark, and before the column lost us, Olson stood up in the back of his truck, took his helmet off, and allowed a large overhanging tree limb to knock him unconscious. Our part of the column got lost because Olson's truck turned onto a side road to attend to him, and the trucks ahead of and behind it didn't know about it. When he didn't wake up, his truck—still pulling

a howitzer—went back to where Lt. "Buster" Whidden had
seen an evacuation hospital.

Battalion reported that he had a fractured skull but was
going to live. It was, without question, self-immolation. They
were sure he was trying to get out of combat, not attempting
suicide. Olson finally revealed why he wanted to be the radio
repairman so badly: someone must have told him it was a safe
job—as close to noncombat as you could get. He had planned
to be a coward before he left home. The captain received one
more lesson in how poor he was at judging character.

This village was so far back from the front that we could
barely hear artillery, and the flashes in the night sky were the
only times we saw signs of battle. We were right where the Luftwaffe wanted us, however, and they strafed us all of the four
days we spent there. Luckily they did no damage.

Not having been in the chow line when the Me 109s
strafed the first time, I was not as terrorized by it as those who
were. Olson was not the only guy in the battery who was scared
enough to want to hurt himself. Riley, a gunner corporal, shot
himself in the foot the second day we were strafed. He tried to
pretend it was an accident, but nobody believed him. Then
our battery idiot, Gus Crisantheos, while on guard duty on a
dark night, called, "Halt!" three times and, getting no answer,
fired four shots at what he thought was an intruder. It turned
out his intruder was a blanket hanging on a line and blown by
the wind. All four shots missed—from seven yards! This was
the second time Gus's weapon was discharged; the other time
was by accident because he had a round in the chamber and
the safety turned off. The captain was furious with him and
threatened to take away his ammunition if it happened again.

Chapter 8

During the time we spent in that small village, we were twenty or more miles behind the front lines. The entire combat team that included our battalion was in division reserve, preparing us for being the point in the Seventh Army's attack on the border. We were to be the first troops from the VI Corps to enter Germany. Ruotolo told us this on the way up to join the 2nd Battalion of the 411th Regiment.

Rocky drove us to a small city, Neiderbronn. We went into a nice apartment house at the edge of town. Ruotolo slept in the only bedroom, and Frank Lawrence and I slept on the floor in the living room. There was a bathtub, so we all— except Rockwell, of course—had a bath. Rocky insisted he had to sleep in the jeep. We spent the following day in the apartment while waiting for the battalion to arrive. Frank and I wrote at least ten letters, and Rocky, outside in the jeep, reread some of his romance magazines.

After dark, the infantry battalion lined up to begin their attack, right outside the apartment. We were introduced to Lt. Col. William Kasper, who was going to lead us. "We know nothing about these woods we are going into," he told his men. "Keep noise to a minimum, and hold your hand against the back of the guy ahead of you. I don't think there will be any moonlight to see by."

This battalion had more than 200 riflemen in three companies, and about 300 men in all, so our column was long, and it was ten minutes or so before we fell in at the tail end. There was no path at first; we simply followed a small trail made by the men in the lead. The terrain sometimes changed suddenly, and we had to slide down a slope or climb one, so we often lost touch with the back of the person ahead of us but always remade contact immediately.

Outside of the interval in the vineyard in Barr, we had never been in the real role of forward observers before, even in training. I was excited. The dangers we were about to face were necessary, not like one of Tonto's capers when he tried to make himself a hero.

Colonel Kasper's orders were passed back in whispers from man to man. At one time the message was "Keep absolute silence; we may be behind enemy lines." I pictured us being cut off—a lost battalion, like in World War I. I wasn't terrorized the way I was under a strafing or when having to scrunch down and await the end of a shelling. This seemed adventurous. I did feel the chill of the night air more acutely, however.

After sliding down one of the slopes, I fell on my back and almost lost my radio from the canvas strap. I thought I heard the men go to the right. Frank was behind me and fell into me, so the two of us had to regroup. When we had our equipment all together, I started to the right, with Frank's hand on my back. We held our heavy radios and battery packs up and trotted. When I didn't hear the crunch of footsteps ahead of me after thirty seconds, I stopped and whispered, "I think they must have gone the other way."

Frank now was in front, and we pulled our radio and battery pack up again and broke into a trot to the left After five minutes, we couldn't find the column, so we retraced our steps. Now I began to panic. If we truly were behind enemy lines, we could well run right into a German sentry and get shot or captured. But we kept trotting, though the radios were getting heavier, and we were running out of breath.

"Who goes there?" A sentry! Ours! Thank God! Ruotolo realized we were missing and sent a guy back to find us. They were taking a break while waiting for us.

We came out of the forest after an hour or two, and the moon came out about the same time. We could see where we were going for a change. The terrain was hilly and relatively treeless. We were in farmland, and we located a road going from north to south, so we now were on the right track on the colonel's map. All of us breathed sighs of relief.

We hiked until three in the morning, by which time that blister where my radio rubbed broke, and the tear in the thigh of my pants was four inches long. I have no idea where our planned objective was, but we were bushed, and Colonel Kasper knew it.

We found a house and barn on the road, and the colonel saw it as a place for us to spend the rest of the night. Most of the battalion slept in the hayloft of the barn, and we forward observers got to stay in the house, sleeping on the floor with a couple dozen majors, captains, and lieutenants. Even the colonel slept on the floor, being too much of a gentleman to chase the French family out of their rooms. I realized I was finally seeing a *real* officer. Infantry officers were superior to artillery officers, I was beginning to believe.

All the battalion's hard work that night turned out to be wasted: in the morning we slept until nine, and a column of trucks was passing the house when we looked out the window.

We spent another day trying to get ahead of the rear eche-lon. The following day, we found the front lines again. A run-ner from Regiment brought a fresh set of orders for the colonel.

During the day, the infantry cannon company forward observer had kept close to us. He was Sergeant Tucker, who had been one of Battery B's cadre in Louisiana, and I sus-pected he was one of the guys who robbed me. He was a tall, nineteen-year-old, prewar veteran then, and he strutted inso-lently around us recruits. I had disliked him thoroughly. Funny how being together in an attack can change things: Tucker and I became close friends that day, and we never looked back. We became brothers.

Just before dark, the battalion reached an empty *gasthaus*, a large country inn with room for the entire battalion, and the colonel decided this would be a perfect stop for the night.

Tucker, Frank, and I stood around, smoking and talking outside the inn, getting rested from the ordeal of hauling that fifty-pound radio and twenty-five-pound battery pack. Tucker, who was only carrying a one-pound walkie-talkie, had helped by alternating with Frank and me. We heard an engine coming down the road and looked around for a sentry to stop what sounded like an approaching motorcycle. The motorcycle was upon us before we saw any help.

The rider was a Kraut soldier, who simply pulled up in front of us and threw up his hands, though we were all unarmed. He was entirely too happy to see us for me to believe he was anything but a German deserter. When the colonel arrived with an interpreter, the Kraut said he was bringing dispatches to his headquarters, which had been quartered here the previous night. Having the dispatches fall into our hands so easily convinced everyone that this was some kind of ruse. We gave the prisoner a couple of cigarettes, and he smiled and thanked us but seemed bored.

Large as the auberge was, we had far too many men for the number of beds. Men slept in the halls, in the lobby, on the floors in the rooms, and some slept as Tucker, Lawrence, and I did—crosswise on a bed, our legs hanging over the side, our backpacks useful as pillows.

In the morning, we woke to find that hard rain had fallen all night, and we set out cross-country in a light rain, expecting to encounter the enemy shortly. One incident that happened soon after we left the inn that day told me more about Colonel Kasper.

We came to the edge of a woods and saw a valley we had to cross to get to another woods. The colonel ordered all men to fix bayonets, and a company CO asked him if he expected to stage a bayonet attack. "Hell, no," he said. 'the sun's out, and I want the Boche, if they're over there, to see the glint. When the sun hits those bayonets, it might take a lot of fight out of them. I'd rather they run than stand and fight." Kasper's attitude was a big contrast to the gung-ho stuff I heard from artillery officers like Major Thompson.

We entered the woods without a fight and climbed to the top of a hill deep in the forest. Mountains were visible to our north through the trees. The colonel told everyone to dig in because we had some waiting to do. The rain the night before had thoroughly soaked the ground, and when we dug, our holes filled with water. Bailing with our steel helmets didn't work. Nevertheless, the infantrymen—men who were used to digging and knew the benefits of good foxholes—continued digging and bailing. After two hours, no one had a hole he could get into without taking a cold, wet, muddy bath.

The enemy must have been able to observe us from over in those mountains, because we got medium artillery shelling just before noon. A man lying only a few feet from me was wounded in the thigh, and medics bravely ran to him, even while the shells were still whistling in. Soon more men got hit, and the morale in that woods was rapidly going to pieces. Why were we staying there?

The worst wound suffered near me was by one poor guy who got hit in the same part of his anatomy as did the protagonist in one of Hemingway's early novels: he lost his manhood. The medics' aid men turned white over that one.

During the shelling, Colonel Kasper, when he wasn't lying facedown, was pacing. It was not his decision to remain there. Finally, when the expected signal by radio was hours late, Kasper sent a runner into Climbach, the town we were to attack.

The runner was back in less than half an hour: the battle for Climbach was over. The town was already occupied by the other part of our pincers movement. Kasper was disgusted.

We entered Climbach, and at the center of the town we met men loading four two-and-a-half-ton trucks with the bodies of dead black soldiers, and an equal load of dead Germans. They had been neatly lined up on canvas on the sidewalks. Their arms and legs jutted grotesquely over the tailgates and sides of the trucks. We knew of no black infantry in the Seventh Army, and no black troops other than the 614th Anti-Tank Destroyer Battalion. So where did these black infantrymen come from?

Ruotolo sent for Rockwell to come get us in the jeep, and we went east of the town to join our battery. It was located in large four-foot-thick concrete bunkers, part of the Maginot Line, part of the reason for the battle.

In as much as I was not actually a witness to what happened that day at Climbach, I will try to tell it as I understood it. The Germans had occupied these bunkers to prevent the entrance of troops from the east. The two companies of the 2nd Battalion, with which we spent the day, were supposed to close in on these bunkers from the west at the same time that 1st Battalion troops attacked from the east—with help from the two tanks. This was Task Force Blackshear, organized by Colonel Yeuell, the 411th Regiment CO. The story goes, he had asked Seventh Army for a company of tanks to attack the Maginot bunkers, but they gave him only the two.

Yeuell, it was rumored, had made a bet, while playing cards and drinking with some other brass, that his would be the first Seventh Army troops to cross the border into Germany. With only two tanks to bring direct fire onto the thick concrete of the fortifications, he decided to use the antitank guns of the 614th. These were towed guns that had to be pulled into position by trucks and half-tracks. This meant that in order to get direct fire, the antitank cannoneers would be visible to the Germans in the bunkers while they uncoupled the guns and dug in the spades of their 5,000-pound antitank cannons before firing them—a very dangerous situation. Major Blackshear, designer of the assault, felt that the two tanks up on the road, level with the bunkers, could keep the Germans busy enough to allow the towed guns in the valley to work.

The all-out effort and extreme bravery of the black soldiers saved the shaky scheme from disaster. The ten-man crews of the 1st Platoon of Charlie Company's four 105-millimeter guns—in mud up to the axles—immediately drew heavy fire from German 88s on a hill above the bunkers. Two of the 614th's guns were quickly knocked out, then a third, but the fourth gun kept firing until it was nearly out of ammunition, and a brave truck driver carried ammunition into the muddy valley until he bogged down twenty yards short of the last gun firing. The tank destroyer (TD) men kept firing until the infantry troops on the flanks of the bunkers finally chased the remaining Germans out. The Germans had a company of riflemen in the woods behind the meadow who attacked the anti-tank guns, and the 614th soldiers, though armed only with carbines and automatic pistols, were up to repulsing them. They killed more than they lost, but the death count was large for both.

Colonel Kasper, a West Point man, explained some of it to me. The refusal of Seventh Army to send a company of tanks turned out to be lucky for the task force, Kasper believed. The German commander of the forces defending the fortifications fully expected tanks. Furthermore, he anticipated that they would move into a hayfield opposite the bunker, so he positioned a platoon of infantry in the forest behind the field. Foot soldiers getting behind tanks have a big advantage: they can rush the tanks and climb atop them to throw grenades in the slots undetected by the tankers until it's too late. The Molotov cocktails used in Russia, were a good example of this. But the unexpected towed guns, with the soldiers on foot carrying automatic weapons, were too much for the German platoon. The grit of those black men also surprised the Krauts. Hitler and his henchmen had conditioned their soldiers to feel superior in courage to non-Teutonic peoples, so when they attacked, they expected the black antitankers to run or surrender. Colonel Yeuell and Major Blackshear went in like fools and came out like geniuses (my opinion, not Colonel Kasper's).

One known hero of the battle was a half-track driver. As the Germans rushed him from behind, he turned in his seat and mowed them down with his .40-caliber "grease gun." He killed eight.

Another story, which was never confirmed, involved our Captain Pultz. Pultz was sent on the task force after he volunteered for the job. He rode down the road on a tank, with a radioman from headquarters who also volunteered. They were to call for artillery as soon as the firing began near the bunkers. Supposedly, when the firing began, Pultz got off the tank, then ran and hid in a shack a quarter mile to the rear of the conflict. For whatever he actually did, he was given a Bronze Star Medal.

After the war, Charlie Company of the 614th got the Presidential Unit Citation, and eventually, in the nineties, a Major Thomas from Detroit was awarded a Medal of Honor posthumously.

Chapter 9

After visiting with the battery, Ruotolo took us back into Climbach, and we went to a house and got a room. We wrote letters the rest of the day. I had to write thank-you letters to a bunch of my mother's lady friends who sent me a dozen fruitcakes for Christmas.

You had to write to people who wanted to send you something, telling them you wanted whatever it was they wanted to send. Then they could show your letter to the postmaster and be allowed to send their gifts.

Mom taught a bunch of middle-age ladies how to make real old New England hooked rugs, and she probably talked about me at the rug-hooking sessions, so those gals all wanted to send me something. I kept Mom happy by requesting fruitcakes, which I hated. The arrival of all those cakes reminded me how close we were getting to Christmas. The weather was not at all wintry, but it was December 17 when we got to the Franco-German border.

Tonto told us we were going to sleep half a mile from Germany that night. I was restless, thinking the fighting would be ferocious from now on. I was sure Hitler would command his troops to fight to the death. In the weeks since York's death, I had let go of my certainty that I was going to die, but that night, on December 17 at the German border, depression returned: I expected to die again.

Next morning, we overslept and had to skip breakfast. The 2nd Battalion had already headed up the road toward Germany. We ran to catch up, only to find they were less than a quarter mile away from town. The soldiers, those not lying prone along the roadside, were in a house at the top of a slope. Colonel Kasper was inside, so we went in too.

It was a bunker, made to look like a house. The walls were four-foot-thick steel-reinforced concrete, and every window was actually a one-and-a-half-inch steel plate. This was part of the Maginot Line, a fake farmhouse that was built to serve as a bunker in war and an immigration station in peacetime. The colonel was on the second floor peeking out through the slits in the steel window plates, and he seemed upset.

Frank, Tucker, and I looked out the slits and saw what had Kasper so disturbed—two dead GIs. They were scouts, the two riflemen who walked 10 yards apart, 100 yards ahead of the column. I thought it was chillingly unfair to assign men to go ahead to near-certain death, treating humans like penguins that get pushed off the ice to see if killer whales are in the water. We were told that scouts have a ten-second life span when the shooting starts. How uncivilized the U.S. Army is, I thought, to allow such a suicidal strategy.

Tonto wanted to immediately call for artillery fire on whatever was holding up the advance. Kasper agreed. "The Boche have the same kind of building over there we have here," he said. "This place is almost impervious to shells. It has a steel roof. If you can't hit that house, there are troops in trenches over there on both sides of the road."

We conducted fire for half an hour, and according to Tonto, we hit both the house and the trenches.

Kasper told his company commanders to try to advance again. We watched as several men were immediately cut down.

Kasper had to call a halt to the advance, and Tonto begged to fire more artillery. This time, when I turned on my radio, I heard a German oompah-pah street band playing military marches: we were being jammed. All communication with Fire Direction Center was out. Forward observers and field artillery suddenly became useless, so Kasper—knowing that tanks had been used the day previous—sent a runner into Climbach asking for a tank.

While we were waiting, several soldiers came in through the back door as we stood smoking on the stoop. Tracer bullets let us know the Krauts wanted no one to come along that road. Then a lone soldier came and fell on the road right beside the stoop.

I thought he had been hit by the tracer fire, but a rifleman beside me knew the guy and hollered at him. "Hey, John, come in here where you're safe." John moved but didn't respond.

"Come on, you don't need to get up; just crawl in here," his friend urged. John looked up and choked out, "I'm scared!"

Another infantryman helped the rescuer, and together they half dragged the poor man down to the basement, where Colonel Kasper was having a conference with his company commanders. The badly frightened soldier produced gurgling sounds in an attempt to cry, his sobbing becoming spasms.

Kasper left his captains and put his arm around the boy. "It's okay, son," he said. "You're safe here. Do you smoke?"

The boy gurgled an affirmative.

"Give him a cigarette, somebody."

The cigarette didn't relieve the guy's choking, and with all the other guys in that cellar bug-eyed with sympathetic pain, the colonel asked two medics to take the shell-shocked guy back into Climbach to an aid station. "This man needs hospitalization," Kasper said. "Be sure and tell them I said so." He then gave the terrorized soldier another hug. "You'll be okay, son. God bless you."

After the boy was gone, Kasper asked, "You men who know that soldier . . . has he done that before?"

"Yes, sir," a doughboy said, "he does it any time a shell comes near us."

"Has he been sent to an evacuation hospital before?"

"Yes, sir. They just keep sending him back."

"Damn it, that's disgraceful. That man isn't a coward. He should never have been put in infantry. He can never do this stuff. He endangers us all, and he might have to go to a mental hospital. He could even lose his mind completely if they keep sending him back."

I tried to imagine how Major Thompson would have acted in the same situation. Colonel Kasper treated that frightened soldier with intelligence instead of posturing. I was not surprised when I learned that Kasper was a West Pointer.

The tank arrived, and Kasper directed the tank commander to put a round into every room in that house. The tank rolled to the top of the ridge and fired a number of rounds into the house-bunker. Yellow-brown dust exploded from the walls. I was watching through a slit in the steel, and I saw four or five men run from the side of the building.

The tank backed down the slope after a German 105 shell burst a few feet from it. Colonel Kasper then ordered the battalion to move forward.

Machine-gun fire erupted from the trench, and the men advancing were quickly pinned to the ground. Kasper had the tank come back atop the ridge and fire its .30-caliber machine gun at the trenches.

The tank delivered a withering five minutes of almost continuous fire at the trenches. It then backed up, and Kasper told his captains to wait and see if some of the men still alive over there decided to surrender. A lone figure climbed from the trench, held his hands atop his helmet, and staggered toward us.

The new prisoner turned out to be an old man, shuddering with fear as he dug a safe-conduct pass from a cuff all German soldiers had on their sleeves.

All resistance was gone from across that field. When we got to the trenches, we saw four or five dead German soldiers, a testament to the power of a tank against foot soldiers—even those dug in.

We left the road and began following a well-worn footpath into the woods. Two newsmen joined us as we came to a narrow stream where the entire column was waiting for Colonel Kasper to order them to jump across. The reporter and cameraman from the International News Service were there to photograph the first troops from the Seventh Army to cross that stream—the official border of France and Germany. I found out later that we beat the 45th Division by half an hour.

An hour later, we entered Bobenthal, our first sight of an occupied village in Germany. Towering over that town were the Hardt Mountains (sometimes spelled Haardt). It was a tiny burg, with a single onion-domed church and about fifty houses, most of them on the south side of the Lauter River. The Lauter was swift and about seventy feet across—too wide to jump and, though shallow, too deep to wade.

The enemy hadn't bothered to blow up the little bridge, so we crossed it, just as an old man with a shaggy mustache came down the road flicking a twig at two cows. I wondered whether he was a Nazi. He reminded me of Gramps, my farmer grandfather in West Brookfield, Massachusetts.

The Hardt are a small range, covering about fifty square miles, and they are not tall—in altitude ranging from 1,000 to 1,500 feet—but they are extremely steep. The Nazis found that steepness good for their Siegfried Line defenses and built concrete bunkers atop and around these mountains.

We settled into a house beside the bridge for the rest of that first afternoon to write letters and then spend the night. There was not a stick of furniture, a rug, a stove, or anything else to show that anyone ever lived there. We learned later that two-thirds of the people of Bobenthal fled to keep the German lines between themselves and their invaders.

Ruotolo was very excited by the prospects of heroic deeds we would need to perform the following day. When Ruotolo was in such a mood, Frank and I shuddered; nevertheless, we brought in our bedrolls and slept on the floor in that house by the bridge. Because there were no people in the house, Rocky came in too.

In the morning, we set out to catch the battalion before daylight. We found the men lined up on a road a mile north of Bobenthal. They looked nervous as they were being instructed by Colonel Kasper at the foot of a mountain.

He told them that today was going to be the most important day the 103rd Division had faced yet and could open the way to a quick conquest of Germany. This battalion was important to the division, because we were going to attack a bunker dug into a hillside on a flattop mountain called Hill 426.

"We have to conquer that bunker," he told them. "One way we *can't* do it, is to move across that open field . . . they'd cut us to ribbons. Company G is going to move around the side of the mountain from the left, and Company E is going around the right. Fox Company will be in reserve down here. When we need 'em, we'll call 'em up."

He wanted his forward observers to be right behind the first platoon. The path up that mountain was a series of steps. Though they were formed from slabs of rock and appeared almost natural, the Germans had made them—not so much to allow us to get up there so they could kill us, as to allow their own troops to get up or down on the same day. We had to climb those steps, one at a time. We'd walk up steps six inches high and shinny up others that were as much as two feet high. That day, those steps made mountain climbing only a tiny bit easier than scaling a sheer rock cliff. For Frank and me, carrying radios and battery packs on canvas straps, it was torture and had our thighs bleeding. The battalion took at least two hours going up and rested often. The December temperature was in the fifties, so we sweated quarts.

The enemy had plenty of time to zero in on the top of the steps where we had to climb out. Soon after the first men in the column got to the top, mortar shells whizzed down past us to explode in the valley below or on the mountain behind us. We knew the first men up were having shells land right on top of them.

Colonel Kasper wisely assigned some of our medics to go up near the front, instead of keeping them at the rear. Soon they passed us taking wounded down the steps.

We forward observers went up right behind the colonel and a company commander. A soldier a few steps behind us used the term "Jerry," and Kasper stopped and looked back at that man. "They are not Fritz or Heinie or Jerry, soldier. Nazis are not comical, not even Krauts. They are Boches—primitive barbarians. Killers! Criminals! Miserable, nasty, uncivilized brutes who dishonored the German nation by selecting a madman to lead them with his mindless anti-Semitism. Call them Boche or Nazi. Never say Jerry in my presence."

Before we got to the top, Ruotolo had already determined that this would be the ideal time to conduct fire with heavy artillery. The 240-millimeter howitzers were huge guns that could hurl 100-pound shells ten miles and produce a hole ten feet across. Fire Direction Center could get us such fire from Seventh Army artillery, and Ruotolo had been itching to call for fire from them since we landed in France. I sort of liked the idea myself, and Frank did too.

At the top, most of the infantrymen were on their way around the perimeter of the mountain when we set up our radio and called for fire from our 105s, for purposes of adjustment. It took ten rounds for us to see a burst near or atop the barely visible bunker half a mile away. Then Ruotolo called for 240s to fire on the same coordinates.

We waited twice as long as it took for fire from the 105s, but finally I was able to relay the message, "On the way."

We heard the shell going over, and it sounded much like our small artillery. The boom was much louder, but we saw no burst.

"What happened?" Lawrence asked.

"It went way over," Ruotolo said. "Let's wait and see if we see smoke." We waited a full half minute before a tiny wisp of black smoke rose off in the distance.

Ruotolo should have quit right there. Those big guns had too large a dispersion area to be able to adjust on a target smaller than a town or an airfield. They could kill anything within a quarter mile of the burst. But he was being Tonto again, so he called, "One thousand over."

We never did see that round; it burst near the road at the bottom of the mountain. Ruotolo was about to make another sensing, when a soldier came running. "Colonel Kasper says to cease fire," he said. "That last round nearly hit some of the men and jeeps in our motor pool parked down below."

Kasper, no longer believing Ruotolo could break open the bunker with artillery, had us fire a barrage of smoke shells to blind the men in the bunker, and then he attempted to attack them from the sides.

The attack was a bust. I can no longer remember the number of 2nd Battalion troops lost in that attack, but it was bad. Colonel Kasper was numbed by the failure.

The men of the battalion were all assembled on the south side of the mountain, where a wide ledge gave them a place to dig foxholes, and Kasper told them they could dig in.

An hour later, the colonel regretted that order. The men were busy with axes cutting down trees four to six inches thick. Two or three men worked together to cover the six-foot-deep holes they were digging into the side of the mountain. "I hate to see them working so hard getting things safe," he said. "When they get their underground city built, it'll be hard to move them back into attack mode."

Nevertheless, Colonel Kasper ordered the battalion to stage another attack on the bunker. When the attack had been shot to pieces, and the medics could not even go to men who lay screaming within several feet of the concrete fortress, Kasper had his head in his hands. The only way we were able to aid the attack was with a smoke barrage under which most of the survivors were able to retreat. We felt helpless. Ruotolo was getting even more restless.

I heard Captains Stagg and Greiner, both of them company commanders, volunteer to try to attack the bunker from behind. Kasper sent Greiner with a platoon—or what was left of one—to go down the mountain fifty feet, circle around behind the bunker, and climb up behind it. He was hoping they could then climb to the top, lean over, and drop grenades in the slots.

We waited for the men on that mission for an hour, then heard shooting, or what we thought was shooting. Half an hour later, Captain Greiner came out of the woods looking pale. The men following him looked at their feet and carried their rifles hanging down.

"We lost six men up there," Greiner said. "They rolled grenades down on us. Potato mashers without the handles. They expected such an attack and zeroed in the exact distance those cans had to roll before they blew. The guys who got to about six feet below the bunker had their heads blown apart."

Instead of feeling the frustration the battalion men and officers were feeling, the situation fired up Ruotolo's imagination. Having been around him for a month, Frank and I could see the wheels rolling—*here was his chance to do something to get his Medal of Honor.* "I still think 240s can blow that thing open," he said, his eyes blanked out, his voice dreamy. I think he knew Kasper would never allow it.

When Ruotolo gave us an option—stay on the mountain overnight or go back down to Bobenthal and sleep on the floor in the empty house by the river—even though we knew how torturous it was carrying the radio equipment up those huge stone steps, we favored going down. Mild as the days had been, this was December, and at that altitude, the night was certain to be frigid.

Rocky was waiting for us in the infantry motor pool at the foot of the mountain. He had been there when the 240 shell hit nearby, so he took us to see the hole that huge shell had made. It looked like a bomb crater, easily six feet deep and fifteen feet across; trees nearby had most of their branches blown off. "The guys down here were cursing you guys," Rocky said.

We found the battery east of Bobenthal, just across the Lauter. The Signal Section guys were sleeping in a man-made cave on the side of a mountain. I got my mail and found more fruitcakes sent by Mom's lady friends. Guys who liked fruitcakes quickly took them off my hands.

The battery had taken counterbattery fire early that day, and Captain Pultz quickly moved them to this place. It was the first time the battery ever got shelled by the enemy.

We went back to the bald-top mountain before daylight. A motor-pool sergeant introduced us to five totally green rookies. "Take these guys up," he said. "They're from a repple depot in England. Tell Captain Stagg of George Company they're his."

During the climb up, the rookies were silent, and Frank and I could see they were scared silly. We tried to think of something to say to reassure them but couldn't think of anything that wouldn't be a lie.

Chapter 10

The battalion was all dug in and under cover of big logs. It was just like the colonel had said the previous day: they now had a city of log dug-outs and seemed content to stay that way.

Major Thompson had come up from the artillery and had a telephone line brought up with him. What did he think he could do that Ruotolo hadn't already tried?

The newest thing the enemy was using was arching machine-gun fire. Periodically all that day, they sprayed tracer fire over the slope and in among the 2nd Battalion troops, like a gardener spraying water on his lawn. Getting out from under the safety of those logs was to invite sudden death, either from the machine guns or from the artillery fire the Krauts were regularly aiming at the trees. One doughboy had already died that day from a tree burst that sent shrapnel through the top of his steel helmet after penetrating his four-inch-thick log roof.

That day, I got one more example of what a jerk Major Thompson was. He went to the top of the rise to conduct artillery fire on the bunker. "Just because you couldn't do any damage to that thick concrete with 105s, Donn," he told Ruotolo, "doesn't mean heavier stuff can't do it. I'm going to use the 384th and see if that can't do it."

I never went to OCS or learned anything significant about artillery, but I knew the 384th's 155s weren't going to break up four-foot-thick concrete walls: Thompson was grandstanding. I enjoyed coming around him just to see him pretend he didn't recognize me. I knew my presence irritated him, and I enjoyed seeing a major jealous of a lowly PFC.

Thompson was applauded by Ruotolo as he adjusted fire on the bunker. The major had his own communication man, so I stayed down the hill and waited for the results of his fire mission.

When the major called, "Fire for effect," one of the rounds came in short, right into the 2nd Battalion's foxhole city. Thompson called, "Cease fire."

I had a phone and had spliced into Thompson's line. Major Hawkins at Fire Direction was defensive about the short. "Now, Tompy," he said, "are you sure that was one of our rounds? The Krauts have artillery too, you know."

Though by now he knew a man was killed, Thompson laughed about Hawkins's question. "Hawk," he said, "that round came from the same direction as the other ones. One gun somewhere in the battalion is firing short. Could be a defective gun, or maybe some gunner is not on his aiming stake. Have the execs back there check 'em."

Hawkins grumbled, and it was half an hour before the guns resumed the fire for effect, but when they did, no more rounds came in short. Fire Direction offered no explanation as to how they had improved. We had an enemy to defeat, but the upper tier of officers seemed more concerned with protecting their turf.

I liked Major Hawkins, but he was as capable of being silly as all the other officers at headquarters. In every house or tent where Fire Direction set up its switchboard, a home-made sign was hung over the entrance: "HawK's holE—YOu fINd 'eM— wE ShOOt 'eM." What really embarrassed me about that juvenile sign was the way so many of the officers in the battalion acted proud of it.

As I expected, Thompson and Ruotolo tried to pretend that the artillery had been effective, but when the infantry tried to rush the bunker after the mission, the results were the same as before—more casualties. I watched Ruotolo suck up to the major. Thompson was clearly insulting him just by being there, and the lieutenant had to pretend he wasn't aware of it.

Thompson fired another mission an hour later, and I was within hearing distance as he gloated over its success. "Listen,

Hawk, you ought to have seen this," he said on the phone. "I located a Kraut slit trench over on a mountain near here. They were all taking their morning dumps, and we caught 'em with their pants down! I think I saw one Kraut jump right in there with the crap. You'd have laughed your ass off."

I hated being in the same army with that guy.

Ruotolo had Frank Lawrence and me come up to the flat area within sight of the bunker, and I suspected he was trying to impress the major with his bravado. I immediately began to dig a foxhole under a tree just to the edge of the open field. The ground was soft, and I dug down three feet in half an hour. For some reason Frank didn't follow my lead; perhaps he was impressed with Ruotolo's bravado and wanted to be just as daring.

Because the digging was so easy, I decided to go down another foot—a decision that was about to save my life because of what happened next. Just as I completed my extra deep fox-hole, a beautiful German shepherd dog came running along the perimeter of the mountaintop, his tail wagging, his tongue hanging out in a doggie smile of friendliness. Wanting to pet him, I called, "Here, boy. Here, boy." He headed toward me but veered away when he was a few feet off.

Suddenly a young lieutenant saw the dog and yelled, "Shoot him! Shoot that dog! He's a spy dog from the bunker over there!"

I turned to see if he was talking to me. He was looking at two infantrymen. They stared at the officer, appearing as unready to follow that command as I was. The dog caught the tone of the officer's voice and broke into a trot, then into a sprint, heading directly for the woods. The lieutenant drew his .45 and fired.

The dog fell and rolled down the slope, yelping in pain, then scrambled to his feet. The lieutenant shot again.

The dog fell once more, screaming in terror as he got up and continued toward the enemy bunker. I instantly hated that lieutenant. Spy dog? My eye!

"I told you men to shoot," the lieutenant shouted at the two men, "and you deliberately disobeyed me. What the hell's wrong with you? Can't you see what that animal was doing? He was scouting our positions, so tonight he can lead a patrol over here."

I thought he was as full of shit as a Christmas turkey and just had a mean streak he needed to use.

I went thirty feet or so from my new foxhole to talk with Frank and Lieutenant Ruotolo. I was not at all surprised to hear Ruotolo support the lieutenant who shot the dog. "The Krauts could follow that dog over here and slit the throats of guys in the foxholes tonight," he said.

A shriek announced an incoming shell. We dove to the ground. The shell—which we quickly identified as German 105 artillery—landed halfway to where I had dug my hole. I then did a stupid thing: I ran to the hole and barely dove in ahead of a shell that exploded so close my feet could feel the percussion through my combat boots. Many soldiers died making that same dumb move.

I was lucky, but that deep foxhole later saved me.

Those first two or three shells were the German observer's adjustment rounds. In the next hour, I learned that the target of that enemy forward observer was my hole: I was the one he wanted to kill!

Shell after shell burst within yards of me. I was covered with dirt and certain the next one was going to come right into the hole with me. "*There are no atheists in foxholes,*" I thought. Was it a cliché?

God could have nothing to do with this stupid war if he was a just God, I decided. And if he was not *just*, then why did all those religious folks worship him?

After the first ten bursts or so, Ruotolo and Lawrence began yelling at me. I stood up to yell back at them, only to have the next shell burst even nearer than before. From that time on, I wanted them to stop the yelling.

One burst hit only a few feet away, and it nearly buried me. I felt a sharp pain in my knee and was sure I had been wounded. I saw no hole near the pain, so I scooped away hand-fuls of dirt and rolled up my pant leg. My knee was bleeding, but when I wiped the blood away, I found only a tiny pinprick. That last shell had sent a grain of sand with such force it pene-trated the thick wool of my trousers. The grain of sand hurt like a splinter of wood in the finger does.

The shelling on my foxhole lasted—with only short rests for reloading—a full hour. Midway through that hour, I realized why: to that German artillery observer, I was the guy who killed his dog, a dog probably loved and petted by an entire bunker.

That stupid, stupid lieutenant! Now I had to be punished for his stupidity.

Around noon, after half an hour had passed with no shelling, I looked up to see Frank Lawrence above my hole. "You okay?" he asked.

"Yeah," I said, "but I may be a little crazy. Get the hell in here. They aren't through yet. They want revenge for that dog."

Frank jumped in the hole with me. "You think this was all over the dog?"

"Why else fire at one foxhole, when there's a whole city of 'em just over the hill?"

"God! You're right. They think you did it!"

We left the hole forever half an hour later. Before we ran over the slope to the battalion, I inspected how close I came to death. My radio atop the hole had been ripped open at one corner, and the slender tree directly above me had a half-round groove one foot above my hole made by the side of a shell. Two inches to the right, and the fuse of that shell would have hit dead center on the tree and exploded into my head, instead of making a shell hole on the ground two feet away.

I never did go into my idea about the dog with Ruotolo—he was unlikely to believe it.

We went back down the mountain for the second time well before dark. I think Ruotolo knew I was shaken by my ordeal.

Halfway down, we heard a strange sound coming from the mountain next to us. A mule with a large burden on its back appeared on the side of the mountain, and Ruotolo knew why: "They're bringing up a mule-pack artillery unit to see if they can't get direct fire from old world war 75s to penetrate the bunker," he said.

If 240s couldn't do it, I thought, then how could little 75s do it? Maybe they hoped to be lucky and hit right on the observation slit. Good idea if it worked.

Soon a young lieutenant met us as he came up the slab rock steps. He was the officer in charge of the mule company. "The mule you just saw there was Sergeant Cora," he told us. "She's the best mule we got. Sharp as a razor, but stubborn as a mule, ha ha. She got away from Andrew, and he's got to catch up to her before she gives away what we're trying and they shoot a mortar at her."

Andrew appeared a few minutes later and yelled over to his officer. "She got spooked by a shell goin' over, sir."

"You just better get her before dark, or it's your black ass, Andrew . . . hear?" The lieutenant turned to us and said, "I raised that mule myself and I love her to pieces. Mules are sweeter than horses, and we race 'em back home in Oklahoma. Cora's made me a lot of money. I may have to go over there, if that damn Andrew can't catch her. She'll come to me sure."

There were more mules on the road at the bottom, and more black mule soldiers. I wondered why they were going up so late in the day.

We went back to the battery, and that's when I first felt the "high of survival." At one time, I couldn't stop laughing as I told the Signal Section about the shelling I took over that dog. What I was experiencing was close to delirium, and I tried to stop cackling but couldn't. Some of the guys looked scared by my jag.

I woke several times in the night and felt sick to my stomach and very depressed. In the morning, I was chipper again.

All of the emotions I felt then, I learned later, were common to soldiers, sailors, and airmen after close calls with death.

That morning, as we rode in the jeep toward the foot of the mountain, Ruotolo blurted out his plan for the day. "Guys," he said, "we may have to go on a suicide mission today."

I nudged Lawrence. "How?" Frank asked.

"I think we can crawl up to within fifty feet of that bunker and conduct fire with 240s."

I was speechless. The silliness of this plan was embarrassing. I could think of no ready answer. All I said was, "Count me out, Lieutenant."

In the days, and weeks, and years since, I have thought of hundreds of smart things I should have said to that childlike lieutenant. For example: "Only the 'suicide' part of it is sure to work, sir, but I doubt those 240s can hit you before the Krauts do."

But alas, I just sat there while Rocky sped up the jeep in terror; he took such stuff seriously. Frank apparently thought the idea of a suicide mission was so foolish he made no comment.

"Of course, I have to get Battalion's okay first," my Yale-freshman officer said, "and they probably won't give it. But we have to think of something. Do either of you guys have an idea?"

"Sure," I said. "We have an air force that could wipe out that concrete with one medium bomb. But the wisdom of the army is such that they'd rather bomb civilians in cities. So . . ." I knew Ruotolo was sensitive to criticism of the army, and my comment was meant to hurt his feelings a little: the army could do no wrong if you were a Tonto-Ruotolo.

At the bottom of the mountain, the officer who had sent the young guys up with us the previous day stopped us. "You hear what happened to those five repple depot guys you took up yesterday?"

"No, what?"

"Two of 'em got killed, another's wounded."

Atop the mountain, Colonel Kasper was uneasy. "We've got a stalemate here, and neither Division, nor Regiment, nor the

Seventh Army knows what to do. I could neutralize that bunker in minutes if I had a flame thrower. You think they'll give me one . . . ?"

Someone came up the mountain with copies of *Stars and Stripes*. The news was all about the big counterattack the Germans were staging up north in the Ardennes. By noon that day, the order came up to stop any more attacks on the bunker. We had to go to the aid of those troops up there.

The French First Army was going to relieve us, and the 103rd Division was going to move north. The 2nd Battalion had lost seventy of its riflemen and had not done what those men gave their lives for. To my knowledge the mule platoon had not fired a shot—and had not even found Cora.

Chapter 11

The artillery pulled out that afternoon. Tomorrow the infantry would also be leaving Germany: all so sad, after losing all those men getting there. Ruotolo, Frank, and I were being left behind to orient the French forward observer, who was to arrive in the morning.

That night we went to a *gasthaus* in among the mountains. There were no beds or furniture of any kind in the entire small hotel, but a medical unit had used the building and put army cots in the large lobby of the place. Frank and I were pleased to meet a medical major who was as nice a guy as Rebman. He got out his whiskey allotment and gave us each a shot before we turned in for the night.

In the morning, we had to climb the mountain again. The French lieutenant spoke good English but seemed puzzled by what he was expected to do. He was relieving a battalion of infantry with only a company, supported by less than a full battery of artillery. I gave him five packs of cigarettes from the supply Ray York had left in a machine-gun ammo case.

By midmorning, we set out to catch up to the division. The roads were chock-full of jeeps, trucks, half-tracks, and tanks, all going north. In Saverne, the man directing traffic was Skip Horner, the tenor sax man from my college swing band. Skip was in the division band, which put away its instruments and road-marked in the combat zone. I hollered at him, and he recognized me, but we didn't get a chance to speak.

I worried about the Luftwaffe all day. They could have killed thousands, had they made a raid on the motor columns going north. It turned out I should have been more concerned with the two guys sitting up front—Ruotolo and Rockwell. The motor column was going along bumper-to-bumper, and those two guys were never known for patience. When he was impatient, Ruotolo became garrulous. His subject was always his ambition—what he wanted for himself. Rockwell always depressed the clutch and raced the engine when we had our frequent slowdowns.

We had to listen to Ruotolo brag that he was in line for a promotion to first lieutenant, which would give him the highest rank of anyone from his class at Yale. He had memorized every word from the *Yale Review* he got in the last mail call, and apparently it reported news of promotions of Yale men so the Eli alums could get bragging rights.

We were in a lane of jeeps with officers from the 411th, and the line was moving only about fifteen miles an hour. I believe Rocky never uttered a swear word in his life, but he was grunting with frustration about the pace of the motor march and the fact that he couldn't pass the slow traffic ahead.

Suddenly a two-and-a-half-ton truck appeared attempting to pass our column on the single outside lane as we were going up a slight rise. We were already less than a jeep length from the vehicle ahead of us, but Rocky raced to close up, nearly touching bumpers.

At that moment, with the passing truck right beside us, a Sherman tank appeared at the crest of the hill, coming downhill toward the truck and closing fast. A soldier sitting in the passenger seat of the truck, looking desperate, signaled Rocky to back off and let them in.

"Don't let him in, Rocky," Ruotolo said.

"Let him in, Rocky!" Frank and I yelled. "Let him the hell in. He's going to run head-on into a tank, for God's sake."

The time for Rocky to back off was gone quickly, and the truck had no place to go but to run us off the road. There was a scraping of metal, and we found ourselves on the way into the ditch, skidding sideways. Our jeep then turned onto its side, and Ruotolo lurched from his seat onto his face as we continued over onto the cloth top. Rocky fell on top of Ruotolo, but, as luck would have it, they were thrown clear. Frank and I were jammed in so tightly by our radio and bedrolls that we simply remained upside down in the rear seat. Because of the real-life slow motion, the thin bars holding up the canvas top somehow held, which saved all of our lives.

Before Frank and I could scramble out of the turned-over jeep, Ruotolo was running toward the truck, which had stopped, along with dozens of other vehicles. A sergeant—the man we'd seen signaling—came running toward us. "Is everyone okay?" he asked.

"Sergeant, what the hell did you think you were doing?" Ruotolo yelled. "Give me your name, the name of your outfit, and the name of your driver. I'll have you court-martialed!" Ruotolo had a small notebook in his hand.

"Sir! Sir!" the sergeant said. "We're the general's kitchen truck. We *had* to pass the column. We're trying to get the general a hot meal."

Ruotolo's face fell. Morally indignant one second, in the next he was brought face-to-face with the stupid stubbornness of himself and his driver. He quickly recovered. "Just the same, sergeant, I have to make a report of this accident."

While the lieutenant was writing things in his notebook, Frank and I were turning the jeep back onto its wheels with the help of a dozen soldiers from the crowd that had stopped. The trailer had only turned on its side, and the tarp had kept everything in place, so nothing spilled out. On the jeep, we had to push the metal supports back to move the canvas top close to its original shape. The windshield had a crack across its width; it would be there the rest of the war. Ruotolo had a severe scrape on his right cheek, and I think he darn near fractured his wrist.

When we were once more moving along with the column, I couldn't help but point out how I felt about what happened in that "accident." "You know, if we'd been killed," I said, "those guys in that truck would have been in deep trouble. Sort of reminds me of the epitaph: 'Here lies the body of Doctor Grey. He died defending his right-of-way. He was right, *dead* right. But he's just as *dead* as if he'd been wrong.' We sure were *right,* not letting that truck in . . ." Frank grinned at me, but I didn't get the rise out of Ruotolo I was hoping for: he kept looking straight ahead, dabbing at his face. Rocky didn't even grunt.

We didn't catch up to the battery that day. We stopped in a *gasthaus* that had been partially destroyed. We were on the third floor sleeping on the floor. Sometime in the night I heard a guitar playing some good jazz riffs. It seemed to be coming from the floor below. I went down to investigate and found a guy picking away. He grinned when I came into the room. "Not really my instrument," he said. "I play piano, but . . ."

I went out to the trailer and got my wire brushes out of my duffle bag. I found an old padded seat to use as a drum, and we jammed for a while—just guitar and drum. It didn't sound too bad. We played "Sunny Side of the Street," "Rossetta," and "Pennies from Heaven," some of my favorites, with which he was in agreement. He even played a stop-chorus so I could do a hot brush solo, complete with foot stomps to simulate bass drum accents.

In the morning, we set out again after bumming a hot meal from some rear-echelon company that was staying in that town. Hot breakfasts were uniformly the same throughout the army, but once in while a unit had a mess sergeant who really could cook. That mess sergeant did something to the GI powdered eggs with cheese and wine that was soul-satisfying. I remember that breakfast after all these years—that and the jam session in the wrecked *gasthaus*.

We rode all day in a column that was less crowded than the day before, and Rocky, having learned a lesson, drove with less groaning. Ruotolo kept talking about stopping a tank attack—his latest ambition.

I had lost track of the day of the month and all dates, so when we ran into heavy snow and zero temperatures just after dark and Ruotolo announced, "It's Christmas Eve, guys," we were all surprised. The weather had been like September ever since the snowstorm back in November in the Vosges. The snow we passed all day was about six inches deep, even before we ran into this snowstorm, so we knew the cold and snow had been here before we arrived. The eighty miles north made a big difference.

We came into the village of Farbersville, just as an air burst exploded over the main street. I thought about the Star of Bethlehem and how different this was from the biblical eve that was probably being celebrated back home. Our uniform overcoats didn't keep us nearly warm enough, so we got blankets from our trailer and were snuggling under them.

Ruotolo went into a house that had a unit designation sign out front. He returned to tell us he had found out where the battery was located. We wandered around some, and finally found it just before midnight. The men were sleeping in a bombed-out barn that had two separate mangers still standing, though the center with its hayloft was destroyed. Two large cows lay a few yards away from the barn, their legs sticking out in frozen stiffness, casting sad blue-black shadows on the full-moonlit snow.

Ruotolo went to the nearby farmhouse to find the officers, and Frank, Rocky, and I went to the barn to sleep with the men.

The cannoneers were sleeping in the right-side manger, and the signalmen and drivers were in the left. The men had lanterns to light the straw-strewn compartment, but they couldn't use their heaters because the heat might thaw out the three huge pigs sharing the manger with us.

We spread out straw that was inches thick on the concrete floor, and our shelter-halves and blankets made for reasonably comfortable sleeping that Christmas Eve. I slept less than a foot from a half-ton sow.

In the morning, the men soon saw all the damage to our jeep, and they marveled that we had survived the crash. Rocky walked as far as he could get from us, as we told how his and Ruotolo's silly stubbornness had nearly gotten us killed.

There was a holiday air in the manger that morning as men unwrapped the last packages of gifts from home. A truck took the Catholics from the battery to a mass that was being observed at battalion headquarters.

The kitchen crew made a special Christmas Day dinner of turkey, stuffing, and mashed potatoes, and though it was not great, it was better than the Thanksgiving meal, where the turkey had tasted like fish and made a lot of us sick. We forward observers were not surprised to see Rocky refuse the turkey, instead going off to the side and eating a cold can of C-ration meat and beans. He did gather a handful of Christmas hard candy and stuff it into his deep jacket pockets.

Right after our dinner, a corporal came into our manger and set up a portable organ. When a chaplain followed him a few minutes later, we were taken aback. The Catholics, though they had already been to mass earlier, also took part in the church service that afternoon. Hymnbooks were passed out, and everyone sang. Even Len Harris, who was Jewish, sang. With the temperature zero, Len could hardly be expected to wait outside until the service was over, and he was good-natured about it, saying, "My rabbi wouldn't mind. I haven't had much chance to sing lately, and they were nice songs."

The next day, the supply sergeant had Christmas gifts from the army for Rocky, Frank, and me—lots of new gear to keep us warm in the zero weather. We got faux-fur vests to wear under nylon zip-up jackets with hoods, thick mittens with slots for trigger fingers, and if all this didn't get us warm enough, we now had wool-lined tanker's coveralls to wear underneath.

But the best thing of all: we would no longer have to carry the radio equipment on canvas straps. Too late to prevent the calluses on our thighs or the rips in our pants, we now had curved plywood backpacks on which to strap the radio and battery pack. These were originally designed for mortars, but some genius saw that they could make the toil of FO radiomen less trying. Frank Lawrence and I did an Irish jig, with the equipment on our backs, for the supply sergeant's benefit.

The lieutenant did not want to take an extra day to relax after Christmas, so on December 26, we went to his latest stupid OP. On the way there, he got enthusiastic about the news carried in the latest *Stars and Stripes*. "We've got a new secret weapon, and it's in artillery!" he said. "It's called a Prosit fuse, and it will go off fifteen feet above the ground. Think what that will do to infantry who feel safe dug in."

"But didn't we already have a fuse that would burst above ground?" Frank asked.

"Yeah. But this fuse will automatically explode at the exact same number of feet every time. Our time fuse is not reliable. This one uses the same principle as radar."

"How is it secret if *Stars and Stripes* tells about it?" I asked.

"It's no longer secret. Our battery expects to have some in this week."

He had managed to find an OP even more dangerous than the one near the occupied village that got Ray York killed. This time we were at least a mile ahead of the infantry outpost line. (I'm sure the officers at headquarters were tickled silly when he told them about this one.) Just north of Farbersville was an open stretch of land that spread for miles in every direction. The danger Frank and I noticed immediately was an enemy trench less than half a mile away, and we could see soldiers in it when we arrived. The town behind the trench was small, but we knew the enemy occupied it. Ten miles away lay the city of Forbach, with a railroad visible to the naked eye. On it were busy steam engines—the kind of targets Ruotolo immediately relished.

"Look, guys," Ruotolo said, "you don't have to dig fox-holes. The French dug them back in 1939, when the Krauts first invaded here. All you got to do is scoop out the snow."

That was the only thing good about this OP. It was in a thicket that grew along a ridgeline, and scrub brush and skinny trees were the only cover we had. I told the lieutenant, "Those guys in that trench can see us as easily as we can see them. So do we want to stay here and have them shell the hell out of us?"

"Not if we keep down in these foxholes, they won't see us."

I knew better than to make him promise he'd do it. Getting shelled seem to be too much fun for him to expect him to resist exposing us to them. I will say one thing he did that was new: he got into a foxhole for the first time. Over the months we had been in France, I was learning how to manage Ruotolo . . . sometimes. I just wished it could be always.

The ridge rose only about twenty feet above the huge area we were observing. A tower that had once been part of a castle was a mile away, and Ruotolo fired on it that first day. He also fired on the Forbach railyards. It was a unique experience to be able to see all his targets without needing binoculars. Riding back from this OP gave us a chance to hear him rehearsing the tale he was going to give the brass at Fire Direction. The castle tower was being described as an enemy OP, and though neither Frank nor I saw any sign of hits on it, he characterized his adjustments as destroying it. The locomotive in Forbach, he also said he destroyed, though Frank and I watched it steam away before the first rounds exploded in the railyard.

The lieutenant was not being dishonest, I told Frank that night. He was talking himself into believing anything he needed to believe to construct this image that the war going on in his head offered him: he was "Tondo the War Hero" in that image.

We stayed that first night back in Farbersville in a flat above a barbershop, for which Frank and I were grateful. Sleeping next to dead pigs was a good thing to avoid.

Being in a cozy apartment, we all wrote a number of letters. I'm not proud of what I did that night, but I sneaked a peek—while he was away at the toilet—at what Ruotolo was telling the folks back home. "Dear Folks," he wrote, "Another inning in the game of war we are playing . . ." That's all I got to see, but it was one more adolescent concept of his that kept me in a permanent state of dread. Bad enough to face death, wounding, capture, and fright on a daily basis, but never feeling secure about your leadership just made things worse. No telling when he would actually take us on a real suicide mission without warning. Comparing war to baseball was less than acceptable in a guy who could have been a junior at Yale that year, I told Frank Lawrence.

Before going to the OP, we went out to the barn where the battery was staying and we came away with another prize—kapok-filled bedrolls. "They're warm enough to keep you toasty at twenty below," the supply sergeant told us. Ruotolo decided to use them that night, so in spite of our nice room over a barbershop in Farbersville, we slept 100 yards back from the OP that night. Even Rockwell was ordered to sleep atop the snow with us.

The kapok was magnificent. I put my wool socks under me and they were bone dry in the morning. But not everything about that night was so great. A fresh crater from a mortar round was still steaming about fifty feet away, and it was that explosion that had woken us up. The enemy had seen us, and we had to gather up the bedrolls and move out of there before they adjusted fire and came closer.

Rocky went back to his jeep, but Ruotolo decided to take us to the OP. But first he decided to reconnoiter on his own. He took the M-1 rifle from the trailer and left Frank and me behind while he stalked the OP. He came running back seconds later. "There's a Kraut patrol in the thicket, about fifty yards this side of the OP," he said. "They're the ones who fired the mortars at us. Come on, let's go and get rifle-grenades. We can wipe them out with one shot."

"Yeah," I said, "and they can wipe *us* out if we miss. Have you ever shot a rifle-grenade?"

"Well, we ought to do something."

"How about we go back to the flat, and we all get haircuts from the downstairs barber?"

That idea was too good for even a *Tonto* to refuse. The Krauts had blocked our return to that OP, so the lieutenant's PFC radioman kept him from getting his section wiped out that day. We all got haircuts except Rocky.

Did that day's experience send our FO section in search of a safer OP? Not on your life! The sun came out gloriously, and wave after wave of DC-3s flew over to parachute food to the men of Bastogne. The Battle of the Bulge was about to end, and Tonto took us back to the thicket, after the enemy had obligingly let us know we were fools if we went there.

All day, he kept saying that a tank attack was expected, and all units in the European theater of operations (ETO) were warned to be prepared.

The Battle of the Bulge was—for some of those not tragically involved—a godsend, because it proved that the enemy was still capable of being dangerous; otherwise men such as Lieutenant Ruotolo couldn't think of themselves as heroes, a huge need for their egos.

Brig. Gen. Roger Wicks wanted to see this latest OP of a forward observer who was gaining fame within the division artillery he commanded, so I was sent back to the road to escort him up see us. I had been the general's orderly four times back in Texas, and it didn't surprise me when he recognized me. Wicks was a former West Point football coach and thus wasn't uncomfortable with enlisted men. "Well, young man," he said, "so you got to be a forward observer. What's this OP like? Am I taking a huge risk coming here?"

"We get shelled fairly regularly, sir," I said. "But they only seem to do it once a day, and we've already had our shelling today."

"Okay. I never look forward to getting iron thrown at me. Can we get there without being seen?"

I assured him that I would try to lead him to the OP with the least risk. I didn't lie to him that we could get there completely under cover.

He spent only five minutes and didn't say much. He had to have seen how dangerous this place was. I went back with him as armed guard, and as he got into his jeep, he shook my hand and told me to be careful. I think he didn't really approve of the OP—not that it did any good.

In mid-January, we went with George Company on an attack to straighten a tiny bulge in the lines we had inherited from the Third Army in central Lorraine. Since the near disaster in the Ardennes, bulges were unpopular with Eisenhower.

From a position on a cliff 100 feet above a valley, we watched an infantry platoon advance into a small settlement half a mile ahead of our outpost line. Rocky left our flat above the barbershop in Farbersville and joined the infantry motor pool, a mile back. We had hardly settled into foxholes when we heard a loud grinding sound coming toward us. I pushed myself up to see what it was and quickly dove back down—the grinding was from some sort of shell we had never heard before. It passed over our heads and seemed to explode 100 yards behind us. We later found out that shell was a giant mortar projectile that had lost part of its fins and gone end over end, hence the grinding sound. It had such a huge explosion that what we thought was right behind us was actually a mile back in the town where Rocky was. (Unless there was another such rocket that Rocky told us about later.)

We went back to watching the attack on the village below, where three riflemen were sent forward to scout a farmhouse on the side of a hill. As they drew near it, we heard the sound of a German burp gun and saw the three scouts flop to the ground. Everyone on our cliff was sure they were killed. They lay still for several minutes, and the G Company commander cursed. He cheered moments later when all three got to their feet with their hands up, then cursed again as they walked into the farmhouse and surrendered. Getting captured was something infantrymen hated only a mite less than death.

The captain then moved us from the cliff down to a farmhouse only a few hundred feet directly below the house on the hill where his men were captured. Frank and I laid down a phone line, because we knew radio sending and receiving was poor from valleys. Ruotolo forgot to tell us we might be on this attack more than one day, so we had left our nice new kapok bedrolls behind. Guess what? We were going to spend the night, but only the basement of the house was heated, and the outside temperature was zero. Ruotolo got to go to the basement, but Sgt. Frank Lawrence and PFC Bill Hanford had to stay upstairs.

Frank and I looked in all the rooms and found a bedroom with four mattresses but no blankets. "Why don't we lie on one mattress and pull another one on top?" Frank suggested. It was better than nothing, but just barely. I had to pull down hard on the sides of the upper mattress to get warm by a few degrees, but when I fell asleep, I let go and woke up with my teeth chattering.

Our phone rang, and I answered. It was Fire Direction: Major Hawkins was checking the line. When the major could hear my teeth chattering, I told him we'd left our warm coats behind because we had to carry so much stuff.

"Have you seen the Willie and Joe cartoon in today's *Stars and Stripes*?" he asked. "It shows Willie and Joe on each side of a couple of French peasants in a bed, and the man says to his wife, 'Mama, we have been liberated.' That ought to cheer you up."

Major Hawkins was always a good guy. Too bad he had to have that "Hawk's Hole" sign to irritate me every time I saw it.

Somehow we survived that tooth-chattering night, and in the morning Ruotolo took us into the center of the cluster of houses that were all there was to this village—a dozen houses on a hillside. As we began climbing the narrow footpath, an explosion sent us to the ground. It was less than twenty feet from us, and we thought we were being shelled, until we saw GIs dynamiting to make foxholes in the frozen turf.

The house we moved into was deserted by its owners, as were all the houses on this hillside. Apparently nobody wanted to live in no-man's-land.

We had run a line into our house, but the first time Ruotolo wanted to call for artillery fire, the line was dead. I was sent out to find the break. It was easy to find a break in that thin rubber-covered line; all you needed to do was to pick it up and run with it in your hand, and when you come to the break, you'd be empty-handed.

The break was less than 200 yards away, next to a rusty, burned, overturned Citroen auto. I had barely knelt to fix the line before a ricochet zinged off the car past my ear. It's easy to know you are in the sights of a sniper when that happens, so I got on my belly to finish the splice with shaky hands. Another ricochet zinged off the Citroen before I finished, so I ran in zigzags back to the house and had Ruotolo fire a barrage at the forest where I was sure the sniper was.

We left that house early that afternoon. The infantry had straightened the line successfully.

That night, back in the flat in Farbersville, we heard the RAF bomb Saarbrucken. It sounded like a giant timpani drumroll, bomb after bomb falling, powerful enough to rattle the earth under us, though we were at least twenty miles away.

At six the next morning, we were hustled back to Alsace: the tank attack Ruotolo had talked about finally took place near the city of Sessenheim. Frank and I had thought it was something he made up. But riding south, we learned that Seventh Army had been putting out intelligence reports anticipating it ever since the Allies chased the Germans back out of the Ardennes. With an officer like Ruotolo, it was hard to separate truth from fiction.

Ruotolo had been called to battalion headquarters in the middle of the night and briefed at a hurried conference. Now he filled us in, as we rode toward the Hagenau Forest region. Two days before that, the German Army had crossed the Rhine eighteen miles northeast of Strasbourg in an attempt to cut off the VI Corps troops that had taken our place in the Saar when we moved north at Christmas. The first day, in a two-and-a-half-hour battle, the Krauts had knocked out eight of our tanks, and the 3rd Battalion of the 411th had lost seventy or more men. "One company had only twenty-eight men at chow last night," Ruotolo told us. "Then yesterday, the Krauts staged a counter-attack, but our guys held. Now we're going to stop them from their third attack with a pouring on of artillery."

We arrived at a row of houses that I seem to remember as small frame two-story boxes, and Ruotolo chose the middle house in the row. The family was cowering in the basement, and who could blame them: the roar of battle was raging to our east, toward the Rhine in that part of Alsace. We raced to the second floor, running a line of the thin telephone wire with us. Ruotolo and Lawrence positioned themselves at the only two windows in the room that looked toward the battlefield, so I couldn't see the action taking place out there. We immediately called in a fire mission on distant Sessenheim. The battle was all taking place between here and the town, but no targets were clearly seen, as both our troops and theirs were scattered unevenly across miles of open space.

When Frank let me look out his window, I could see the fields where the battle was raging. It was about ten square miles of open land crossed by telephone poles and fences, with a few small clumps of trees. Two tanks were barely visible. They were large, so I assumed they were Tigers, and they flashed blazes of fire every second or two. I couldn't see any soldiers, but I knew they had to be out there, as the air above the fields had a cloud of black smoke that couldn't all have come from the tanks. Also I could hear the almost continuous rattle of machine gun fire—a mix of the *ratatattat* of ours and the *brrrrup* of theirs—and the single bangs of rifle fire.

I knew Ruotolo was frustrated by not being able to call for fire on the tanks, and he had no way of knowing if the rounds of artillery from our guns were doing any damage to the Germans back in Sessenheim. We must have been directly in the path between our howitzers and our targets, because we had the sizzling sound of shells passing over us from our rear whenever Fire Direction called, "On the way."

Being in a house while directing fire brought a false sense of security: those tanks and batteries of 88s from the forests were sending death in streaks in every direction, so an accidental hit on our house was always a possibility.

We weren't in that room looking at the battle more than two hours, before Fire Direction called and told us to get out of there—the division was pulling out.

Now Tonto had to take one more risk; this had all been too tame for him. He walked out the door he'd been looking through to a small platform atop a wooden fire escape. He stood there for several minutes with his binoculars, sweeping the horizon one last time. Inviting a German observer to spot him, I thought.

We were loading our equipment in the trailer in front of the house before Tonto's latest folly brought results—a direct-fire shell crashed into the room we had vacated only minutes before, and the right side of the house trembled and crashed open before our eyes. Tonto seemed blessed: that none of his stupid risks had got him killed was amazing . . . but those poor Alsatians in the cellar.

On January 22, our division was ordered to move back to Alsace. Frank Lawrence and I were being sent ahead to be road markers. That order was obviously another of Captain Pultz's bits of vengeance directed at me. At chow, just before leaving, we stood next to the chow truck talking about how mad we were. "Some of the cannoneers were on vacation while we were up with the infantry," Lawrence said, "but the captain chooses to send us on a crappy detail."

"Yeah, and Ruotolo says nothing," I added.

Captain Pultz suddenly materialized from behind a nearby shed. "I heard that, Lawrence and Hanford. You think of yourselves as some kind of heroes, don't you? Well, I don't buy that garbage."

Frank and I waited for what he was going to say next, while Pultz chewed on his food and a new dilemma he had just created for himself: how was he going to punish us for our insolence? FOs were off-limits to courts-martial for anything short of cowardice, and Frank and I were in good favor with headquarters. We were feeling a power surge from Pultz's tongue-tied grasping. "War is dangerous," he said, sounding much less sure of himself. "But just because you see more than your share of it doesn't give you the right to be so smart-assed. So shut up and do what you are ordered to do." He offered no explanation for why he chose to send us, because he had none.

The entire division was in wild retreat that day. French civilians threw garbage at us. They had good reason: they were going to be behind German lines again and were afraid of the consequences, especially to some men who had worn FFI armbands. Who could blame them? There seemed no reason for the retreat—neither to them nor to the men retreating. General Patch had decided our position was untenable, and Eisenhower had agreed with him, so we were moving back to the lower Vosges.

Our road-marking duty was over around midnight, and Frank and I got picked up by the supply truck at the end of the column. We slept the remainder of the night atop ammunition cases, without benefit of blankets. The following morning, we pulled into the little Alsation town of Bauxviller. Ruotolo was there to meet us, and despite the fact that our entire combat team was in reserve, he wanted to take us to find an OP.

I rode to the new OP ready to explode. From the way his lips moved, Frank Lawrence was just as angry. After sending Rockwell back to the battery, we climbed a naked hill in the middle of nowhere. Once more, he had chosen a dumb place to observe from, just because it was dangerous. Two months' experience had taught us this was insane behavior—no FO in the ETO did this sort of thing more than once—so I decided to say something.

"Look, Lieutenant . . . Why are we so far forward? We could be captured this easy . . . " I snapped my fingers. "Do you want us to spend the rest of the war in a prisoner-of-war camp?"

"Don't talk nonsense," he said. "We have the best FO section in the battalion. I think we've the best section in the division. Our reputation is all over the division. Sure, we take risks. We're soldiers . . . here to win a war."

I shut up. No use talking. Tonto was immune to good sense.

We spent the day as usual, firing at ghosts. Despite our being out in the open, with no means of cover whatever, we were not fired upon. I came to the conclusion the Krauts hadn't caught up to us yet. Our retreat was too quick for them.

After chow, I got hold of Lawrence. "Look, *mon ami*, let's go and find our own billet. We can go to the edge of town and sack in where Ruotolo can't find us in the morning."

"I don't know . . ."

"Come on! What can he do to us?"

He shrugged and went along with it. Tonto-Ruotolo was wearing down Frank as much as me. Besides being dangerous, our lieutenant was boring us both to death. We found a vacant apartment in a small apartment house less than fifty yards from the block of houses where the battery was staying. Our ten-in-one box of rations gave us no reason to go to the battery for anything. Even Rockwell didn't know where we were.

The concierge woke us before daybreak. "*Kommen sie! Kommen sie! Feuer! Feuer!*" She ran to the window.

I could see the reflection of flames on the window of the shed across the road. "My God! She wants to tell us the town's on fire! Look at those flames, Frank."

We pulled on our pants and ran out to the corner. Huge flames shot into the air from behind the block of buildings where the battery was staying. "We must have been bombed with incendiaries or something," I said.

A couple of local men were pulling an ancient fire rig toward the flames. One of those pull-carts with handles at each end for the firemen to pump up and down. It could have come from a Mack Sennett comedy set or a museum. Easy to see this rig could never douse flames the size of these. Nor could the bucket brigade a corps of soldiers and townsmen had set up down the street toward the fire.

"Let's get in there and help," Lawrence said.

"Let's not waste our time," I told him. "Buckets aren't going to do a thing." From this corner, 100 feet or more from the flames, I could see it was the barn where we ate dinner the night before from our chow truck. In minutes, those flames were going to jump across the courtyard and catch the house adjoined to it. (The houses in most villages in rural France and Alsace are joined by long sheds and enclosed by high fences, creating a courtyard in the center.)

"That's where our kitchen truck was parked," a gunner corporal told us. "But they got the truck out, and all the kitchen crew is okay too. Five guys jumped out a window of the shed and landed on the canvas top of the truck."

While Frank and I were watching the fire, Ruotolo found us. "Where did you men stay last night?" he asked. "I looked all over for you."

I beat Frank to the lie. "We were sleeping in a barn near the one that's burning."

"Well, I wish you'd let me know where you go from now on. We can't stay here and watch this fire; we need to get some C rations to eat on the way to our OP. Intelligence says there may be a tank attack in this sector."

We spent the day on our naked hill and saw nothing. Ruotolo fired a checkpoint registration and was disappointed because he had nothing to brag about to headquarters.

On the way back to the battery, he said, "I want you to stay where I stay tonight. I need to know where you are. You should know that. This is the second time this week I've been disappointed in you, Hanford."

I'm a weenie. I put up with nearly anything, but even a weenie has a breaking point. He just hit mine. "You're disappointed in *me*?" I said. "Well tie score, Lieutenant. I've been disappointed in *you* an entire war. You let Captain Pultz send us—your valued forward observers—on crappy details after you've kept us on a stupid OP, where we get bored out of our skulls and are kept in constant danger, because you make sure the Krauts know where we are so they can be sure to shell the crap out of us."

"Now, Hanford, don't go ruining everything. You're spoiling the best FO section in the bat–"

"In the battalion . . . in division artillery . . . in the 103rd Division . . . in the U.S. Army! You really believe that!? Want to know something, Lieutenant? Every last frigging FO section in the ETO has a lieutenant, a sergeant, a T/5 driver, and a T/5 radioman. This—the best FO section on the planet—has a radioman who's a PFC. Is it *you*, and *you alone*, that makes this section so great? Good officers look out for their men. They don't let COs with a grudge send their men to road-mark and sleep on ammo cases in freezing weather, when cannoneers never get sent anywhere."

Having said my piece, I shut up and was immediately sorry. Lawrence patted my shoulder. Rocky raced the engine. Ruotolo just sat there.

We got clear back to the battery before Ruotolo said, "I'm sorry you feel like that, Hanford."

At chow that night, I saw Ruotolo talking for an hour with Pultz. That they were talking about me was certain. I must admit, it had me a little worried. Officers have absolute power—in theory—but I learned that when they want to exercise it, they just might find a superior rank standing in the way. Even a five-star general can be overruled by the president.

I'd hated it when I was told, back in Texas, that I was being assigned to be a forward observer, but now, after a few months, I found out that once I had survived some dangerous assignments, I gained more power than any PFC can possibly expect. Short of cowardice, I could do no wrong.

Still, when Pultz walked toward me after chow, I expected something bad to happen—at the very least, a chewing out. Then came one of the biggest surprises of my life. He held out a small packet. "Tomorrow, Hanford," he said, "you'll have the day off to get ready to go on a three-day pass to Paris, and you'll probably want to sew these on before you go." The packet had two sets of T/5 stripes. *The best FO section in the U.S. Army no longer had a PFC radioman.*

My excitement over being one of the first men in the battery to get such a pass was squelched somewhat when I learned who my passmate was to be: Gus Cristhantheos, the battery idiot. Some guys said he was the dumbest guy in the ETO, and I agreed with them.

So why was he being given a pass to Paris? Captain Pultz took away Gus's ammunition after his carbine went off accidentally a third time and put a bullet through another guy's mess kit in the chow line. And this, after Pultz expressly ordered him to keep his gun chamber empty and the safety on at all times. Yet here was Pultz making dummy Gus one of the first two men going to Paris. Something smelled.

I spent the next day trying to make my uniform more presentable. I sewed up the rips in the trouser legs and boiled my jacket in soapsuds, with the help of a peasant lady who did the boiling in return for a cake of GI soap she used to do her own laundry. A big stain—one I got from an egg I pilfered from a French henhouse and then forgot was in the pocket—was still there, but the jacket looked better after the nice lady ironed it for me.

The fire was explained to Frank and me, while the burgomeister of Bauxviller walked around smiling and practicing a few words in English he was taught by cannoneers: "This is war, and war is hell," a GI translation of "*C'est la geurre.*" The kitchen crew had been sleeping in the shed between the house and barn and were heating their dormitory with a stove one of them made from an empty shell case filled with gravel and gasoline. A guy coming off guard ten minutes before morning reveille decided to go up to the loft where the cooks slept and wait for breakfast until the first sergeant roused them. He sat close to the shell-case to keep warm, then nodded off and kicked it over, sending flaming gasoline all over the floor in the shed. The entire kitchen crew then bailed out a window onto the tarp on the kitchen truck.

Cajun Joe the medic was already working at getting Purple Hearts for the men who got cut by glass from the broken windows.

A 240-millimeter howitzer. It could fire a 360-pound shell more than fourteen miles.

An artillery crew of black soldiers prepares a gun for action.

An American howitzer unleashes its fire at night.

A crew firing its gun.

A crew loads a shell.

A battery of 105s, like those the author observed for.
They could fire a shell seven miles.

A 105 crew in action.

The ruins of a town after aerial and artillery bombardment.

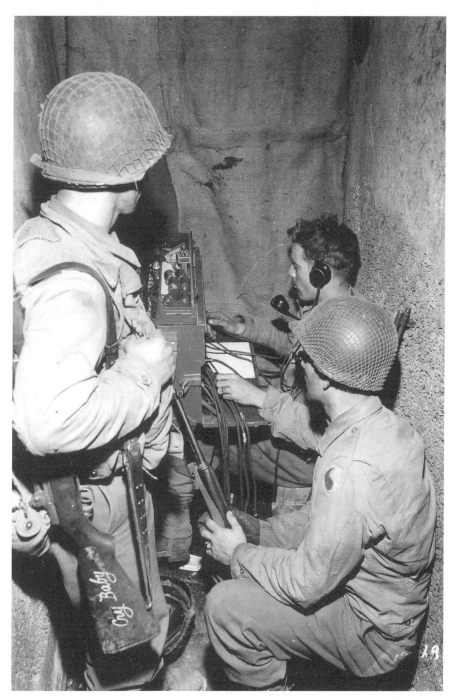

An artillery switchboard.

Cleaning shells.

A 240-millimeter howitzer being transported.

Chapter 12

The truck to Paris stopped at noon for us to relieve ourselves and eat our C rations. We were so far from the front we couldn't even hear the sound of guns.

I finished my canned beef stew as a French bicyclist rode past, his tires sizzling on the wet pavement. He looked straight ahead as if we weren't there; soldiers peeing in the ditch were too common to notice after five years.

With Gus still urinating, I saw my chance. I shinnied over the tailgate and sat next to the headquarters first sergeant. "Got my sleeve all soaked and muddy sitting back there," I said. "Thought I'd move up."

"You ain't kiddin' me," he said. "You just want to get away from that little guy you're with."

"How'd you guess?"

"I'd do the same thing. What's the story on him, anyways?"

I told him how Gus had his ammunition taken away after his carbine went off in the chow line and put a bullet through another guy's mess kit. "It was the third time," I said. "Does that tell you anything?" Just then, the sergeant nodded toward the tailgate to warn me Gus was climbing in.

"What was you guys sayin' about me?" Gus said, sliding in next to me. "I seen that guy makin' a signal. You think I'm stupid or somethin'?"

Right then, the truth wouldn't do. "Well, we were watching you down there," I said. "And Sarge here says, 'The girls in Paris are in for a treat when that guy gets there.'" Sarge gave me a nudge of admiration.

"Whatchu mean? What girls?"

"Paris girls, Gus."

Gus still wasn't sure he understood, so he sat there mulling it over—scowling and smirking as his thoughts wavered. "These Paris girls . . . they're the same like regular French girls?" he said at last. "They go for big ones and like that?"

The truck was fully loaded by this time, and Gus had them roaring with laughter. He didn't like it.

"Yes, Gus," I answered. "Paris is even in France, Gus. We are on our way to Paris, France. Now try to go to sleep like me. We need to save our energy for tonight."

We were entering the Paris suburbs before I figured out just why Gus was sent with me. The headquarters sergeant told me that three of the guys on this truck had to be FOs, because he heard Colonel Caesar telling the battery commanders he wanted the first men sent on pass to Paris to be one FO and one cannoneer from each gun battery, along with the first sergeants from service and headquarters batteries. Pultz and Ruotolo were caught in a dilemma, and they solved it by sending the cannoneer most likely to ruin Hanford's pass—namely, the battery idiot. That way, they punished me for my insolence at the same time they were obeying the colonel.

The trucks entered Paris around three in the afternoon. The pavement was dry, and the rain seemed to have bypassed these streets, making this January day more like April or May.

Half an hour later, our two-truck convoy reached its destination. Next to our truck, a half-canopy jutted out almost to the curb, with a sign: "HOTEL AMERICAIN."

The officer in charge, a service battery lieutenant, lined us up on the sidewalk in front of the small, shoddy hotel.

"Okay, listen up, men," he ordered. "Those guys on the first truck are staying in the hotel behind me, Hotel American, okay? The guys on the last truck will stay across the street at the Grand Hotel Doo Terminus. My French isn't too good, so maybe some of you know better how to pronounce it. There are no restaurants in Paris to speak of, so y'all got to eat over there in the Terminus where the Red Cross runs a canteen. Y'all can have dinner there in one hour.

"Find out about entertainment at the desk of the Terminus. Assemble here in three days . . . Go AWOL, and you'll be charged with desertion. I need not remind you—for AWOL here in France, you can get shot. Use the prophylaxis stations; don't go getting something you'll regret. They can give you a map of them at the desk of . . ." He waved his arms, conducting us as we finished his sentence in a unison shout: "THE TERMINUS!"

I heard a wag in the crowd—there always was one in any gathering of soldiers—"He didn't say where they was selling the VD. That's what *I* need to know."

Gus and I gathered our bedrolls and field bags and went into the Hôtel Americain. It was even grubbier inside than on the outside—which is saying something. Half the men had to stay outside, because there wasn't room for them in the dinky lobby. It kept running through my head what an insult this was: we keep rescuing the Frenchies' butts in wars, and for that—they name a crummy hotel after us.

A little guy with an Oliver Hardy mustache, glasses smaller than quarters, speaking zero English, beckoned us. "*Allez avec moi à vos chambres*," he said. This to a gathering of men who knew little or no French. But most of us understood.

Not Gus. "What'd he say? What'd he say?"

"Goddamn it, Gus. What's it look like? Follow the man."

When I found out I was on the second floor and Gus was on the third, I thought my luck was changing. Furthermore, the antiquated elevator—too small for the crowd but in working order—was right beside my room, making it easier for me to escape from the little pest.

"This is bull, Hanaford," Gus said. "Tell him I wanna be in your room. I don't wanna sleep in no room alone."

"My French isn't good enough, Gus. Besides, it wouldn't do any good. These rooms were assigned before we got here. You're holding the man up. Go up and see your room. Then we'll go and eat, okay?"

It was painful to accept, but I was finding I hadn't the heart to dodge the little guy right away. I think the captain and

Tonto knew I was too soft to get away from a troubled child like Gus, so they sent him as my punishment. But I resolved that tonight was the last time.

At dinnertime, I led Gus across the Rue St. Lazaire to Le Grand Hôtel du Terminus. "Jeez, how come they didn't put us in here?" he asked.

"Luck of the draw, Gus. This place is big, but it looks and smells like it's seen its best days too."

Nothing in the large lobby looked to be less than fifty years old pre–World War I. Knowing that my father's veteran friends from 1918 may have sat on these couches stirred something in me, but the musty smell kept it from being pleasure. We followed the crowd into the dining room.

"Wow!" Gus said. "This is okay!"

"If you like eating in gyms," I said. "No, I take that back . . . it's nice. When's the last time we got to eat off tablecloths? Checkered ones at that. And waiters in black ties and white aprons . . . and wine!"

We were served soup as soon as the wine was poured. It was GI vegetable soup, but it was doctored a lot with garlic, wine, and other stuff. Gus wouldn't eat it. "Friggin' soup. I hate soup. I only like Campbell's tomato," he said, pushing the bowl away. I swore to myself.

When the next course arrived, I already knew what Gus's reaction was going to be. It had a crust, a beautiful crust, and inside was army C-ration beef stew, the better kind that came in the ten-in-one rations.

Gus's reaction was immediate: "Beef friggin' stew! I ain't gonna eat this swill."

"Look at it this way, Gus. You got a fork to eat with instead of an aluminum spoon you carry in your shoe that gives you the GIs. You heard the lieutenant—the only place we got to eat is here. Taste it." I tasted mine. "It's great. They flavored it with spices, wine, and cheese. You can't help liking it. This is France . . . known the world over for great cooks. This wasn't prepared by an army cook. It's delicious. Have a sip of wine."

"I hate wine."

I gave up. I wasn't going to let the little bastard ruin this for me. I ate and enjoyed the food, and to hell with Gus. The waiter even brought me a second helping.

After coffee and a cigarette, I left the table feeling sleepy from the wine. Gus had eaten all he was going to eat when I was halfway through, and he drank no coffee. He couldn't go to the john without me along to keep him from getting lost on the way back. Could have been anyone, but they send Gus Crisantheos, Battery B's ten-year-old, for me to baby-sit.

Out on the Rue St. Lazaire, I took a deep breath of the springlike air. On Christmas Eve we had been in Lorraine, and the Krauts were firing air bursts into snowy subzero skies. A month later, we were having spring. Too good a night to let Gus ruin it. I saw the metro sign and led him across the street.

At the top of the metro steps, Gus asked, "Where we goin'?"

"I don't even know, Gus. I thought we'd take a subway ride to get our bearings."

"Can we find where the girls is at?"

"Wish I knew. We can try."

"Maybe I kin help yez dere." The gravel voice belonged to a big buck sergeant who came out of nowhere. Big enough to be the heavyweight fighter he looked like—broken nose, snaggle-toothed mean look. I sensed trouble.

"We was wonderin' . . ." Gus began.

"I heard yez. I kin help yez wid dat. Where yez wanna go is Pig Alley. Dis here subway—da locals call it metro—goes right dere. I know dis Paris like da backa my hand."

New York, corner of Broadway and Forty-Second, I'm thinking. At that corner, nothing comes without a price tag.

"Da metro's free for GIs, so yez'r in luck dere. But I got a little problem, myself . . ."

Oh oh, here comes the hooker . . .

". . . See . . . I left my cigarettes back in my hotel room," the big guy said, "an' I'm stayin' way on da udder side a town, know what I mean? So I'll have ta ask yez for two packs a smokes, I'm ashamed ta say." He hesitated. "Dat's from eacha yez. Can yez spare 'em?"

I brought an entire ammunition case full to Paris, thanks to the foresight of Ray York, a nonsmoker. Ray bought cigarettes on the ship and then hoarded his pack-a-day allotment until his death. I gave the sergeant four packs from the dozen I'd brought with me from the hotel and held Gus's hand back so the guy wouldn't get more than he asked for.

"Dat's very kinda yez. Jis' for dat, I'm gonna go 'long wid yez. In case yez don't unnerstand my directions."

Just before the metro car slowed for the Pigalle station, the big buck sergeant—who'd identified himself as Harold— leaned over and whispered in my ear: "Listen, Corporal, you been real square wid me, so I wanna be square wid you. I dint leave no cigarettes in no hotel room. I'm a ayewall from da batlah-bulge, an' I'm stayin wid dis French broad, know what I mean?"

"No need to explain, Harold."

"It's okay. I trust yez not to git no MPs after me. See, I kin tell yez'r combat soljers like me." He took a labored raspy breath. "See . . . my outfit was up dere in Bastogne. We got the shit kicked outa us up dere, an' I had alla dat goddamn war I could stand, know what I mean?"

"Okay, mum's the word, Harold," I said. Harold's uniform seemed spotless, like a Paris commando's, know what I mean? He smelled like vomit, and I was sure happy when he backed away a few steps before I choked.

So . . . there were worse guys to be in Paris with than Gus, after all.

I think it's worth noting that a man like Harold was not unusual in post-Bulge Paris. Many desertions took place in the confusion of that epic battle, and though the Americans serving were from what was later identified as "the Greatest Generation," 23,000 men were convicted of desertion in World War II, and many of them wound up on the streets of Paris. Gangs of deserters ran black-market operations with hijacked supplies meant for our embattled troops. These thugs in uniform, while driving a stolen army truck, once got into a running gun battle with MPs on the Boulevard Lafayette. They even murdered the provost marshal of Paris, the city's military chief of police, within weeks of the time I was there.

At the top of the steps at Pigalle, Harold gave us one more set of directions and asked for two more packs. "Dis here's da Boulevard Roach-a-swar. Da side street's Pig Alley. Dere's babes on bot' of 'em. But da ones on Roach is best, least I think so."

I was never so glad to see another man's back as I was that night seeing Harold's broad ass disappearing down the metro steps into a sea of khaki.

A carnival filled the strip running down the middle of the Boulevard Rochechouart— the street Harold called Roach— and Gus got excited. "Hey, Hanaford, they got dodgem cars. You like dodgems?"

I liked ramming Gus's car as hard as I could, and Gus got a chance to ram me back. We took five rides and left the little cars, stumbling around, nearly out of control from laughter. It was the first fun I had with Gus, but how many "dodgems" could there be in Paris?

We walked around the carnival awhile, ate a paper cone of french fries each, and then I led the way across the street to Chez Emille. It was a horseshoe-shaped bar. A mix of servicemen sat there, with and without girls. I was unsure whether this was a pickup joint. Only one way to find out. I ordered a cognac.

"I don't know what that is," Gus said. "Can I have a taste of yours?"

When the drink arrived, I gave Gus a sip. He made a face. "Yuck, that's awful. Do they got Coca-Cola in Paris?"

When I caught the bartender's eye, I beckoned. "*Avez-vous le Coca-Cola?*"

"Hey, I coulda said that. It's the same in French as it is in American. Coca Cola! I didn't know that first part, that *alley-voo* or whatever."

Gus could sometimes entertain by just being himself. *Hinky dinky alley voo.* Gusisms, tonight's show.

I poured a drop or two of cognac in Gus's Coke, and before he could complain, I said, "You won't even taste it, and it'll loosen you up."

He scowled.

A pretty girl across the bar seemed to be smiling at me. Teenagery, soap and water washed, not a dab of makeup— couldn't be a pro, I thought. So before I knew it, I smiled back, and she began circling the bar. Now what should I do?

"Whatta you know, Gus?" I said. "I think I just got me a girl."

"*Bonjour, m'sieur,*" the girl said. "Hello, soldier."

"*Bonjour, mademoiselle.* You speak English?"

"*Un petit peu.* A leetle. I try. *Est-ce que vous parlez français, m'sieur?*" Her lips pursed beautifully on the word *peu.*

"Hey! She speaks American. She said she speaks a little. Whyn't you give her to me? Please, Hanaford! You know how to get a girl and I don't. I can't speak no French. Please! Please!" His facial grimace matched his whine.

"Look, Gus, she and I have already connected. We like each other's looks." I turned to the girl and decided to try my GI pamphlet French again. "*Comment vous appelez-vous, ma cher?*" What's your name, sweetie? Right out of the book.

She understood. "*Je m'appelle Nicole. Est vous, m'sieur?*"

"*Bill. Je m'appelle, Bill. Enchanté, Nicole.*" I shook her hand as instructed in the pamphlet. Her hand had the size and the feel of a child's, and she had a little-girl smile. I thought a more mature woman would be sexier, but I felt possessive of this girl at the same time.

"Please, Hanaford, give her to me," Gus whined.

"Will you shut up for a second, asshole? She doesn't belong to me, so how can I give her to you, dammit? Just look across the bar, and when you see a girl you like, smile like I did, and then you'll have girl of your own, and won't you be proud." *Waste of breath!* "Look at that girl with the orange hair, Greek. Just waiting for you to smile."

"I don't want no orange-hair girl. I like this one."

I turned in disgust back to Nicole. "*Avez-vous une camarade pour mon ami?*"

She smiled and nodded to someone across the bar. A blond stood up and started toward us. Wrong gal. Too old. She has a wig!

Gus emitted the squawk I expected. "Hey, I don't want no old hag like her!"

"Woman of experience, Gus. She'll teach you all the tricks in the book. You had your chance. All you had to do was wink or smile. I told you."

Gus pouted all the way out of Emille's. He wouldn't look at the woman, though she was flirting her head off trying to please him. Suddenly the woman had enough of Gus; she turned back. Nicole intercepted her, speaking rapidly, and the older woman returned, looking more resolute and less frightened. When she took his hand, Gus pushed her away, but she kept walking beside him.

I won't go into the rest of it, but we did what most GIs did when on pass in Paris, and Gus was a pest throughout.

Chapter 13

I set my mental alarm clock for six o'clock and was out on the street while Gus slept. I raced across the street to the Terminus for breakfast and picked up directions to all the tourist spots. I found what I wanted most, a place to have a decent shower. Directed to go one metro stop to L'Opéra, I was to find the American Express office there, then go two blocks west to the former Hôtel de Paris, now the Rainbow Red Cross Center—there I'd get a shower.

I stopped at the American Express to book a bus tour, and I bought a gift of Bellodgia perfume to have shipped to my mother.

Next to the opera house—famed for its phantom—was a real Grand Hôtel. Though not the one from the movie with Greta Garbo (that was in early-Hitler Berlin), this Grand Hotel was truly grand, not shabby like Grand Hôtel du Terminus, and this Grand Hotel had the famous Café de la Paix on its sidewalk. There were actually people eating outside in the balmy sixty-degree weather . . . in January!

Seeing these places I knew only from movies and songs gave me a lift. I enjoyed it all the more knowing Gus wasn't along to spoil it. I went down the Boulevard des Capucines humming a song that was popular in my high school days: "At a Perfume Counter on the Rue de la Paix."

Before I got to the Red Cross Center, I passed the Olympia Theater and saw that Maj. Glenn Miller's orchestra was playing here, so I stopped to look at the marquee. Miller's orchestra was listed there as the AEF Orchestra, and Sgt. Ray McKinley was directing. I knew that Ray McKinley played drums for

Miller's service band and had been a bandleader in civilian life, but why he was now the leader of this band was puzzling. Tickets weren't for sale at that hour, so I crossed the street to the Red Cross Recreation Center.

This facility was doing things right. I had a hot shower while my cruddy uniform was being sponged and pressed. In a way, I didn't want all the stains and rips to vanish; they let knowledgeable people know I wasn't a "Paris commando." The Paris-based soldiers looked sharp in their short British jackets (later called "Ike jackets" after Eisenhower adopted the style). When those guys looked at me, I saw recognition, and I didn't know if it was contempt or envy. I know I had mixed feelings about them.

A caricaturist sketched me, after my pants were pressed, and I went back to the American Express Office to go on the tour.

I was unique among the passengers on that tour: everyone else had a companion to talk to. I sat there by myself and silently absorbed "Tourist Paris"—Tour Eiffel, Place de la Concorde, La Madeleine, Sacre Coeur, the left bank, and all the rest.

We had to stop once, near Lafayette's tomb, for the driver to get out and stoke the stove at the left rear of the bus with the blocks of wood that fueled this wartime vehicle. That in itself was memorable; for when was such a measure ever needed before, or after, except in this god-awful war? But the most important thing I learned on the tour was that I hated being so alone. Like it or not, I was going to have to lose to the captain and Ruotolo and spend the rest of this pass with Gus in tow.

Back at Hôtel Americain, as I walked through the door, the first thing I saw was Gus seated on the lone bench in the tiny, musty lobby with his head in his hands. I felt like a damned heel.

"Where you been Hanaford?" he said.

"I took a bus trip. Saw the city. I thought I ought to let you sleep. Don't tell me you didn't go out?"

"I was scared I'd get lost. I don't know nothin' about Paris," he whined. "Why'd you leave me alone like that? You're a dirty guy."

"Come on, Gus, let's go across the street and get dinner. I'm famished . . ." Suddenly I realized something. "Don't tell me you haven't had anything to eat yet?"

"No. I didn't want to go over there alone. I told you. I ain't ever been to Paris before."

"Jeez, I'm sorry, Gus," I said in the best conciliatory tone I could muster. "I thought at least you'd eat. Well, I'll make it up to you. I got us tickets to the Folies Bergère for tonight."

"What's that? What if I don't wanna go?"

"Naked ladies, Gus. Don't tell me you don't like seeing very beautiful naked ladies dancing?"

The following day, I took Gus on the Paris bus trip, so he'd be able to tell the guys back in the battery that he'd seen "Paree." He complained constantly. "What's all this? Who wants to see all these goddamn churches, and them parks and like that?"

I had wanted to see the Glenn Miller band, but Gus didn't, so we returned to Place Pigalle, and this time I found him a pretty girl, but he still wanted to trade her for the girl who chose me.

It wouldn't have done a scintilla of good to tell Gus that if he behaved, there were two officers who wouldn't have anything to gloat about when we got back.

Chapter 14

The trucks took us back to Alsace the next morning, and on one of the stops along the way, I got a copy of *Stars and Stripes*. The big news was the disappearance of Glenn Miller. He had disappeared way back in December, but the news was hushed up for some dumb reason. Like the Krauts had something to do with it?

We stopped in Saverne, Seventh Army headquarters, to be given a short arm. The news we got there was a surprise. Battery B had moved from Bauxviller to the city of Ingviller, and Gen. Anthony McAuliffe, hero of the Bulge, was now in command of the 103rd, replacing "Cheerful Charlie" Haffner.

Ingviller was a small city, too small to be found on a map, but big enough to house most of the 411th Infantry Regiment.

I wrote a letter to my mother describing Ingviller and comparing it with Bauxviller. (I wasn't allowed to tell anything about the burned house and barn in Bauxviller, as this letter had to be censored by Ruotolo.) "Both of these burgs probably look exactly as they did in the Middle Ages," I wrote, "but Ingviller seems to have an even more medieval look, though it has a business section dominated by the tall shaft of a modern brewery. The stork nests on many of Ingviller's chimneys seem to fit the architecture as though the storks themselves designed the buildings."

Battery B's CP was in the office of a lumberyard on the extreme southeastern edge of town. Gus and I reported in and found Captain Pultz and Lieutenant Wallace seated at adjoining desks. Wallace, who was called Wimpy or Uncle Tom by the

cannoneers, was trying to draw on his forever-unlit Meer-
schaum pipe and making puffing noises.

The captain returned my salute and affected a smile. "Welcome back, you Parisians. Well, how was it?"

Wallace giggled. I was never sure he listened to anything
when he had that damn pipe between his teeth. Maybe he
didn't really think what the captain said was funny, just remembered something that was.

Gus let me answer for him. "Terrific, Sir," I said. "Paris is
the wonder city of the world.

Of course, none of the museums or the Eiffel Tower are
open, but Gus and I had a good time . . . became almost brothers." This time it was Gus's turn to giggle.

"Well, that's nice to hear," Pultz lied. "I'm told I may be
going there myself soon, so I may call on you men to tell me
some fun places to go. You'll probably want to find your sections now . . . and, oh yes, Hanford—I have some news of special interest to you. We'll be losing our forward observer
tomorrow. Lieutenant Ruotolo is being transferred to headquarters battery, and his replacement has yet to arrive."

I knew better than to celebrate in front of the captain, so I
said, "Sorry to hear it. Where are they . . . my section?"

"They haven't found out yet; they're on an OP. You'll have
to wait for them in your new digs."

He sent me across the road to a small cluster of houses. I
could see the guns were dug in in an open field behind them,
so as usual, the cannoneers weren't as well off as us; they had
to sleep on cots in perambular tents. That beat pup tents, however, where they had to sleep on the ground.

These houses were relatively new, different from anything I
had seen before in France. They were corny by U.S. standards,
but modern for Alsace, I guess. Our flat was on the bottom
floor. An Alsatian couple with their six-month-old baby lived
upstairs, but I didn't learn that until later. I was alone to survey
our new living quarters, a typical one-bedroom, one-bathroom,
kitchen-dining-living-room apartment. The location of bedrolls
showed me that Ruotolo had the only bedroom. Frank and I

were given the main-room floor, and Rocky had a bedroll in the entryway, making this a first for him—he was actually not going to sleep in his jeep. Voilà! We had a bathtub and plenty of charcoal briquettes. The final luxury I discovered was a room full of furniture. (The couple who had lived here before us had to flee ahead of our army, because they were Nazi immigrants from 1939.) We had become celebrities with the best accommodations in the battery.

I was soaking in the bathtub when my section got back.

Ruotolo was teary-eyed the next day when saying good-bye. He held both Lawrence and me in bear hugs before Rocky drove him away. Half an hour later, I began to worry, so I told Frank what was bothering me: "If he wears out his welcome at headquarters, which seems likely . . . then bet on it, he'll be back here, pronto."

"All I know is . . . he's gone," Frank said. "Don't always be expecting the worst."

Our new lieutenant arrived the following day. Captain Pultz sent someone from the CP to get us. Frank and I hurried over, praying we would get a better guy than the one we had lost.

The new officer was easily the biggest man we'd ever had in the battery, though not as tall as six-foot-five Byron Krump, with whom I often played catch. Before he said a word, I knew he was a gift. His smile was broad . . . and real! "Lieutenant Gilman, this is your FO section," the captain said.

"I already know about these guys," Gilman said. "They told me at headquarters I was inheriting the best FO section in the division." (He had met Ruotolo, of course.) Though he could have crushed us with his handshake, he held back, but made it firm enough to convince both Frank and me that this was more than we'd prayed for—an officer and a gentleman, the real article at last.

The captain took Gilman back to the CP for something, and Frank and I danced around the table with joy over our new-found good luck. That evening, Gilman brought his bottle of Scotch and put it on the table in the apartment, inviting Frank and me to join him in a drink to celebrate our new family. We spent the next several hours finding out things about each other.

He was a graduate of Auburn University, where he had played tackle on a nationally recognized football team, and he said he would appreciate all the help we could give him in forward observing. His soft southern accent was fun to listen to— entirely different from the country-western nasal twangs we were used to hearing from most of our down-south batterymates.

It took only two days to have the balloon burst. Gilman was supposed to go to Battery C. Once more, we got called over to the lumberyard to meet his replacement. George Apfel, our switchboard operator, who came to get us, didn't help us expect much. "He looks crabby, this one," Apfel said. "I sure wish we'd been able to keep that big guy."

The captain introduced us: "Lieutenant Bonnet, this is Sergeant Lawrence and Corporal Hanford."

Lt. Andrew Bonnet didn't even look up, simply stuck out a limp hand and said, "Gladameetchah." Then turned and said, "Captain, where's your chow truck? I haven't had my lunch yet."

Two guys—Frank Lawrence and Bill Hanford—scuffed their feet on the way back to their new quarters. I said, "We seem to be stuck with another one. This guy may make us wish for Tonto to come back."

When Bonnet finally did come to the house, he had Rocky carry in a huge bedroll and duffle bag, then spent an hour in the bedroom, without thanking Rocky or acknowledging our presence. We were glum.

He came out of the bedroom carrying a bottle of whiskey and said to me, in a growl, "How old are you, Corporal?"

"Twenty-four," I said.

"What month's your birthday?"

"January."

"Mine was last October. Respect your elders. You drink?"

"Yessir."

"There any glasses in that cupboard? Get a glass." He turned to Lawrence. "How old are you, Sergeant?" He went through the same routine with Frank. When he asked about Rockwell, who was out in the hall, he was told Rocky never had drunk nor ever would. "Good!" Bonnet said, "I like my drivers sober. Leaves more for the rest of us."

Despite Bonnet's brusqueness, he was getting off to the same start as Gilman—sharing his booze. I never saw Ruotolo share anything. Things were looking up!

We sat and drank until late. By the time we finally hit the sack, Frank and I knew a lot about Bonnet. And I knew a few things I didn't want to know. I was drunk enough by the end of the evening to still believe much of what he said. By dawn, however, I began to weigh his claims, and I was convinced he had a drinking problem.

He said he had played football at Texas A&M, where he was a single-wing quarterback whose job was blocking for John Kimbrough, A&M's famous running back. Shoot! This guy was only a pound or two heavier than I, and I was never silly enough to play anything rougher than touch football. He really messed up when he claimed to have slept with Jane Russell while in California to play in the Rose Bowl. I had an encyclopedic memory of sports, and I knew A&M never played in any Rose Bowl, so Jane Russell's reputation was unscathed.

Bonnet's other claims: His wife was the queen of the Drake Relays, where he met her when he was competing in the mile relay, running the anchor to lead his team to the world record. And his mom had been campus queen of the University of Texas, his father's college. "Two queens in one family, how 'bout them apples?"

As if that weren't enough, he said his father-in-law was a general and the commanding officer of the 15th Service Command and had kept him stateside at his daughter's request, until Bonnet found out and volunteered for combat, making his wife furious. "This's the only war goin' on, so I wasn't about to miss it."

I never discussed my doubts with Frank, because he was dizzy with admiration, and I knew we were blessed to have Bonnet instead of Ruotolo, so why spoil it?

Sergeant Potter, the radio repairman, had me go on an errand with him while Frank and Lieutenant Bonnet were at an orientation meeting at Battalion. Potter had met Berthe and Albert Weil, the couple living above our flat, and he liked them enough to accompany the wife through sentries posted by the antiaircraft battery on the dirt road behind us. I agreed to go along with Potter and the woman that morning.

Berthe was a prototypical Alsatian *hausfrau,* frumpily dressed in the earth-colored woolens common on rural women in France, as well as in Alsace. I imagined how she'd look with lipstick, rouge, and a nice dress—not bad, maybe even pretty. She had a sad smile frozen on her plain pale face, but it was easy to see she was devoted to her six-month-old baby girl, and that her gratitude to Potter was real. She had cousins in the adjoining hamlet, peasants who could supply eggs, sausage, milk, and potatoes—foods excessively expensive or unobtainable in Ingviller.

"I won't be able to go along with her tomorrow," Potter said, "So you wouldn't mind going with her if you don't have to go to an OP, would you? Her and her husband'll invite us up for dinner soon. And get this . . . they got a source for black-market steaks!"

I wondered how he knew all this, because I guessed neither of them spoke a word of English, and Potter never learned any French or German that I knew of.

Berthe and I took turns carrying the baby. The milk and egg town was merely a cluster of houses and barns, all joined with a common fence. The leathery purple-faced people who sold Berthe the groceries were pleasant to her but seemed to avoid eye contact with me. That made me even less sure that most Alsatians were friendly to the Allied cause, despite the FFI we'd seen in Barr.

The night after I took Berthe for groceries, Potter and I went upstairs to the Weils flat, and though they were stiff and formal at first, we enjoyed the evening. The steaks were tough, but to palates bored by several years of GI food, chateaubriand wouldn't have tasted better. We paid for the steaks, of course, but the cost was small enough for me to believe Berthe and Albert made no profit. We drank apple wine before and after the meal and Berthe served us open-faced mirabelle plum tarte with crème-fraîche topping.

We went to our first OP with our new lieutenant to the east of those where Ruotolo last took us, and Bonnet found high ground with good cover—evidence he had been well instructed at Fort Sill. Frank and I were both pleased. Now we had to see what he would do if we got shelled. Better yet, we had to see what he would do if we saw nothing . . . *and* got no shelling. Our first OP turned out fine—we looked for six hours into a pretty little hamlet where even civilians seemed absent. Where there were no people, we had learned, there were sure to be Krauts.

The second day on the same OP, I was the careless one—I smoked too close to the OP, and the Krauts saw it and fired a mortar shell at us. Now we got our next chance to pass judgement on our lieutenant.

"Is that all they shoot at us? Pop guns?" he asked.

Frank answered for me: "Those pop guns do most of the killing, next to rifles," he said.

"Then maybe we ought to get out of here," Bonnet said.

On our way back to Ingviller, our new officer said, "This doesn't seem like much of a war."

"We haven't gone forward with the infantry yet, sir," I said.

The 103rd Division—along with the entire Seventh Army— remained in a static position for six weeks. During this lull, the captain, having discovered that Bonnet and Lawrence played respectable bridge, brought Wallace and his god-awful pipe over to our flat for nightly two-hour sessions, which he critiqued for an hour after. I usually snoozed on the floor a few feet away.

I went up to the Weils' for steaks about twice a week and played checkers with a jeep driver named Templin on days our section didn't man an OP.

Each night, from the first of March on, we heard trucks and half-tracks pulling into positions behind us. We knew these were artillery batteries attached to Seventh Army or VI Corps.

They were building up support for the attack we felt certain was coming any day. Andy would be getting his chance to see war soon.

Bonnet got his first true scare the first week in March. We were sent to town, where the 411th Regiment had located themselves as close to the main line of resistance as I'd seen since St. Martin back in November. On the main street of the town were trucks, tanks, jeeps, and foot soldiers milling around with headquarters signs in front of most of the houses. I sensed this was some kind of preparation for the coming offensive, and it made both Frank and me uneasy.

We went to the outpost line to make our OP, as this was high ground and less than a mile from woods occupied by the enemy. It was the strangest OPL I ever saw: the riflemen had a dozen foxholes atop a treeless hill that had to be plainly visible to the Krauts. We had barely gotten there and dug our own holes before we were fired on. The doughboys seemed calm about it, so we stayed there. We were shelled about once an hour, and nobody made a move to change to a less vulnerable position. We saw no sign of the enemy, to Bonnet's disappoint-ment, but we spent the day there until Frank and I suggested that this was a stupid place to be. Bonnet respected our expe-rience and agreed to go back into the town. "But let's not go too far from that OPL," he said. "They may need artillery, if the Krauts decide to attack."

We found a deserted house about 200 yards away and brought in a telephone line. It was a balmy springlike day, and I went out on a porch and was whistling the last chorus of Count Basie's "One O'Clock Jump" while beating time on a railing, when the air was filled with shrieks—sounding like 100 shells coming toward us at once. Screaming meemies! I recog-nized them immediately. I ran back into the room and dived under the bed, where Frank had already scrambled ahead of me. We shook like fish in a net.

"It's a counterattack!" I heard Bonnet shouting. "Get on the phone, Hanford!"

I climbed out from under the bed as the shrieking seemed to have ended with giant explosions to our rear. The phone was dead. I had used it just an hour ago, so I knew it was not the batteries. We were helpless: I couldn't even call Rocky to bring the jeep.

Fortunately, it was only a short walk back into town, so all of us walked back. The main street was in turmoil: jeeps and trucks were already in a traffic jam, and soldiers were running toward the exit to town. I held the phone line in my hand as we walked but found no break. I also kept looking for the destruction left by the Nebelwerfer rockets, but again I found nothing.

It took an hour of near panic to find the break in the phone lines and the destruction from the rockets. By some kind of freak of war, the rockets had hit a huge conjunction of wires at an intersection, and nearly every line into that town had been broken. We found Rocky in the traffic jam and were able to get back to the battery in time for evening chow.

On March 12, we were sent to meet with the 2nd Battalion's George Company, with whom we would be going into the coming offensive. It was in a wooded area east of Ingviller and a mile south of Greisbach, a town we had watched from OPs during most of the past six weeks. The George Company CO was Captain Stagg, whom I knew from the December offensive. He told Bonnet we would be going forward in a very few days in Operation Undertone, and he was looking forward to it. I decided that infantry officers were a different breed; unlike Ruotolo, they weren't show-offs, they just wanted to win the war.

The next night, after two restless days, we were invited upstairs to the Weils for a farewell dinner. This time they had the whole section, as well as Potter. (Of course, Rockwell refused to go along.) After half a dozen or so meals with the Weils, I had learned a few words of Alsatian German, so I did most of the communicating. The apple wine flowed freely, and by the time the mirabelle tarte was served, Andy Bonnet was bombed, having downed half a bottle of bourbon earlier. He decided to make the toast. Unexpectedly, he stood and raised his glass: "Heil Hitler!"

The silence following fairly crackled. I avoided looking at Berthe and Albert for fully half a minute; when I did, they were both flush-faced, and Berthe was close to tears. Potter and Lawrence were red-faced, and I knew I had to say something.

"I wish you hadn't said that, Andy," I said.

"Why? I was being funny . . . wasn't I?"

"No, sir."

"How do you apologize in Kraut? I didn't mean any harm."

"I don't speak either French or German that well," I said. "Try saying, '*Je m'excuse*.'"

"Okay. *Jay mscuse*. How's that? That's French, isn't it?"

The Weils, showing they understood his terrible French, both said, "*Merci, vous êtes excusé*." But the damage was too deep to undo so easily. All the sign language, broken French, and bastard German we'd been using to communicate was no longer of use. We were a bunch of deaf-mutes without a mutual language, as Frank, Potter, and I tried to thank our hosts for what should have been a fine evening. We did our best, and Berthe seemed to feel our embarrassment and tried to defuse it, but nothing was working. We hugged both of them and they said, "*Bon chance*," several times.

I almost fell on the stairs, finding myself twice as inebriated as I actually knew myself to be: the embarrassment had made the alcohol in the mild apple wine as potent as cognac.

Back downstairs, Andy hoisted the bottle he had left on the center of the table and said, "I can hardly wait until tomorrow," then tipped the bottle back and took a huge swallow.

I said, "I only hope I'm alive the day *after* tomorrow."

Chapter 15

We were awake at five the next morning, filled with expectation and fear. Lieutenant Bonnet looked more than a little hungover. He downed a few swallows left in a bottle of Old Crow before he combed his hair.

I worried he was going to stay half oiled when we got out where quick thinking was all that could give us half a chance to stay alive. Beneath all that worrying was apprehension. Could this lieutenant do the job well enough to keep Ruotolo from reentering our lives?

I told Frank, "We got to keep a close eye on Andy. Let's try to make him become a bigger hero to Battalion than Tonto."

"That may happen, only if we can keep him sober," Frank said.

A sudden shock awaited. Word came over from the lumberyard: Frank Lawrence is to report there prior to going on pass to Paris. Bob Sudlow would take his place with our section until Lawrence returned.

Frank was happy, and Bonnet and I had to try to be happy too. I could see in Frank's eyes that he understood the pressure this put on me. I was going to be the only man in the section with experience on an attack, and my officer was dependent entirely on Texas A&M and OCS training—that is, if he was telling the truth about Texas A&M.

Sudlow was a nice guy, but I hardly knew him, though I was the guy who invented the section's moniker, "Super Sudlow," which I borrowed from the popular radio singing soap commercial: "Super Suds . . . Super Suds . . . Much more suds with Super Su-u-uds."

As Rocky drove us away to meet George Company, it was almost like leaving home. Ingviller had been our base for six weeks—in war, an eternity.

The riflemen of G Company were lined up for their last hot breakfast in the woods southeast of Greisbach, the village to be bombarded before the jump-off. Captain Stagg greeted us: "You guys didn't eat, I hope? Because we got one helluva mess sergeant."

"I'm not hungry," Bonnet said, "but my men might be."

"This may be the last hot food you'll have for some time, Andy," Stagg urged. "This guy is a genius with government-issue food. You got to taste his hotcakes, honest."

Bonnet agreed to try, just to please Captain Stagg, and though I wasn't hungry, I knew I ought to eat.

"The sump's full of the genius's hotcakes," Sudlow muttered. "So who's hungry besides the captain?"

The thrown-away pancakes said a lot about the kind of day the doughboys were expecting, though the eyes of those I saw showed no emotion at all.

While Sudlow and I were sitting on a log trying to swallow the gummy cakes and greasy bacon, I moved over to make room for a young lieutenant to sit beside me. He looked like a Boy Scout and smiled as though he expected me to recognize him.

"You don't know me," he said. "I'm Mel Wright, and it's okay to call me Mel . . . everybody in George Company does. I came over as a PFC. Two-thirds of our officers are field commissions. See that short, chubby guy there? That's Putt-Putt. Used to be our supply sergeant. Was Putt-Putt then, and he's Putt-Putt still. Reason we got so many battlefield commissions? We lost lots of our platoon leaders on the mountains in the Saar back in December."

Sudlow and I threw half our flapjacks in the garbage sump. Bonnet didn't taste his; he threw them all in the sump and stepped behind a tree to take a nip from a half-pint bottle he must have brought from the States. (Andy Bonnet's recipe for preattack breakfast: Four Roses, to taste.)

The sun was getting higher. "There's going to be a dive-bombing attack at zero-six-thirty hours," Captain Stagg announced, "followed by a shelling from every gun in the VI Army Corps. All of it on little Greisbach over there."

He had barely finished his announcement when someone shouted: "Get down! Get down!"

Every one of us hit the ground hard, and we covered our heads. My mind conceived some sort of counterattack. I hugged the ground until I heard an explosion. It was small. Not as big as a mortar blast. I stayed prone until I heard laughing.

When I looked up, Captain Stagg was running toward a red-faced soldier brushing himself off next to a stonewall across the road from us. "What just happened here?" the captain shouted.

I didn't hear the answer, but when Captain Stagg came back, he told Bonnet that a rookie fresh from the States had tried to hang a hand grenade by the loop holding the release pin—a big mistake. "He was quick enough to pick it up, toss it over the wall, and yell for us to get down," Stagg said, grinning, "So I think he's going to work out."

The hand-grenade incident loosened things up, and the nervous infantrymen became animated for a while, but as six-thirty neared, the woods south of Greisbach became quiet again. I checked my watch and saw there were two minutes to go. I began counting: one thousand . . . two thousand . . .

Precisely on time, I heard the hum of planes, flying level. The sound turned into a roar as the planes began diving. The roar became a rumble as they passed the trees over our heads and we could see them: P-47s spitting lines of tracers, one after the other. Each plane released bombs that looked like aspirin tablets but shook the earth when they exploded, and no tracers rose to challenge the planes. A cloud of pink blossomed from the rooftops of little Greisbach, and the enemy ack-ack guns finally began throwing up black puffs of smoke into the pink, but the planes continued to dive right in and through the black puffs. We, who had been shelled by artillery, couldn't help but see how much more terrorizing an aerial bombardment had to be for those under it.

The roar of planes and the thunder of bombs exploding had barely ended when the shriek of hundreds of cannon shells roiled the air above the trees, and the P-47s moved five miles east to continue their destruction on another village. When the artillery shells began hammering Greisbach, a cloud even bigger than that left by the planes began rising. Flashes followed, as black smoke turned to white, to pink, back to white again. The howitzers were firing high explosives mixed with phosphorus: the high explosive for destruction and the smoke for its effect on morale—to boost ours and damage theirs.

A giant mushroom gray mass grew to 50 feet . . . to 100 . . . then to 150 feet or more, while the ground quaked beneath us. I couldn't believe any human could possibly live through such a pummeling. If his head and body survived, could his hearing? Bonnet said, "This is more like it. This is war!"

I looked at Sudlow to see if he was holding up and could see nothing unusual. His body was tense, but so was everyone else's, and his face showed nothing.

We could hear the town five miles east getting pasted like Greisbach. We had to wait for two more such pastings along the front for the offensive to begin. Battery B was providing all the FOs for the 2nd Battalion, which was attacking in company strength instead of the way it had in December. Lt. Buster Whidden was with E Company on our right flank, and Lt. Kenny Rebman was with F Company, farther to the right.

Captain Stagg gathered G Company on the road. "Okay, men," he said, "The first thing I want to impress upon you is . . . keep moving! They want to pin us down. We can't let 'em. If they can get us to stop coming forward, they can bring big artillery down on us, so keep moving!Crawl, if you must, but keep moving. When we get to the stream over there, we got to wade across. We'll stop long enough for you to wring your socks out. Keep your weapons and bandoliers high, so we don't have wet guns and ammo."

We got to the stream quickly, and the first men to wade into the icy water complained and shivered. No one hesitated. We were so numb from fear that the water almost felt warm. Lieutenant Bonnet took Sudlow's and my carbines and also our pistol belts, because we had to hold the radio and the battery pack out of the water, which was up to our waists at midstream.

On the other side, I sat on the cold ground and took my shoes off, held them upside down, and poured out a stream of water. I had fresh socks but no change of shoes. No good to change socks and then step back into wet shoes. I wrung out my socks and put them back on, damp and yucky.

In less than five minutes, the entire company had made it through the stream, and the men had wrung out their socks and were back on their feet. Minesweepers were in front, the scouts right behind, with Captain Stagg only a few yards behind them—one brave captain.

"We stay in the middle of the column, Lieutenant," I said to Bonnet.

"Why the middle? Why not the rear?"

"The rear will get hit with most of the mortar fire. The Krauts fire the first rounds as far away from their own troops as they can, and they may adjust quick enough to hit the middle if we stop too long. A smart doughboy taught me that."

Within seconds after we moved to the middle, the first mortar shells slithered overhead, falling to the rear, as expected.

Suddenly the column stopped moving. What the captain had feared was now happening: the men up ahead were on their bellies and not advancing.

The next mortar burst was only fifteen feet to our left. Luckily we were already flat on our bellies. "They got the range," I said. "See what I mean?"

I saw no fear in Bonnet's eyes.

Enemy machine-gun fire began chattering up ahead, and when the guns quit firing, word was passed down the column: "BAR [Browning automatic rifle] men, machine gunners, up front, pronto!"

"I hope no Kraut observer sees how far left those last rounds landed," Bonnet said—already thinking smart. If the enemy mortarmen decided to do a sweep back this way, some of the next ones might hit right on top of us.

The column began moving again. The BAR men had done their job.

Greisbach was half a mile to our left, and a ridge with small trees and brush was to our right. We started to pass small white scraps of paper. "Watch your step," an infantry lieutenant said. "Those scraps mark mines detected by our sweepers."

Some medics passed, carrying a wounded man on their stretcher. Probably a minesweeper or scout, I thought.

Several shells screamed overhead and landed far to the rear, as word came back: "FO up front. We need artillery fire."

Bonnet looked pleased. I knew this was bad news, but Andy was to get his second lesson in war. We moved rapidly, crouching low, then were motioned to lie on our bellies and creep, as we got to the slope where the captain and a couple of BAR men lay. I had the radio on my wooden backpack, and Sudlow had the battery pack on his. We stopped well back, where we could get into a crouch without being seen by the enemy, and began putting the two radio parts together.

Andy crept forward and got his field glasses on the target area identified by Captain Stagg. He rolled onto his back, looked toward me and calmly said, "Fire mission. Enemy machine guns . . ."

I pressed the button on my mike and repeated his words. We had radio communication—not always automatic.

We lay there waiting. The first round came whistling over a few minutes later. I couldn't see where the shell landed, but from the reaction of the officers and the BAR men, I could tell the first round landed nearly on target. This too was something that happened because of the remarkable accuracy of the maps made by the French.

After satisfying Fire Direction by making unnecessary procedural corrections with two more rounds, Bonnet had me send the "Fire for effect" command.

When the fire came, it included all sizes and kinds of artillery, with 105s, 155s, and more sizzling over us into the enemy. All those trucks we'd heard pulling into our rear during our six-week respite bought us artillery to spare, and Fire

Direction was using it generously. The Germans were finished, I thought. No one could live very long through that sort of barrage.

We returned to the middle of the column as soon as the infantrymen started moving forward again. Having barely reached the middle, we saw a rifleman shooting into the trees on the ridge to our right. "Krauts. I seen one of 'em peekin' over the bush there," the soldier said.

"There's one of our companies on the other side of that ridge," a lieutenant said. "You're sure it's a Kraut?"

"It's a Kraut," the rifleman said. "I know what a Kraut looks like. Sonuvabitch was right behind that big bush there. I wanna shoot a rifle-grenade in there. That okay, sir?"

"Yeah. Go ahead, if you're that sure."

I knew Lieutenant Whidden was over there with Len Harris and Bob Wilmoth, so I worried.

I wasn't sure the rifleman knew what he saw. We watched as he fixed the grenade on his M-1, knelt, placed the butt of the stock on the ground, and fired.

He got a burst right on the bush where he'd said the Kraut was hidden. It was all by instinct, like an accurate throw by an outfielder.

Bonnet pulled out his .45, took aim at the bush and fired. Shell cases popped from his pistol as he fired six times.

"Did you see the Kraut?" I asked.

"Nah, but I trust that doughboy. He says there's a Kraut behind that bush, I believe him."

I'd have said something sarcastic to Tonto, but not to Andy Bonnet. I was disappointed again, like last night, but I still liked the man; I just wished he hadn't taken so many belts of Four Roses. He put his pistol back in the holster like a cowboy after a shootout, as the infantry lieutenant stared in disgust.

George Company continued forward into a shallow clearing. I checked my watch. We were thirty minutes into the advance. We heard a lot of small arms firing on our right flank, followed by the sound of a shell whistling at us from our rear— our own artillery. A screeching whistle, even from that direction, sent us to the ground automatically. Then a shell burst on top of the ridge separating us from Easy Company on our right. It was a phosphorus shell. The FO over there was Lt. Buster Whidden, and he was being cautious.

More warning whistles brought more smoke shells right in among us. Bonnet said, "Buster's having a problem. He should have adjusted in the opposite direction."

That should have tipped us off. I was stupid not to set up the radio right then and call over there and let Buster know his smoke shells were landing in our midst.

Only minutes after the last smoke shell landed, we heard a loud rush of whistles.

Incoming shells were upon us before any of us could dive to the ground. It sounded like a hundred. Buster was firing on us with high-explosive shells!

I grabbed Lieutenant Bonnet by the shoulder and pulled him forward into a dry stream bed beside the ridge, and Sudlow came right behind.

Andy shouted to be heard. "What the hell're they trying to do to us?"

Shells crashed everywhere, by tens and twenties.

I squeezed out of my backpack and unstrapped the radio, and Sudlow did the same with the battery pack, while death screamed and exploded over and around us. We lay on our sides, trying to couple the two pieces together, none of it easy with trembling hands. Instincts told me all of us would die before we got the artillery stopped.

What I wanted to do in seconds was taking minutes—minutes that could save men from dying. Together we pushed the two cable plugs together so that ten needles from the radio plug fit into the tiny holes of the battery plug. Then I screwed the outer ring of the two fittings together. All this we did with ice-cold, trembling fingers.

The screaming of the wounded could be heard over the air-rupturing whistling of incoming shells and the steady, concussive, earth-ejecting explosions. This was the same massive shellfire that had pounded little Greisbach minutes before, only this time without the mushroom cloud, yet medics ran through the deadly bursts to aid the wounded.

Once I had the cable together, I had to unfasten the telescoping antenna from clamps atop the radio. It took twice the normal time while lying on my side. My own battery was killing our men while I fumbled.

I tried to screw the threads from the antenna into a coupling on the corner of the radio. The threads could not come together! In desperation, I jumped to my feet.

"Get down!" Andy yelled.

I ignored him and grappled with the antenna and coupling until the threads finally meshed. Now I had to remain standing while I pulled the telescoping sections to the very top. Panic slowed me down. But it got done!

The earth came up to meet me as I dove for low ground.

I pressed the button on the mike, then realized I couldn't remember the day's call sign. To hell with it! "Cease fire! Cease fire!" I shouted. "This is Baker Battery! Cease fire!"

I waited for a reply on the loudspeaker, not at all sure I had made contact.

"Identify yourself," came from the loud speaker. Len Harris's voice! Thank God!

"Harris, dammit, this is Hanford. Cease fire!"

"Farm Dog Baker . . . Cease fire!" Harris called. "Cease fire . . . Cease fire . . ."

When I heard Fire Direction repeat the transmission, I clutched the ground and covered my head. Now all that mattered was survival. Bob Sudlow, Andy Bonnet, and I lay in the dry streambed and hugged the ground, fearing the last dozen shells might still kill one or all of us.

The horrendous noise stopped after many minutes, and now the screams of the wounded and the shouting of the medical aid men echoed everywhere.

There weren't enough medics, and I was tempted to go help.

"You don't go anywhere," Bonnet said. "Keep that set on and see where they decide to fire next."

As Andy suspected, Harris came back on with another fire mission. This one, Andy heard on the speaker. They were still calling for fire far too close to us, so he had me call another cease fire, and I saw a look of disgust on the face of a young infantry lieutenant who heard me. After all this death, did the artillery still need to be told to cease fire again? Artillery was the enemy at that moment in this valley, and I was ashamed of being an artilleryman.

Several of the dead were within ten feet of us, and we had to look at what our failure caused this company. To add to the shame, I found my call sign written in ink on the sleeve of my jacket.

An hour after the tragedy hit George Company, all of us were in the woods, fifty yards removed from the bloody corpse-filled clearing. And now the German guns took over. The firing from those guns killed a few more, and everyone was stunned and shaking. All the courage and will to fight were gone; we were like prizefighters who had taken too many vicious jabs to the chin, staggering us and setting us up for the kayo punch. We lay on the ground, hoping a tree burst wasn't coming next.

The Krauts must have been low on ammunition, or I'm sure they would have poured it on until G Company was zero. With the end of their barrage, Lt. Andy Bonnet stood in front of me: "Kick my ass, somebody. I'm the silly turd who thought he had to see war. Come on, Bill, kick! You too, Sudlow, I deserve it. War is stinking rotten dung."

A nearby lieutenant said, "Andy, forget it. What you saw today is just the beginning. You think today was rotten? Wait till we get to Bobenthal."

All around us, men were quickly digging. Captain Stagg hadn't ordered the men to dig in, nor had he said the attack was over for the day. He didn't have to. The Krauts had fired on us, so they knew we were here, and they would fire on us again. Foxholes were loved by infantrymen—with good reason. Deep enough, they saved lives.

Sudlow and the lieutenant also got out their entrenching tools and began digging. I had brought no shovel with me, because I'd anticipated we would get to a town before nightfall, and the radio on my back was weight enough. I asked Bonnet if he wanted me to dig his foxhole for him, hoping to use his shovel to dig mine when I got through.

"I should dig yours," he said. "You saved our butts back there. Why aren't you digging your own?"

"Got no shovel."

"Go get the one on that dead guy over there." He pointed to a sergeant lying facedown ten feet away—one of the ones killed by the Krauts.

I had already seen that possibility but had not been able to. I couldn't even look at the guy, much less touch him. I decided to be truthful. "I can't do it," I said.

Sudlow put down his shovel. "I'll get it," he said.

I pushed past him. "Okay, okay, okay!" I said. I forced myself to go to the dead body. I tried to take the shovel from the canvas carrier that fit right under his backpack. Halfway through, I had to stop and turn away. I gagged, and my eyes began running. Sudlow started back toward me, and I went back to the dead guy, determined not to vomit. The shovel carrier came loose from his pistol belt this time, and I turned away quickly. Twenty minutes later, I had dug down four feet with the small entrenching shovel. Such a deep dig was made possible because of the mild early spring we'd been having. Back home on March 15, the ground would only be unfrozen the first couple inches.

The digging was a way of forgetting the terror we had just gone through. I thought how lucky I was not to be a rifleman from George Company and have to look at my dead comrades lying out there, or have to hear the suffering cries of the wounded—guys I had known for two years in training. FOs like me were mongrels, neither cannoneers nor riflemen, halfbreeds fighting beside infantry strangers while calling the distant field artillery home and family.

Captain Stagg finally told everyone to dig in for the night. It was barely past noon, and the enemy had held up our advance. We would have to start over in the morning.

Across the rest of the front, I was sure the Seventh Army was more successful: the sounds of small arms and artillery echoed all around us the rest of the day.

Sudlow and I decided to move away from the first holes we had dug to make a single narrow slit trench in which to spend the night. We were in flat terrain between two hillocks, each with a large man-made cave dug by the Krauts. The officers, including Bonnet, were going to sleep in the cave to our right, and the medics made the one to our left a temporary aid station. Badly wounded men, who had to be kept sedated, were in there awaiting removal to field hospitals by the division medical battalion. One man's leg had been blown off, and the medics used most of their supply of morphine on him.

Sudlow and I had not brought bedrolls or blankets, so we scrunched together into this hole, barely wide enough for one. We intended to keep warm by using each other's body heat. We did go to sleep like that, but we were able to sleep only two or three hours at a stretch before the cold woke us, then we had to turn with great difficulty and alternate warm sides.

Shortly after dark, we found out how close we had come to the enemy artillery positions. They sounded like they were less than 100 yards away. Horses whinnied, whips cracked, and a few trucks ground gears and roared engines just beyond the trees where we had dug our first holes less than half a day ago

The sedatives wore off in the hospital dugout before dawn, and men in pain moaned and screamed. That Sudlow and I were able to sleep at all was remarkable; it could happen only in war.

When all of the company was up and ready to move out, I heard Captain Stagg talking to the other officers. He was past angry: the division medics had refused to come help move the wounded back to roads for ambulances to get them, because they were afraid to walk through the minefields, even though they were told about the white scraps of paper put down by the minesweepers.

We could see how much damage our shells had caused by how much shorter George Company's column had become as we began moving. There were less than 100 men, I guessed.

We came out of the woods onto a wide footpath slanting down a hill toward a road, where three tanks were coming to meet us. The tankers were smiling and waving at us, and we could see they were black men. We cheered as they drew nearer, and the tankers pushed out their chests pridefully.

They waited for our column to cross the road and begin going up another hill, before they moved into the path we had just come down. As they neared the top, a loud explosion occurred, and the second of the three tanks seemed to be hit by shell fire. We watched from the hill we had just climbed as men poured out the second tank's hatch and ran to nearby foxholes left by the Germans. They had barely jumped into the holes before the remaining tank crews opened their hatches and followed them.

The men around me were guessing that enemy tanks must have spotted them from some distant hills off to our right, but no conjecture anyone was able to come up with seemed possible.

Within minutes after the dozen tankers had left their tanks for foxholes, four or five of them climbed out and motioned the others to come along. By that time, we decided the second tank had exploded a land mine that the first one somehow missed. This was confirmed by the tankers, who went to the second tank and began messing around with a broken track on the left side.

A jeep soon came down the road, as we sat there watching the drama unfold. The jeep had a white officer, who stood up when he got to the bottom of the path and motioned for the men to come down where he could talk to them. He was in the process of interrogating one of the men, whom I judged was the ranking NCO, when we had to leave the scene behind us. Somehow we got the impression that these tankers were raw rookies, and it was not going to be easy to get those tanks moving again.

Chapter 16

We reached a small village before noon, just as it began raining lightly. Easy Company came into the town at the same time, and our paths crossed as the roads merged at a fork. This was the company whose FO was Lieutenant Whidden, who called that disastrous fire on G Company. George Company stopped and let them pass, and E Company then went down what appeared to be the main street in this hamlet, which paralleled a creek.

The two company commanders talked briefly, and Whidden, Harris, and Wilmoth came over to see us. Bonnet turned his back to Whidden, but I wanted to talk with these men whom I considered friends. Through it all, Lieutenant Whidden was a friendly person; for example, he actually encouraged us to call him Buster after he came to us as a replacement for Allison. I knew he—or Easy Company's CO—had mistaken us for Germans. Even so, the tragedy was as much my fault as his after I saw the smoke shells, and I told him as much. All three of them patted Sudlow and me on the shoulder.

Captain Stagg then had us wade the creek even though his company already had men being treated for trench foot. Small bridges were too easy to booby-trap in Stagg's opinion. Across from the town, we were in among trees too sparse to be called a forest, but despite the bridge, the village had no houses on this side. We watched as Easy Company trod along the paved street and turned a corner leading out of town and soon disappeared. Less than a minute later, we heard the sizzling of a large artillery shell coming over us to crash on the road. This artillery fire had to have been pre-arranged because no observer could possibly have seen that road through the trees behind us. Yet another two shells crashed within twenty feet of the first one. I worried that the enemy knew where we were and might even have a brave observer inside the town calling on fire very near his own location. Were those four shells "overs" that just needed a slight adjustment before our side of the stream would be fired on?

Not long after that, a tiny old women came along the road, skinny loaves of bread sticking up from a leatherette shopping bag. We hoped the Krauts were through with targeting the road, but a warning shriek told us another round was coming in—and the old lady seemed to be walking right into it! *Boom!* It landed less than twenty feet from her, and she fell to the pavement. At least a minute passed, and the old lady remained face down. All of us thought she was dead.

We cheered when she got to her feet, brushed herself off, picked up her bag, and started forward again. Then we held our breath as another round screamed above us. This shell landed fifty feet or more behind her, but she dropped to the ground again like a trained soldier. She got up immediately and bravely continued on her way.

But it wasn't over yet. The next shell seemed to hit at her feet, and this time, we were sure she was dead. She lay perfectly still for five full minutes. When she got up this time, I held back tears. We were even more amazed when she still took her time brushing off and gathering her things from the ground. "Run, Grandma! Get in your house!" someone shouted. She finally went in a house a few feet from her last fall. We all applauded.

Captain Stagg kept us in the woods across from the town for several more hours, and the artillery never did fire on us. When we went back into the village, we used the bridge. I have no idea what convinced the captain it was safe or why we went through the creek in the first place.

There were more houses in that village than we saw at first, most of them back down the other road from the fork. George Company was ordered by the division to remain there for the night to guard regimental headquarters. We FOs were excused from guard duty—one benefit we had when we were up with the infantry. All of us needed dry shoes and socks after having waded through two streams in forty-eight hours. The house we were billeted in had a coke-fired potbellied stove, and we all put our shoes close to it and dried our socks on a line above it. *Stars and Stripes* had run several articles on the dangers of trench foot. They showed men having amputations when their feet were badly frostbitten. The Russian Army, the article told us, assigned each soldier a foot-rubbing partner, and should one of them get trench foot, his partner would be court-martialed. Lieutenant Bonnet, Frank, and I all examined each other's feet and were surprised that we had come through the wading so well.

We were kept back only one night. Bonnet told us he thought General McAuliffe gave George Company this as compensation for having so many men killed by our own artillery. Perhaps, by so doing, we avoided some firefights in places where the Krauts stood and fought to keep us from overrunning them, but we now found ourselves behind most of the Seventh Army. We marched all day and were still behind most of the rear echelon by nightfall. We found barns to sleep in near towns we had passed through the previous December: Zinzwiller, Neiderbronn, Woerth, and Lembach. In Neiderbronn, I couldn't help noticing the magnificent modern three-story hotel that I thought might have been designed by Courvoisier, an architect whose work I had studied in college. Neiderbronn was where the 2nd Battalion began the December advance through the forest, and we had missed seeing the hotel then because it was east of town while we saw only the west.

Four days after leaving Ingwiller, we finally crossed the bridge over the Lauter River, having returned to Bobenthal, the village we had dreaded for two and a half months. Nothing had changed. The house next to the bridge was still empty. Lieutenant Bonnet took us in, and we unloaded our field packs. The infantry motor pool was there, and Rocky soon found us. He knew where the battery was located.

Lawrence was back from Paris and was elated to see us, having heard about the disaster near Rothbach, with darn few details. No one was sure whether all of us survived. The entire battery rushed upon us and wanted to know how Sudlow worked out and if we blamed Whidden for firing on us. The gunner corporals hated thinking that they had pulled the lanyards to fire on our own men. I can't remember what I told them, except the toll of eight dead and eighteen wounded. They said Battery B fired nearly twenty rounds before the cease-fire order stopped them. They had been ordered to fire forty, so we had stopped about half. Andy said he was going to put me in for a Silver Star for it. We figured that if every battery in the battalion fired that many, G Company was hit with sixty or more rounds in about seven minutes.

Andy and I said good-bye to Sudlow, who showed his relief at not having to go back with the infantry; then we had Rocky take us back to the house beside the river. Rock even came inside the vacant house, and we all slept on the floor.

We awoke before sun up, having been startled by an explosion outside the house. Rocky was standing on his feet, his eyes popping. "They been coming in for an hour like that," he said. Extreme fatigue had kept us asleep. We needed no order from the lieutenant. We got our bedrolls gathered up and were out of there in less than a minute.

Rocky drove us in the opposite direction from where we had headed in December. We traveled west along the Lauter River toward the town of Neider Schettenbach, and we found G Company assembled on the road about a mile from Bobenthal. We were going to have to climb another mountain like the one 2nd Battalion scaled the first time we were in Germany. Captain Stagg had come down with the flu. I can't remember the name of his replacement, but this lieutenant shook hands with Andy and acknowledged Frank and me with a nod. He then told us what awaited us on this mountain.

We were to face an obstacle worse than the fortification on flattop Hill 434. He told us this mountain had an abatis—in this case, giant trees blocking the road—that we had to cross just to get to the pillbox where the Krauts were positioned. The mountain had the same chiseled rock steps as Hill 434, and the climb was slow. This time, Frank and I had our backpacks, so at least our thighs weren't getting rubbed raw. The distance up was shorter than back in December, but it was warmer, so we perspired more. All but the replacements knew what to expect, and there was less griping.

The climb before had been nearly half a mile, but this time, it was half that. We reached a shelf on the top step that was several hundred yards across in a tall hardwood forest. We had no shells raining on us during the climb, and this was a very different mountain, with more than half of it still above us. Without more rock steps, the hill above us was too steep to allow us to climb any farther. A cliff about twelve feet high was at the base of the upper section of this mountain, a natural barrier to the top. I wondered why it was so important to chase the enemy off such hills. Why couldn't we just isolate them by moving around them? But I didn't ask—I was a common soldier and didn't need to know.

Frank drew my attention to two man-made caves at the very top of the stone steps, very likely dug by the Kraut soldiers put on guard here while they waited for us. We got on our knees and crawled in. Each was about ten feet by ten feet inside, with a three-foot-high entrance. Frank said, "I'd like to spend the rest of the war in here."

There was a path going west through an ever-widening plateau. We moved stealthily over several hundred yards before coming into a shady glen about a quarter mile across, covered with stumps and logs. So tall were the trees in this mountain forest that little sun got to the ground, so there were no seedling trees or even weeds.

We went through maybe three quarters of a mile of similar hardwood forest before we came to the abatis. When we got there, all I could see was a cluster of huge trees cut down near the base and allowed to fall helter-skelter across a swath 100 yards across. These hardwoods were six to eight feet in diamater and probably 200 feet tall before being cut. The swath

went from the base of the mountain to the top, where
Siegfried Line bunker awaited us.

Only the company commander and a few of his officers
saw what was so ominous about the abatis. One soldier wondered why we couldn't just crawl under those logs until his
commanding officer pointed out that barbed wire that had
been nailed to the trees before cutting. "We have to crawl over
'em," the officer said. "Some of them will put you twenty feet
in the air, making us like ducks in a shooting gallery . . . and
those Krauts don't miss slow-moving targets."

"Then how will we cross it?" the soldier asked.

"Here's where our FO comes in. Andy, can you see that
bunker up there?"

"Yeah, barely . . . gray slab. That it?"

"That's it. Fire a registration on it, and then have Fire
Direction give us ten minutes of smoke up there. We should be
over the logs by the time they're through firing. We can rush
the bunker through the smoke and hope to get a grenade or
two in the slot before we all get slaughtered by machine guns."

I think I saw Bonnet blink hard and swallow before he said,
"Gotcha." Then he turned to me and said, "Battery adjust."

We fired six rounds of HE before Andy was certain he had
the right coordinates. Then we got Fire Direction to send
phosphorus. The first smoke shell hit right in front of the
bunker, so Andy called for forty rounds. As soon as we had the
area up there blanketed in smoke, the company moved into
the abatis. It took at least five minutes for most of the men to
be well onto the giant logs, and then the medics followed.
After we called the cease-fire, we had Fire Direction give the
mission a number, so that when we had to call the same smoke
mission, all I had to see after that was "Fire Mission . . . barrage
four one . . . smoke."

If the company was forced to withdraw, the company commander was to shoot up a flare to signal us to fire smoke again.
If they didn't call for it after the last men with the red crosses
on their helmts disappeared, we were to start into the abatis
ourselves. I dreaded that, because Lawrence and I were handi-

capped by the two sections of radio we would have to assemble if they needed us after we got into the abatis and onto those huge logs. We couldn't assemble the radio on top of those logs, could we?

About ten minutes after the company began climbing over the abatis, the enemy opened up. It sounded like fifty machine guns firing at once. The air on that mountain vibrated from the ear-splitting chatter, multiplied by echoes. At the same time, mortar shells began falling on the logs immediately in front of and behind us.

The flare went up.

Those guys in the abatis needed us, so we had to remain where we could keep radio contact and endure the shelling. We knew we were lucky to be back here out of the giant logs, but that didn't make us less scared.

Soon, after the last riflemen had climbed the last log, medics came back with men on stretchers, aided by other guys. It was a struggle to hoist the stretchers over the huge trees, and two men would have to alternate on each end to keep the stretchers as level as possible. The medics would barely get a wounded men back before they had to leave him for the volunteers who continued carrying him back to the ambulances waiting at the bottom of the rock steps. The medics then returned to the abatis for the less urgent wounded whom they'd been forced to leave behind.

I didn't see how the rock steps could be negotiated, but I knew it was going to take extraordinary effort. I don't think there was ever a time when I more admired the guts of those medics and the riflemen who volunteered to help them. I even forgave the medics who failed us after the shelling near Greisbach.

Before the last man and last two medics climbed over the last log, we had called for our smoke barrage twice, exploding eighty rounds of smoke shells. The Germans had kept a continuous stream of tracers pouring onto our end of the abatis, and we had taken refuge in some foxholes dug by the men who'd been here in December.

George Company took nearly an hour to withdraw, and two more officers were lost, along with twenty-nine enlisted men. These are estimates offered by officers a few days later when a roll call was delayed to avoid letting the men know how badly their company had been shot up. With twenty-some men lost to trench foot and flu and twenty-eight killed or wounded by our own artillery three days earlier, the first crossing of those logs further reduced George Company to three officers and eighty men. (The company had left Ingviller on March 15 with 6 officers and 140 men.) The most senior lieutenant was now the CO, and he had the men begin digging in next to the abatis. Bonnet, Frank, and I dug with them.

I was leaning forward on my tiny spade when I thought I heard a gun go off next to my ear. I looked up to see a soldier pitching onto his face. He'd been digging ten feet from me, and now he had a bloody hole in the back of his helmet as neet as though made by a hand drill. He didn't twitch after he hit the ground. There had to be a sniper across the abatis—a crack shot! Before the nearest lieutenant could react, a second man in the line of men digging nearest the abatis died from a bullet through the heart.

"Get back, everybody! Get back! Sniper! Sniper!" the new CO shouted.

We all moved back a dozen feet. More shots! Two more men fell dead.

We moved back twenty feet. Not far enough! More men killed!

We moved a third time, at least 200 yards back, but by then, nine men had been killed by the sniper. I listened to the officers talking about it. That expert sniper had a smokeless gun, they believed, and a telescope sight; he was concealed cleverly in the trees directly across from us.

Bonnet, Lawrence, and I talked about it. We marveled that not one man he hit was left wounded, and none lived more than seconds—all were shot through the brain or heart. The company began digging their holes near the rock ledge that divided the semiflat plateau from the precipitous upper half of the mountain.

The Krauts up there in the pillbox knew about this place too, so mortar fire came whistling into that area soon after we got there. It must have been zeroed in when the Nazis were preparing the Siegfried Line.

Frank suggested we FOs go back to the caves we had seen at the top of the rock steps. "Good idea," Andy said, "but I think the CO has to find out what Regiment wants first."

We didn't have to wait long. Regiment wanted G Company to attack again. The new CO, whose name I have forgotten, sighed, but what else could he do? We called for the smoke barrage once more before we moved back beside the abatis. Two more medics had come up to join the first two, and each pair of them carried a stretcher. Would they be enough?

We saw the last of the medics climb into the gaps between the huge trees, and then we called the cease-fire. This time, we didn't wait for the flares to get ourselves behind trees where the sniper couldn't kill us. Andy was worried—should those three officers fail to return, he was expected to take over command of George Company. We had already read in *Stars and Stripes* about other FOs who had been forced to become commanders of infantry companies.

The CO had discussed with his officers, including Bonnet, what the men were expected to do after every man reached the end of the abatis. They now had to run up a forty-yard-long slope to the bunker. This slope ws so steep, he told his men, that they'd be moving in slow motion if they stood up to run, so they might as well get on their bellies and crawl, while hoping the smoke would keep them invisible. They might be able to keep lower than the machine-gun and rifle fire and throw a grenade into the slot in the bunker face. In the previous attempt, they stood up, and not one man advanced more than ten feet. Some men might still lay dead on that bloody ground near the end of those logs, he told them.

This time, he wanted us to cease fire when the flare went up. When the last smoke shell landed, the men were to begin crawling. Should the advance fail and need smoke to cover the retreat, a second flare would signal us to fire the smoke barrage again.

This attack lasted longer than the first one, but the second flare went up shortly after the last medic disappeared into the smoke. Arching machine-gun fire fell all around us while we waited.

Again, the CO was shaken when he returned. Seeing the despair on his face made me believe the Nazis had successfully made this defense impregnable to charging infantrymen. I felt the frustration of the infantry officers. They were being expected to do the impossible.

Soon after all of us got back to the place near the stone ledge, the CO told Bonnet that any further attack was off for this day. We were free to go back to our battery. I radioed Fire Direction and had them send Rocky up to get us.

We were glum as we descended the rock steps to the road. This day had been nearly as sad as the day our own artillery fired on us. We talked about how close each of us had been to a man the sniper killed and how it could just as easily have been one of us. Tomorrow it would be the same thing—another failure.

When we got in the jeep, Rocky had news for us. The battery had gone back to the same place where they had been in December, and they were hit with counterbattery fire. Donald Bleile, a cannoneer, was killed when he ran to get into his foxhole as the shellfire began. It was the first death in the battery area, and Captain Pultz was distraught. He called headquarters and told them he was going to move without first sending out a quartering party. The entire battery moved back into the woods, almost to the French border. There, Pultz had them park themselves on the road for two hours, until he found a place behind houses at the southern end of Bobenthal. Even while there, he was certain the enemy had an observer on the mountain directly above Bobenthal who might be able to see them, so he and Sergeant Camden went on another quartering party. They hadn't found a place yet.

Bleile (pronounced bly-lee) was one of the rookies on my train from Fort Custer. He was a farm boy from Indiana who came up to Detroit for work in the war industries and got drafted there. He was also among the ten guys from Battery B who took the two-week basic the army gave us late arrivals that January. We were paired in the physical toughness exercises, so I knew him better than I knew most of the cannoneers. The guy was easily the most quiet man in the battery, but he was never morose like Olson, and everybody liked him.

Before setting down for the night, we had to go to the Fire Direction Center for Bonnet to report on our missions. Headquarters was located in the *gasthaus* east of Bobenthal, where we spent the last night before going up to Lorraine in December. Bonnet went in, and immediately Major Hawkins came out to the jeep to talk to us. He seemed disturbed. "You guys used up our supply of phosphorus. We had to send four trucks from Service Battery to an ammo dump to replenish it."

"That's about all we're good for, sir," I said. "HE is useless against that bunker."

"I know. You weren't the only one. We had nine FOs up on those mountains, and all of you were firing smoke. But don't worry about it. There's lots more in the ammo dump. That's not really why I came out to see you guys." He paused. "Do you remember Lt. Bob Gilman? I think you had him as your FO for only a couple days."

"We sure do," Lawrence said. "Did something happen to him?"

"I hate to tell you this . . . But the day you guys got shelled by your own artillery, Gilman rolled over on a land mine. A bad day around here all around. I can't tell you how sorry I am about all this." He came up and gave us hugs.

Frank and I sat there stunned. Two good guys we knew were dead, and dozens more for whom we felt some responsibility were dead or wounded on that mountain. And we were going to have to go back and do it all again tomorrow. The war seldom seemed more horrid.

Bonnet decided—danger of shelling be damned—that we were going to sleep in the deserted house by the bridge tonight. Rocky could go back to the battery to sleep if he had to. Rocky stayed, and Frank and I got a large swallow of Old Crow to help us sleep. The hard floor of that dusty, spider-infested, foul-smelling house was our Waldorf Astoria for the night. I thought about those poor benighted guys up there on the mountain, depressed for certain and fatigued beyond comprehension, still needed to post guards and sleep on cold, damp ground, all the while in danger of a sudden counterattack during the night.

Chapter 17

While climbing the rock steps on our way up to rejoin George Company, we were glum. None of us was looking forward to watching poor George Company launch another attack on a concrete fortification that we were certain would be futile. The army that was ordering it offered no strategies different from those that had already failed, and now those riflemen—who'd lost faith in their chances and had their courage all but destroyed—were expected to be successful with twenty fewer men.

Though Bonnet, Frank, and I did not have to climb into that abatis and go up there to face murderous machine-gun fire, we felt the frustration of the officers who had to order men they cared about to do it. If only someone had an idea! Where was our Air Force?

When we found the company, they were readying their M-1s and were about to try again.

This time the acting CO was going to try something different: they would advance straight across the abatis instead of going up, the way they had been going. Then they would move up the opposite side of the abatis, with the huge trees over there as protection against gunfire from the bunker, until they were many yards closer. It wasn't exactly a lollapalooza, but it *was* different, so a glimmer of hope came with it. Our function now was to fire smoke as deception: the Krauts would still expect the attack to come from the front.

But going straight across the abatis had new difficulties. When the giant trees to create the abatis were cut, most of them crisscrossed *up* the mountain, as they fell vertically; this left gaps between them in a few places, and the barbed wire was exposed in those areas. Lawrence was the first to point this out, while Bonnet and I were focusing our attentions on whether the depth and thickness of the smoke would be enough to cover the crossing.

"They're going to take as long getting across this way as they did going up," Frank said, pointing to a rifleman who had to have two others help him get free of barbed wire that caught his jacket and bandolier. To avoid these gaps, the men following those first ones, began zigzagging along overlapping logs. The company was soon out of sight, and the Red Cross helmets of the medics disappeared soon after. Bonnet reminded us that there were twenty less men than we saw yesterday.

The ruse seemed to be working, because the guns in the bunker sent their tracers over the tops of logs where our men had gone the previous day. We had to get behind trees and watch for the flare, while the enemy began sending mortar rounds into the trees around us. Frank pointed out a deep hole near us, where a large shell had penetrated the earth beneath the roots of a tree with a huge girth. It had room for all of us, so we got in under those thick roots and found room to spare.

When the sound of the machine guns up at the bunker became more intense, and we no longer could see tracers, we knew our men were close to the bunker. This brought up the flare, signaling another failure, and we called for a dozen more rounds of phosphorus. By now the enemy knew where to aim their fire, and the tracers began arching into the middle of the abatis. Our returning men wisely began recrossing down lower on the mountain.

When the first returnees were nearly close enough to climb out of the abatis, the Germans began pouring their entire arsenal at our side of the abatis with intense and continuous fire from medium (105-millimeter) artillery and mortars, as well as arching machine-gun fire that rattled the trees above us. We huddled in our hole, unable to hear, choking from the smell of cordite, and shaking from a shared terror that numbed our brains and nerves. Would it ever end?

And then there was a lull—not an end, but a decrease in intensity. We were able to hear a voice—a sobbing cry: "Officer! I need an officer! Officer, officer!"

Above our hole, a soldier stood straight up looking down at us, as tracer bullets flew on every side of him and dirt from nearby explosions pelted him. I expected to see him fall dead any second.

Bonnet shouted: "I'm an officer. Get down! Get down!"

"Sir, who are you? I need permission to go to the rear!"

"You have my permission. Now go!"

"What is your name? I need to know who you are."

"I'm Lieutenant Bonnet, the forward observer. I order you to get down. Now get down!"

I yelled at the guy: "Come down here! There's room!"

"I want to go to the rear. I'm scared! So awful scared!"

"Permission granted!" Bonnet shouted. "Now get the hell going!"

"Yes, sir. Thank you, sir!" He now began walking to the rear. Not running, simply walking, not even crouching. He was a zombie.

When he was no longer to be seen, and the incoming fire had intensified again, we all scrunched down and tried to hold on. I was certain we'd see the body of that poor soul when—and if—we were able to climb out of there.

But it did end, as it always did. The heavy-artillery, mortar, and machine-gun fire sputtered to an end, and the men who had cowered in the gaps between the logs finally came out, covered by our third smoke barrage of the day. No further attacks were planned for that day, but the casualty counts from the three attacks already made were alarming. George Company had a mere forty men left, and now there was only one officer—a Lieutenant Schultz.

Schultz gave the men orders to improve their foxholes and hunker down for the rest of the day. He sent a messenger back down the mountain to request that hot food be sent up in marmite cans.

Then Bonnet came up with a plan of his own. "Lieutenant, I'm going to ask Fire Direction to give us a barrage on the same coordinates as the smoke mission. I'll ask for twenty rounds of HE. Even if I can't crack that concrete up there, it ought to have an effect on the Krauts' morale. What do you think?"

Schultz approved it, and it was an easy mission, because we didn't have to leave the safe place near the ledge and risk being shot at by the sniper; we simply called it in. Fire Direction gave us the twenty rounds, and we sat on nearby rocks and listened to the slithering sounds of the shells passing over. The trees shook from the explosions.

When the mission was over, there was a brief respite, and then the Krauts gave us an answer. They fired several rapid rifle volleys into the trees above our ledge. The sounds of bullets hitting the trees gave me a scare. It seemed as if the Germans were mounting a counterattack and were just above us doing the shooting. Something I had always imagined was happening, I thought, and my gun was needed. I tried to put a bullet in the chamber of my carbine but couldn't—it was filled with sand and mud. I hadn't cleaned my weapon in months, and I was mortified. Out of shame, I suppressed an impulse to strip down the gun immediately: it wouldn't do to have those riflemen see me getting dirt out of my weapon.

We went back down the mountain just before dark and had Rocky reluctantly take us to the house by the bridge. A shell had hit the house that day, but other than ripping a chunk off the corner closest to the bridge, it did little damage. After Rocky agreed to come get us before daylight, Bonnet allowed him to go back to the battery for the night.

The three of us finished off a bottle of Southern Comfort that Bonnet produced from his pack, and why not? The future looked bleak: would all of George Company have to die before Regiment or Division could find a better way?

I had a slight hangover in the morning, but I took time to strip and clean my carbine before we climbed back up there.

Second Battalion headquarters had sent Major Greiner up to see why G Company was having no success. This seemed silly, considering that had any other company in the division done better, the division would have broken through the Siegfried Line by now. Frank and I remembered Greiner from the December attack, and we had liked him then; but then he was a captain and not connected to a safe-behind-the-lines headquarters.

We tried all the same stuff as the previous day, and Greiner bravely crossed the abatis with the company. The results were the same, except this time there was no barrage when they returned—no machine gun, no artillery, no mortar fire, nothing. Had we been more knowledgeable in the business of warfare, we might have guessed that the enemy was having difficulty getting enough ammunition, and that this shortage canceled any less-than-essential barrages—the earliest signs they were hurting and ready to quit.

Greiner and Schultz were the only officers on the attack, and they'd lost just ten more men. I heard Greiner assessing things. He told Schultz and Bonnet, who was asked to join the conference, that he thought perhaps the bunker could be conquered, if we just tried something different. He said, "Perhaps you ought to try crossing down 100 yards lower."

"I thought you liked that guy," Bonnet said to Frank and me. "What a jerk! He got sent up here by Battalion to find something positive to report, so that's what he's going to do. How stupid!"

No other attack was scheduled, so I had time to talk with Lieutenant Schultz. I had heard him make some reference to Michigan, so I asked him if he was a Michigander. Not only was he from my state, but he was from my city, my side of town, even my high school, and we had played drums side by side in the Denby High School Marching Band and had taken drum lessons on Saturdays at downtown Cass Tech High School at the same time. We were ashamed that neither of us had recognized the other.

Schultz was given permission to cancel any attack for the rest of the day, but he wanted his FOs to stay up with the company—just in case . . .

We went back to the caves at the top of the rock steps. All of us wanted to have a peaceful place to write letters. The previous two weeks were the longest period in which none of us had taken time to write home.

I took a nap after writing four letters in less than an hour. A loud roar of approaching planes startled us, and I crawled out of the cave to see them as they came near. They were two twin-engine B-26s—Flying Prostitutes, the air corps called them—and they were flying less than 500 feet above the Lauter River. Flak was making black puffs in their path toward Neider-Schettenbach, and I was excited to be able to clearly see the pilot, copilot, and tail gunner as the planes passed level or slightly below me. Some of the ack-ack bursts were exploding less than 100 yards away, and I didn't think about the danger until I heard the crackling of branches in the trees around me over the booming of the antiaircraft fire and the roaring of the planes. I dove back into the cave as soon as I realized how stupid I'd been. Frank and Andy hadn't bothered to come out and still didn't recognize the importance of this moment.

As I lay at the mouth of the cave and watched the B-26s returning from the bombing, I saw smoke streaming from one of the two bombers. They climbed as they flew over Bobenthal, and I saw the fire go out on the plane that had been smoking. I wondered if there might be a wounded crewman on that plane. They had been on what civilians were told was a milk run, but, from watching that smoking plane, I decided there was no such thing as a milk run where guns were firing. I only learned later that they had bombed a pillbox outside Neider-Schettenbach.

This use of bombers was something I had wanted since last December, and it took all this time to bring them. Now when were they going to bomb the pillboxes in the mountains?

We climbed the rock steps for a fourth straight day on March 21 and found George Company in a shady glen several hundred yards back from the abatis and 100 or so yards below the rock shelf where we had our foxholes. The men were on the downslope of the path into the glen, pinned down by sniper fire. Most of them had found a log to protect them from the sniper or snipers, who'd already killed four men. We immediately threw ourselves to the ground, and I found a thick log about two feet in diameter to hide behind.

Apparently the sniper had a perch in the trees on our side of the abatis. He had surprised Schultz and the company as they were assembling in the glen preparing to mount another crossing of the abatis, thinking they had found a place safe from the sniper who had been in the trees across the abatis.

As I lay behind my log, no shots were fired, and I kept trying to think of what we could do to find the sniper or snipers. When I drew a blank, I decided that lying there was stupid, so I got up, gathered my radio backpack, and started back up the rise to the safety of trees.

Bonnet said, "What are you doing, Bill?"

"Getting the hell out of here."

"Good idea . . . Frank, you coming too?"

Then Lieutenant Schultz said, "Let's all go. Come on, guys . . . out of here."

The entire company got up then, and we all ran back into heavier foliage.

Remarkably, when the men got on their feet, no one was hit by the sniper. Perhaps by then the sniper had gone back across the abatis, his mission to kill a few more of us having been accomplished.

Lieutenant Schultz—to obey orders from Battalion—still had to make another attack on the pillbox, but he looked around him and did a count. With four men having been killed by the sniper and six men coming down with the flu the previous day, the company was reduced to eighteen men. He sat on a rock for several minutes thinking. When he had his mind made up, he told his radioman to shut down his walkie-talkie and had his telephone operator pull out the wires from his phone. He looked at Bonnet and said, "You can go back to the caves with your men, Andy. Just come back here in an hour. I don't have enough personnel to send up there any-more."

When we returned an hour later, Schultz had his radioman turn on his set. "Send the following communication to Battalion, John," he said. "'We have attacked and been repelled.' Now everybody rest. You guys from artillery can go back to your caves again."

Whether or not the infantry battalion brass understood the message (army communication procedure would not allow giving casualty figures on either telephone or radio), a new company was sent up the stone steps that afternoon, and George Company was relieved. I think the new company was from the 409th, but I'm not sure.

Going down the steps, Bonnet said, "Would you guys like to have a bath?" He had it all figured out: when he made his report to headquarters, he told them we were going to stay with the infantry, while the infantry was expecting we would be with the artillery.

We were on our way back to Ingviller an hour later. Both Lawrence and I protested that this was AWOL, but Bonnet assured us, "It won't get you guys in trouble, you're just following orders—*my* orders. I'm the only one who can get in trouble. Don't worry . . . we'll be back tomorrow morning, and nobody'll be the wiser."

Rocky knew the way, because we went back along the same route the motor column had taken five days before. I particularly wanted to see the modern hotel in Niederbronn-les-Bains because of my interest in modern architecture. That hotel was untouched when we passed it earlier, but now the right half was a pile of rubble. Bonnet had Rocky stop the jeep so he could find out what happened from several officers who were walking around inspecting.

When he returned to the jeep, he told us the hotel had been blown up by a time bomb. It exploded on the nineteenth, four days after the start of this offensive, apparently expected by the bombsetters to explode with a division headquarters inside. Fortunately for us, General McAuliffe and his staff found other lodgings. Not one life was lost, although a couple of engineers were wounded.

We went back into the flat in Ingviller that we had left six days earlier, to find the bathtub gone. The entire flat was empty of everything. I went upstairs to see what had happened, and Berthe gave me a big hug. "Bill . . . you are alive!" she said in French or Alsatian-German, I can't remember which, but in words I understood. She then told me why the bathtub and furniture were gone. The FFI had taken all of it for a newly married couple, claiming the right to do this because the previous owners were German nationals—enemies of France.

But we would have our baths, she assured me . . . she'd see to it.

Berthe then put on her stove every bowl, pot, pan, and kettle she had, after filling them to capacity. While the water heated, she scrubbed all the scum off a huge zinc tub the Weils normally used to crush the fruit for their wine; this would be our bathtub. The same soapy water was used by all four of us—Rocky was ordered to bathe by Andy—and with another pan of hot water for each of us, we rinsed.

It took a couple hours, but we bathed outdoors beside the house, and we all (except Rocky) were pleased with the resultant clean feeling. Frank and I were pleased to see Rocky's hands come out fairly clean, but on the rest of him, the dirt was too deeply encrusted to make any real improvement. He had not taken a bath since leaving the States, even though the army regularly performed "short-arm" exams, and after each one, he had been ordered to bathe.

Albert and Berthe had us up for dinner, with the usual black-market steaks, apple wine, and Berthe's specialty, an open-faced mirabelle tarte. Rocky again refused the invitation. This time Andy didn't embarrass us. I gave them $20 worth of francs in U.S. Army scrip, as well as at least a carton of cigarettes, to help them pay for the food.

With no bed in the downstairs flat, we all slept on the floor in our bedrolls in the main room, with the exception of Rocky, who slept in the hall as he did before.

Berthe had told me—using our mix of French, Alsatian, and English—about a tragic thing that happened to the little church in Mulhausen (a tiny village not to be confused with Mulhouse, a big city near the Belfort Gap). The Germans had planted a time bomb in the cellar, and it destroyed that little onion-domed church on a Sunday, several hours after mass. The only casualty was the lone parish priest.

We were familiar with that town and that church, for Mulhausen was in a valley below one of our favorite observation posts, and we had used that OP once on a Sunday and had seen the parishioners going to mass. Because they were so brave—holding mass in no-man's-land like that—we had resolved never to fire a mission on that village.

Those bombsetters were ordinary Wehrmacht troops, not SS, and this action was simply criminal, whereas the bombing of the hotel in Neiderbronn was tactical and an act of war. The Nazi ideology under the master criminal Adolf Hitler made criminals of ordinary people in Germany, and not just the criminally inclined members of the SS. The time-bombing of the little church in Mulhausen was proof of this.

We arrived back in Bobenthal early in the morning and were not ready for what we found after crossing the little bridge over the Lauter River: sitting on the town's curbs were hundreds of German soldiers, their helmets piled neatly next their rifles, carefully stacked in cones.

I was curious how a Nazi soldier would take such wholesale surrender, and as I stared into the eyes of a man sitting there, I saw no shame, only a stolid hatred of his enemy, whom I embodied. Somewhere in that mob was the sniper who killed so many of us—possibly with pleasure—but now he sat there knowing his enemy was going to give him better food than he had eaten in weeks.

We found Battery B lined up and ready to go. All explanations would have to wait. The motor march was about to begin, and had we gotten there an hour later, our AWOL would have been exposed.

The truck column started west along the river road to Neider-Schettenbach, and we passed the mountain where we last saw George Company. When I noticed he had his earphones on, I called Len Harris in Rebman's jeep just ahead of us, violating the rules of standard radio procedure. I needed to find out what had happened.

From him, I learned that a salient run by Gen. George Patton's tanks on the Rhine plains behind the Siegfried Line of bunkers cut them off from supplies of food and ammunition. What we just saw in Bobenthal was the 500 German troops who came out of the bunkers with their hands up.

There was a lot more to it than just what I learned from Len Harris. Right after we left to go to Ingviller, the entire VI Corps artillery opened fire on targets beyond the pillboxes and beyond the mountain range, guided by aerial observers, while the Air Force—which I had been wishing for—was strafing and bombing the supporting artillery and ammunition dumps from the Rhine to the Hardt. Then Seventh Army sent Task Force Rhine, consisting of the 1st and 2nd Battalions from the 409th Regiment, riding atop tanks, past Neider-Schettenbach toward a forest-covered supply road discovered in an aerial photo.

It was toward this road that our column was now headed. Though our column moved at a snail's pace, it took less than an hour to traverse the entire Hardt Mountain Range, revealing how small a range it was.

The level of defeat suffered by our enemy soon became apparent, as we passed a dozen GIs busily putting up posts and barbed-wire fences while at least 100 German soldiers stood by, patiently waiting for their cage to be completed.

As we came onto the mountain road that Task Force Rhine had attacked the previous day, we began seeing war destruction unparalleled in our previous combat experience. There were no ditches on either roadside, and dead horses, overturned cannons, and still-burning vehicles of every description lay on the right shoulder, having been pushed there by GI bulldozers. A line of huge dead Percherons and Belgians lay body-to-body, making a bloody horseflesh berm as tall as a man, and it covered the right side of that road as far ahead as we could see. Many live horses roamed free on both sides of the road. Dead soldiers lay in and among the trucks, cannons, kitchen vehicles, and horses.

The task force apparently had run along the open ground paralleling the road and simply mowed down all of these troops, their horses, and their vehicles, making this mound of equine-human-mechanical garbage.

We passed a column of captured soldiers, being herded along by a short rifleman, who were on their way back to the newly built prisoner cage. As I counted artillery pieces and kitchen trucks, I began to think we had captured an entire enemy division artillery unit.

Some of the horses had been set afire by the burning vehicles, and Frank commented on the smell. "I may never be able eat steak again," he said.

Rocky pulled the jeep onto the field, leaned over the side, and began retching. "It's okay, Rocky," Bonnet said. "Get it all out. We can catch up to the column later."

It took Rocky ten minutes to be able to drive again, and when we passed a group of raggedy people watching one of their men cutting a piece from the rump of a dead Percheron—which they obviously intended to roast and eat—Bonnet held a finger to his lips, warning us not to comment. Rocky hadn't seen it.

The bad taste would linger in our mouths until lunchtime had passed, by which time we caught up to our battery on a side road. The captain had received orders for us to begin searching houses and barns nearby. Our section and Lieutenant Rebman's were made into a team and sent to the next crossroad to begin.

A mill was the first structure we came to. It was postcard picturesque, with a working waterwheel and a separate decorative pond with two swans. Showy peacocks strutted and squawked their catlike calls on the large lawn surrounding it.

Our two-jeep party of searchers was met halfway to the mill by the miller himself, a middle-age man in lederhosen. He shook hands with several of us and said, "*Guten morgen, mein Herren,*" smiling broadly. I didn't want to shake his hand, nor did either of the officers; he was still the enemy in our eyes, and we didn't trust such friendliness from one of them.

When we got into the mill, we were surprised to see it was actually busy milling flour. The pulleys were turning, grain was dropping into chutes, and bags were filling at spouts. The air was dusty, and the smell was sweet and chalky. All of us were quickly absorbed.

Chuck Howard spun on his heels as a pretty girl in a brown dirndl skirt with a tight-fitting white blouse began descending steps from a loft above the mill room. As she left the dusty room, he started to follow her. "Look out, Chuck," Lieutenant Rebman said. "That one's too young. Back off."

"She's got a bosom, she's old enough," Chuck said. He continued following her as she left the mill. But he was back moments later. "I guess you're right. She looks like eleven in the daylight. They develop young in Germany, I guess."

The search-turned-educational-tour continued, as the miller showed us several smaller rooms with bags of assorted flours piled high.

The girl returned, holding Rockwell's hand, having brought him away from his precious jeep. Strangely, he was carrying his weapon in his other hand. Rocky was flushed and seemed to be out of breath. I thought I detected excitement, as well as embarrassment. What he was expecting now he had only read about before.

Howard had to comment about it. "I'll be damned! You suppose he learned something from *True Confessions?*"

The two of them disappeared behind the door at the top of the steps, but Rocky burst out an instant later, aiming his automatic pistol at the door. "There's Kraut soldiers up there, and they got guns!" he said. He backed down the steps so rapidly that he fell against the railing and his gun discharged a short volley into the ceiling. Flour dust began raining down in sheets from the pipes above the milling room. We were choking and half blinded, but all of our search party aimed their weapons at the loft—all but me. I'd left my carbine in the jeep!

I put a thick post between me and the steps. The girl appeared on the loft holding her hands palms-up in a gesture of fright. "*Bitte! Bitte!*" she begged.

"Hold your fire, guys," Bonnet said between coughs. "I think Rocky's army wants to surrender."

I came out from behind my post and saw what Bonnet was talking about. A seventy- or eighty-year-old man in a *Volkssturm* uniform was coming onto the loft, shaking in paroxysms of fright, with his hands held high. When he saw we were not going to harm him, he began tugging at something in the fold of his sleeve. (The "safe-conduct" leaflets fired by our artillery were kept in nearly every wise German soldier's sleeve for just such a moment.)

Chuck Howard and I went upstairs to search for any other soldier who might be up there and found none. A search of the miller's house also turned up none.

This incident was ironic. On the ship coming over, Rockwell had told Ray York that as a member of the Hutterite faith, he would let himself be killed before he would kill another human being. Yet after he'd been scared a few times, Rocky traded his carbine with a tanker for a grease gun, because it fired more rounds faster. And now he had almost killed an old man trying to surrender. Rocky demonstrated that no man can know how a war will make him behave until he has lived in it.

Chapter 18

There was an atmosphere of celebration throughout the battery, especially within the three sections that had gone up into the Hardt Mountains as forward observers with the three infantry companies. With the Siegfried bunkers behind us, we were sure the worst was over, if the war was not already won.

To our surprise, the guns were put into position to support an infantry attack a few miles from the Rhine River. The Seventh and Third Armies had captured 100,000 enemy troops in the Saar Triangle, which led us to think all opposition was gone. And now here we were, readying to fire across the Rhine.

For two days, Battery B fired at unobserved targets across the Rhine. All of us presupposed we were going to be in for a bloody river crossing. To our relief, the VI Corps put the 103rd on corps reserve and turned us over to military government, which wanted us to do a search for arms and enemy deserters. This made sense. In most countries occupied by the Nazis, an underground resistance soon formed behind the lines. Eisenhower knew the Nazis were extremist and dedicated, and he had every reason to expect they would resist our occupation. The search for arms was necessary to prevent the German populace from forming guerrilla forces to harass us. As far as soldiers being hidden by civilians, we were only too happy to have deserters encouraged, so we planned to do few house-to-house searches. The 103rd was given a two-day furlough from that task and allowed to celebrate the beginning of the end.

Speyer, a medium-size city on the Rhine, was the center for German sparkling wine, which they—erroneously, as far as the French were concerned—called Champagne. A warehouse full of this stuff was discovered by the 103rd Division, and General McAuliffe had it confiscated to help us celebrate. A bottle was awarded to every enlisted man, and a case to every officer. The celebration began immediately, and an entire division was drunk within an hour after we got our hands on the cheap champagne, which we blasphemously swigged warm from aluminum canteen cups. Over that ten-square-mile area west of the Rhine, it sounded like New Year's Eve in Manhattan, with live ammunition being shot into the air from rifles and carbines. (Strangely, no reports of casualties were announced afterward.)

To be certain the German populace would appreciate our disdain of them, Eisenhower decreed that his army should not fraternize with the enemy. To this end, when we needed a place to stay, we were to tell the people to move out of their houses, rather than moving in with them as we did in France. Part of this decree was immediately scorned, as *fräuleins* welcomed American soldiers into their beds. The day of the champagne celebration, a Wehrmacht brothel was discovered a few miles away from our battery area. Its female employees had remained behind, apparently waiting for the cigarette-wealthy Americans. The *fräuleins* had a few houses in which they worked, and lines formed there throughout our two celebration nights. Colonel Caesar was livid when he found out, and he had the battalion medical officer set up a short-arm station in front of the 928th Battalion Headquarters. As far as Battery B was concerned, it was unnecessary, the entire battery—even Chuck Howard—was too drunk to be bothered with Wehrmacht "camp followers."

The division still had too many bottles of the awful wine, so they issued a repeat allotment. Now every officer had two cases, and every enlisted man had two bottles. For my four-man section, that meant we had nearly three cases remaining after the first drunk. To make room for the wine, Bonnet had us throw out all of the potato-masher grenades and other stuff that Ruotolo had stashed in our trailer.

Frank Lawrence and I were not heavy drinkers, and I think both of us got drunk enough to throw up that first day. After that, the stuff in our trailer was there mostly for Lieutenant Bonnet. He was drunk, off and on, most of the time thereafter.

Three of Battery B's officers had become forward observers in our last offensive, and now a fraternity developed. With six cases and eighteen bottles of champagne between us, less the twelve or thirteen bottles consumed during the first day of celebration, it was inevitable that we would have our own private celebration. Our section's billet in a small village whose name I never learned became the place for our party. From among the drivers, only Nick Longo came to the party; Rocky and David Lease, Buster Whidden's driver, didn't drink, so the champagne was actually divided ten times. That house had a slightly out-of-tune piano, and Kenny Rebman had played in a swing band at Cornell, so I went to the kitchen and found a dishpan for my drum, and using the wire brushes I carried in my duffel, we jammed for half an hour. Then the ten of us sang whatever songs we knew the words to.

None of us got more than tipsy, except Bonnet, who was drunk all the time but didn't always show it. Before the party ended, we all swore to remain friends for life.

Battery B was moved east across the Rhine at Ludwigshafen and then back across at Worms. Finally we settled in a village west of the Rhine and began several days of collecting weapons from nearby villages. Upon entering a town to which our section was assigned, we'd first find the burgomeister. He would then get the town crier to inform the people that they were required to bring their weapons to the village square, where we waited to load them onto a three-quarter-ton truck.

In some towns, the town crier rang a bell; in others, he had a field drum on which he made an uneven drumroll before shouting our orders to the people. I was amazed by the response this got. In one tiny hamlet, the town park accumulated a six-foot-high pile of rifles, shotguns, pistols, swords, boxes of ammunition, boxes of hand grenades, along with knives—including pocket and kitchen variety—and even a couple of letter openers. Today, whenever some gun lover tries to tell me that guns in every household will prevent a totalitarian dictator from taking over America, I laugh. The German citizenry were very well armed, and fat lot of good it did!

We loaded many of the guns in our jeep—a mistake! A drunken lieutenant and guns are a bad combination. Bonnet found ammunition for several rifles we collected, and he fired them at telephone posts as we drove from one village to another. At one time, he fired his own .45 into the ground along the way, and he nearly shot an old woman in the foot when she just happened to be walking where he was shooting. I felt helpless to stop him, and Frank felt the same way. But we knew the war wasn't over, and we didn't want Ruotolo back, so we had to keep our mouths shut about his drunken shenanigans.

Though the war was still going on, Battery B went into garrison demeanor. We found a place to hold reveille and retreat and a flagpole on which to raise and lower the Stars and Stripes.

The howitzers were covered by canvas, and the vehicles were all in a motor park, with the exception of those being used to pick up weapons. The captain wanted to be saluted and told all officers to report any enlisted man who failed to salute. This stuff was hard to bring back for men who had been using first names for the officers who'd allow it, and that included every officer in Battery B except Lieutenant Wallace and Captain Pultz.

Lieutenant Bonnet was made officer of the day after we got back from one weapon search, and he was drunker that day than usual. He staggered in front of the battery and slurred his speech when he called us to attention, producing a few guffaws from the ranks. Once he had to order an about-face after turning us incorrectly to the right. He had completely forgotten the ritual of reveille, but he stumbled around with a silly grin, devoid of embarrassment, while our flag was lowered. Fortunately for Frank and me, the only officer to witness it was Rebman. I think the captain would have had a fit. Frank and I worried that a similar display might give Pultz one more excuse to bring Ruotolo back.

While we were in that village (I think the name of it was Carlsburg), our FO section stayed in a house whose owner came around every day to tend to his rose bushes. He used human manure from a cesspool beside the house, which he brought up with a long-handled bucketlike ladle. Each time we came near him, the fat old guy smiled and told us, "Me nix Nazi. Me nix Hitler."

During our time in that place, I had guard duty twice. My post was a mile down the road where it ended at a junction with another road. I was not to allow any vehicle to pass, and I saw none. (I don't remember any civilian autos anywhere during our occupation.)

On my second night of guard duty, Nick Longo drove to my post and jumped out. "Take the jeep, Hanford," he said. "I'm taking your guard."

He explained that Bonnet paid him to relieve me because he had something he wanted me for. When I got back to the house, I found him in the hallway kissing a pretty nurse. He gave her one more smooch, then turned to me. "Hanford, meet Lt. Anne Doyle, but keep your hands off her, 'cause I saw her first. Anne, this is Hanford, a real war hero."

Lawrence and I were invited by Bonnet and Nurse Doyle to a party being thrown by nurses from a field hospital. Once more, Frank and I would be the only enlisted men on a drinking occasion with officers we barely knew. This time, some of the officers were female. I was expectant. If there were more Anne Doyles around, I wanted to meet one.

Rockwell drove us to a house in the town shared by our battalion headquarters and the evacuation hospital, Nurse Doyle riding up front on Bonnet's lap. We quickly realized the party had been going on for more than a few hours. The room they were using was small and had a carpet rolled back, allowing the waxed wood floor to be used for dancing, and male lieutenants were dancing with female lieutenants, and some nurses were dancing with other nurses. They had a record player and a fair-size collection of Miller, Dorsey, and Goodman records. Lieutenant Rebman was lying on a sofa with his eyes closed. "Buncha bitches," he said, when I spoke to him. "Get drunk. Only way to go."

I got a glass and filled it with scotch. I decided to just sip it and do what Rebman advised— nothing else to do. I couldn't see myself asking a nurse-officer to dance, and Anne Doyle was the only girl in the room that was remotely pretty.

Then Bonnet temporarily broke off trying to coax Nurse Doyle into bed and brought a fat blond captain over to introduce to me.

"This's a real war hero, Cap'n. Don' matter he's not a cap'n too. Meet Bill Hanford from Dee-troit, Michigan. You and him oughta dance . . . he's a real Fred What's-his-name."

I got up and took Capt. Georgia Somebody out on the small square floor, and we tried to dance. Either she was a terrible dancer or she was deliberately being difficult because she was embarrassed to be dancing with an enlisted soldier. When the record stopped, I asked her to sit the next one out. Frank had an even more unattractive nurse in tow, but she seemed to be a good dancer.

I refilled our glasses and sat down next to Captain Georgia. I shared her embarrassment at this mismatch—no thanks to Andrew D. Bonnet—but I was determined to make the best of it.

She soon let me know she'd done better. "Do you have a girl back home, Bill?" she asked.

"I used to. We don't write anymore."

"I have a wonderful major in my life," she said. "He's in ordnance." She pulled a folio from her pocket. "This is his picture. I never leave it off my person."

The snapshot was a bad photo of what looked vaguely like a handsome man. I'm probably being cynical, but I didn't believe this guy could really be interested in this fat, plain, thirty-something woman whose English was so gauche—*I never leave it off my person*? The photo was more of a wished-for man, I thought, but this gal was an army nurse, and I liked it that she had something to cling to. I will always respect doctors and nurses, most of whom care about people.

We danced again several times and drank after each turn on the floor, and the scotch began having an effect. I was surprised when she suddenly came close and put her head against my cheek, and her dancing improved. Several of the couples around us were dancing with both arms around each other's necks, and I could see that the booze was now in charge in that room. Bonnet danced near, and I heard him say to Nurse Doyle, "Let's you and me get married, sweetie."

I didn't initiate it, but Georgia Something and I kissed, and she had her mouth so wide open I could feel her upper lip with my nose. The invitation was clear, but the place for it was not there. Nevertheless, when the party began breaking up, she clung to me desperately.

I was pretty drunk when Rocky came to get us, and I kept thinking how sad it was that a woman who volunteered for the misery of an evacuation hospital should have to be so lonely.

Chapter 19

When we moved the following day, we crossed the Rhine once more at Ludwigshafen and moved to the village of Urgerach, near Darmstadt. Each section had a block of houses to live in, and we ate our meals in the village schoolhouse. The battery CP was in a house where the town's love goddess lived until evicted by us. She had as big a bosom as I had ever seen in a gal so young, and though she was far from pretty, all the guys in the battery lusted after her. Within hours of our arrival in Urgerach, Bonnet had Rocky drive him, along with this girl, to a nearby woods, with instructions to return for him in two hours. Right under the captain's nose, he openly broke Eisenhower's "no fraternizing" rule. For a battery's FO, rules were easily broken, for who would replace him? Even if Bonnet had been less privileged, he could not have cared less where girls—or alcohol—were concerned. Now we knew that our lieutenant was a ladies' man as well as a drunk, but we saw him as better than Ruotolo, so we agreed to cover for him whenever it was necessary.

Twenty men at a time were sent by the battery for three days of duty at a prison about five miles away. This was part of the service the 103rd Division was committed to while under the command of the U.S. military government unit that had preceded us there and had jailed all the German guards. They also raised an American flag on the flagpole in front of the guardhouse.

Military government officers screened the inmates to find anti-Nazi political prisoners, some of whom they found in all German prisons and jails. Six ex-prisoners were now running the prison and were expected to cooperate with us. We were there only as guards. The six trustees were: a Swede, a Norwegian, a Dutchman, a Belgian, an Isle of Jersey Englishman, and an anti-Nazi German, and they all spoke English fluently.

It was not easy to be in this place, even as military occupiers. Between the barbed-wire double fences were snarling dogs. The guardhouse, where we ate and slept, was cobwebbed and dirty, and the cots were lumpy. The regular guards—now our prisoners—had their families in bungalows across the road and lived there when they were off-duty, so they had let the guardhouse flounder.

I became friends with Jean, the Belgian. We shared a passion for "le hot jazz," and Jean had once heard and seen the great Gypsy guitarist Django Reinhardt when he came to Brussels.

The German was made the chairman of the trustees, and I liked him too, but I can't remember his name or what it was I liked about him. I only remember thinking how smart the military government was to select him as a trustee.

The Isle of Jersey trustee, who spoke with a Cockney accent, was too slippery, I thought.

He somehow had permission to leave the prison nightly, and he had a bicycle to take him wherever it was he went so freely. He returned at two or three in the morning, whistling arrogantly. I was sure he had a *fräulein* he was seeing, and that he had to have known her before we got there.

I told Jean my suspicions, and he said he felt the same way: the Brit got to be a trustee only because he was an English citizen. I later learned that there were plenty of Nazi sympathizers on Jersey during the Nazi occupation of that island, and some counterspies were among them.

While we were there, several buses came to take men back to their countries. Strangely, the day before the bus to Antwerp was due, a Belgian escaped. Jean, who knew the escapee, told me the man was going to face a murder trial when he got back home.

I was sent out to search the surrounding fields for the fugitive, along with a cannoneer named Rufus Yosset. Just as his name suggested, Rufe Yosset was a character right out of the comic strip "L'il Abner." He spoke with a nasal twang, sang country songs with a yodel in his voice, and could throw a baseball through a brick wall. (When I played catch with him, my hands stung for hours after.) He was also a pretty good shot with a carbine.

We took a jeep, with me driving. The prison had several hundred acres of fields with grasses as tall as our jeep's windshield. It was a great place for our escapee to hide, so Rufe rode standing up. We moved slowly down a narrow aisle that served as a road through the weeds. Suddenly Rufus yelled, "Stop!"

I thought he saw the fugitive, so I stopped, not expecting him to take aim at the man. I shouted, "No Rufe! Don't shoot!" At that instant, he fired.

"I think I got him," he said. I could see us getting in plenty of hot water over shooting our prisoner, but I started the jeep through the field in the direction in which he fired.

"Probably a doe," Rufus said. "I didn't see no horns." I was relieved.

We found the deer, and he'd made a clean kill—shot it right through the head. It was a doe. A prisoner dressed the deer as soon as we returned, and all of us in the guardhouse had steaks that tasted like Kansas City beef. I didn't know then that the animal is supposed to hang for twenty-four hours to drain all the blood or that deer is supposed to taste gamy.

We never caught the escapee, and with Europe in such turmoil with displaced persons wandering all over, he probably never had to go back to Belgium.

The following day, I was sent out with a prisoner who was going to weed a three-square-acre prison garden. We had no more than arrived there before a woman wandered into the field and began shouting to the prisoner. I yelled at her, " *'Raus, fräulein! 'Raus! 'Raus!*" (In English: "Scram, lady, scram.") She ignored me. The prisoner looked at me and grinned, as though to say, *Try and make her.*

I was nervous. What if she keeps walking toward him? What if he runs? I knew I would have to shoot, so I decided to shoot in the air first. I threw a round in the chamber with a loud clack, to see if that would stop those two. When it had no effect, I fired into the air. They stopped and looked at me. I glared, to show I meant business. Then I walked toward them with my carbine pointing at them. "*'Raus, fräulein, 'raus!*"

The woman finally turned and began walking slowly away. I breathed a sigh of relief. The prisoner sat down and thumbed his nose at me. "*Arbeit, arbeit!*" I yelled, and fired the carbine again. The man got up and began hoeing. I had been tested and passed the test, so my prisoner was convinced, and I was able to go back to a nearby mound and sit with my carbine across my knees. The woman went back to the guards' bungalows across the road.

I thought perhaps the prisoner might have been one of the guards and the woman his wife, and I told the trustees not to send any of us on such an errand again, at least not with a former guard.

When I was on guard later at the main gate, a civilian in a three-piece suit rode up on a bicycle and told me in English that he was a dentist who regularly came to the prison to fix the teeth of prisoners. I told him to go away, but he persisted, so I went and got Jean. He had never seen the fellow before, so he had him show credentials. Eventually Jean said, "Take him back to the main building, but keep an eye on him. Make sure he fixes teeth."

We went into the main prison building, which I hadn't been in before, and we had to pass through a large, high-ceilinged room that might have been a gym. The room was crowded, and one prisoner was playing an out-of-tune piano while the other inmates were singing with gusto. Most of them stared at me as they sang, so I sensed the singing was for my benefit. I wished I knew the words or the melody to the Horst Wessel song I thought they were singing. Being a criminal in a Nazi nation didn't mean the person wasn't also a Nazi, and those men were plenty hostile toward me and they wanted me to know it.

We went to the hospital, where a dentist's chair was located. A prisoner was summoned, and the dentist looked into the convict's mouth but didn't put him in the chair, just picked at his mouth and sent him away. Another man appeared and knelt in front of the dentist and began measuring his inside leg with a tape measure. A few minutes later, a coat with no sleeves was brought. The dentist put it on, and the man made more measurements.

I had seen enough. I walked between the dentist and the prisoner-tailor and interfered. "Let's go, dentist," I said. "This prison is now under the United States military government and is not in the business of tailoring suits for civilians."

"But I haven't seen any patients yet," he said. "The tailoring is how they pay me."

I prodded him with my carbine. "Let's go, dentist. Turn around. No more of this."

We walked through the room with the singers, with my gun in the dentist's back for all of them to see. We went all the way to the front gate with my gun against his spine. As he left, I gave him a kick in the pants. "And don't come back again," I said. Jean said I did the right thing.

That evening, Lieutenant Rebman came into the guardhouse with a grim look on his face. "Franklin Roosevelt just died at Warm Springs," he said. "Harry Truman is now being sworn in. We're going to have a memorial ceremony tomorrow."

In the morning, we raised the flag and then brought it down to half-staff and fired a ten-gun salute. I think Rebman and I were the most depressed by it; none of the other guys were into political stuff, with the exception of Dale Ride, who was very much a Republican. To Dale's credit, he didn't jump with joy; he just patted me on the back and said, "Sorry, Bill. He did a good job leading us through this war."

My group was relieved of duty at the prison after four days, and all of us rejoined the rest of the battery in Urgerach.

Bonnet must have tired of his young femme fatale, because the day we got back, he brought Dale Ride and Chuck Howard to join Frank and me in the living room of our billet, and he wanted to have a game of poker.

"You play, don't you?" he asked me.

"Not well. What kind of stakes we talking about?"

We were going to play for cigarettes, the best medium of exchange in Germany those days, and I had plenty, so I said okay.

Andy had chips, which we used instead of cigarettes. In ten minutes—as I expected—a large pile of those chips sat in front of the lieutenant. Real Texans, among other things, could drink and play poker, and Andy Bonnet was a real Texan.

Around the fifth hand, I heard the door open behind me, and I turned to see Major Thompson standing there, so I jumped to my feet and yelled, "Ten-hut!"

"At ease, men," Thompson said. "Just here to see if your quarters are satisfactory." He paused and stared at Bonnet, who ignored him, pretending to concentrate on his hand. "Are you playing cards with enlisted men, Lieutenant?" the major asked.

"Yeah. Got time for a few hands?"

"I consider that insulting, Andy. I think you know the rules regarding officers gambling with enlisted men"

"Sure, but who's gambling?"

"Oh, *come on*! What the hell are those chips? I consider your attitude unacceptable and extremely discourteous. I expect better from an officer."

"Good! Good! I'm happy to know you believe in courtesy, Major. I'm from Texas, you know, and we value courtesy as highly as y'all do in Carolina, Joe. Now I want to know if your mama didn't teach you to knock on the door before you enter a room. I don't seem to remember hearin' a knock just now."

I wanted to crawl under the table. My own discourtesy to the major the previous November had been attempted subtly—no matter how it came out—but this was blatant. Bonnet was asking for a court-martial. "Why are you doing this, Bonnet?" Thompson said. "I . . ."

"So you'll know better to walk into a room and accuse one of your officers of gambling. Got a better reason?"

"This is conduct unbecoming an officer, and I don't propose to spend another moment listening to this."

"You're welcome to stay and get in the game, Major, but if you must go, be sure and close the door behind you, thank you very much. How's that for courtesy?"

"You'll hear more about this, Lieutenant." Thompson's face was twisted with hate as he slammed the door.

The room was silent for several red-faced seconds—that is, red-faced for all but Andy Bonnet. He calmly lit a cigarette, found a bottle of champagne under his seat, and slammed it on the table. "Whose bid? Git yourselves glasses."

Lying awake well into the night, I fretted over the clash between Bonnet and Thompson, figuring our well-liked lieutenant had just screwed up enough to get himself a court-martial. After an hour of worrying, I suddenly sat straight up.

Nothing was going to happen! Bonnet was a forward observer *... a field artillery forward observer!*

It had been slow sinking in, but in the last months of World War II, with the Luftwaffe in decline, the field artillery had become nearly "rear echelon"; and though the dangers faced by an FO couldn't be compared to an infantryman's, within the field artillery forward observers were doing all the dying, and they were heroes, almost gods. I was learning about *informal* power.

All the power conveyed by rank was *formal* and primarily for the garrison army. But this was war, and in war, evidence of courage was outranked only by evidence of greater courage. Though this shift of power was subtle, Major Thompson had sensed it the night of Ray York's death, and he was still fighting it. When Bonnet mouthed off to Thompson, I think he knew the major only from things I'd said and was showing off for my benefit. He was more oiled than was apparent, as he had the ability to hide his state of intoxication, and both his courage and his combativeness were boosted by alcohol. Nevertheless, his status as Battery B's FO was going to protect him this time. Who wanted to replace him? Would the army foolishly punish an officer by moving him to a less dangerous assignment? Major Thompson was in a bind.

We were fools to expect we would never have to face combat again, but when the phone rang in our billet (we had run a line from the battery CP), and we were told that tomorrow the 103rd Division was returning to combat status, all of us were shocked. We shouldn't have been; the *Stars and Stripes* had daily stories of Seventh Army combat near Heilbronn. The Germans weren't finished yet, though most civilians in our zone acted like it.

We packed trailers, wrote letters, and then just sat around worrying. No one wanted to die in the last days of this war, and the reentry into combat was met with intense anxiety.

The captain had his own dilemma: Division had been sending to all units the wine and brandy they were confiscating from German warehouses. Pultz, fearing another drunken spree, had hoarded it in the house where the battery CO was billeted. Now how could he get rid of it?

At the evening chow in the schoolhouse, the kitchen crew tried to dispense a couple of gallons of grenadine and brandy with just three glasses. In order to get everyone served their share of the liquor, they had us chug-a-lug a medium-size glass of the powerful drink at the end of the chow line. "Get it down, get it down!" the cook shouted. "Drink up, drink up! You're holding the line up!"

The strong, sweet drink began having a very pleasant effect on me before I finished eating, so when I heard a cook yelling that there were seconds on the stuff, I went back and guzzled another. That was a big mistake. I was no longer rational, so by the time I finished eating, I stopped and got a third glass. Out on the street, halfway to our billet, I realized I had left my carbine leaning against a desk in the classroom where I ate, so I went back.

Until my friends told me the following morning, I didn't remember what happened next. I apparently took another drink on the way in and yet another on the way out. When I got back in our billet, I found that the CP had called everyone to come get a bottle of red wine. In my drunken state, I drank the bottle straight down. There was probably enough alcohol in my system by then to bring about my death within an hour. Fortunately, I was helped into the bathroom by Frank Lawrence, who got my head over the bathtub before I began throwing up. They told me I threw up for half an hour, and then passed out. A couple of my friends picked me up and carried me to bed, and surprisingly—thanks to Frank Lawrence—I had hardly any hangover in the morning.

But I slept in the back of the jeep for hours until we were crossing a bridge over the Neckar River in the city of Heidelberg. I was wakened by the guys in my jeep, who didn't want me to miss seeing this storied place.

While still on the bridge, we passed a man on a bicycle who wore round thick glasses the size of quarters. When I was right beside him, the jeep moving nearly at bicycle speed, he looked at me and said, "This is beautiful city, no?" It *was* beautiful, and seemed untouched by the war.

I dozed off and on for most of the day, until we passed through Heilbronn. This must be the most gorgeous part of Germany, with castles and cathedrals on steep hills, and quaint architecture, amid rolling fields that had been cultivated over centuries into gardenlike undulations. The Neckar River had a postcard vista at every turn. The only thing missing was the enemy.

We turned away from the Neckar River into equally pretty lands and came to a hospital that our advance party had selected for our billet for the night. It was only three in the afternoon. The hospital was empty of patients, but a beautiful girl who was an administrator there was still sitting at her desk when we arrived. She was petite and dark-haired, more Italian-looking than German, and the entire battery was acting silly at the sight of her. Of course, the captain had to tell her she had to leave, but you could see he hated doing it. Andy pretended he didn't see her, but fifteen minutes later, I went in a side door and found him with the pretty *fräulein* sharing a glass of champagne. The girl spoke no English and Bonnet spoke no German, so how he did it, I'll never know.

Shortly after I found them with the champagne, he had Rocky drive him and his latest female conquest into the nearby village to her house. Rocky came back after receiving instructions to return as soon as the battery was awakened. Bonnet took two bottles of the wine and nothing else.

The reaction this outright violation of the nonfraternizing edict got from the battery ranged all the way from smiles and applause to jealousy and anger. I could see the captain was fretting about how to handle it. Bonnet was a renegade, and there seemed no way to stop him. He was a drunk, a liar, a ladies' man, and a rebel—an officer who cared not one hoot for the title of gentleman. But the little coterie of forward observers loved the man. Chuck Howard called him "Stud" and offered to trade me his lieutenant, my best friend Kenneth Rebman, for Bonnet, if the captain would allow it. Chuck could be silly.

I had to go with Rocky in the morning. The battery was march-ordering at six o'clock, and I had to hurry into town before breakfast. The hospital-administrator *fräulein* lived in a modest bungalow on a street that looked more midwestern American than I had seen before in Europe. There was even a concrete driveway. I went to the door and rang the bell. Bonnet came to the door after a wait of five minutes. He was buckling his belt, and the woman was standing just behind him in a nightgown. He smelled of booze and had a silly grin on his face, so I knew he was still oiled.

When he finally recognized me through his mental fog, he turned and pulled the girl to him, and they kissed for nearly a minute. Then he turned and winked at me. "Jus' a minute, Bill, I needa say g'bye." He turned to the girl and said, "I . . . love . . . you . . . Marie . . . I . . . come . . . back . . . get you . . . Okay?"

I said, "Ugh, ugh, Kemo Sabe." He turned and winked again.

Chapter 20

The battery spent the night in a barn several miles east of Ulm, an important city of Swabia in the region called Schwarzwald—the Black Forest. Some displaced persons had left piles of their baggage in the hay, and I found a clarinet that I kept, expecting that someday I might lead a band again, and a clarinet for one of my saxophone players to double on might come in handy.

The battery still had not set up the howitzers, so I guessed that our combat team might be in reserve. That afternoon, Lieutenant Bonnet was told to take his section to a town (the name of which I have forgotten) and join a company of infantry on an attack.

We met once more with George Company and were surprised to see sixty men. A few of these guys were replacements, but the rest were mostly soldiers who'd had the flu, trenchfoot, or minor wounds when the company had been reduced to eighteen men back in the Hardt Mountains. Capt. Tom Stagg was there once more, and he quickly recognized us. "Glad to see you, Andy, and you guys too," he said, nodding at Frank and me.

We began trudging along a road in flat treeless farmland, not what I expected in the Black Forest. We could see mountains in the distance, which I now know were the Swabian Jura. This hike was unlike the forced marches we went on back in Louisiana. We were in no hurry, and we didn't know what to expect. Resistance in late April was spotty, according to *Stars and Stripes*. The Russians were closing in on Berlin, and rumors of complete surrender were flying. Some units of the 103rd had been capturing entire companies, mostly preteen boys, *Volkssturm*, and non-Germans forced into service.

The morale in George Company was good. We expected to advance only ten miles a day, in order for our artillery to leapfrog five miles at a time in our support. At one point, we moved into a woods adjoining plowed fields, and a large deer ran right through the column, not more than ten feet from me. The soldier in front of me could have touched the animal if he had wanted to. Not being a deer hunter, I had to be told that the European deer were unlike our whitetails. One soldier near me was of the opinion that hunting might have been *verboten* during the war, or else that deer wouldn't have come near humans so easily.

We walked for at least five hours before we ran into opposition. A Wehrmacht rifle platoon in a copse opened fire at us, and we dropped into a ditch and fired back. The Germans quickly threw up their hands and surrendered, so I felt sure their rifle fire had been merely to get our attention. There were about twenty of them, and I guessed they were mostly Poles or Ukrainians, for whom capture was liberation. One soldier among them wore an entirely different sand-colored uniform that was recognized as Italian. In any company of Americans, it was never difficult to find someone who spoke Italian, so George Company found a sergeant who could talk to the man. The Italian officer told the sergeant that he was a prisoner of the Germans and wanted to join our army to fight them. By this time, we knew that any Italian prisoner of the German Army would have been sent to a stalag at least a year ago, so we knew the man was a liar. One of G Company was sent back with the prisoners, but I have no idea where to.

Arriving after dark in a fairly large city, we located a hotel in the very center. Several other army units must have beaten us there, because Frank and I were forced to sleep in the lobby. When we got up the next day, we found we were sleeping right under a large photo portrait of Hitler. I took my carbine and smashed the frame to the floor, and then crushed the glass with my shoes.

We set out that day on a dirt road through farmland that stretched for miles. Once more we could see mountains in front of us. An hour into that day's march, we came to a bend in the road next to a wooded area with a large building set back in it that we thought might be a *gasthaus*, and suddenly machine-gun fire erupted from the direction of the building. The entire company dived into a ditch, and BAR men immediately returned fire. Captain Stagg was probably expecting another surrendering bunch like the last time we were fired on.

After a few rounds of mortar fire landed on the road, Stagg asked Bonnet for artillery fire, and Frank and I connected up the radio and battery pack, while still in the ditch. But when I tried to make radio contact, I heard nothing through my earphones; the radio seemed dead. I tried wiggling the various cords and reconnecting the cable, but nothing worked. Either the battery was dead or the radio was in need of repair.

When I told the captain my fix, he told Bonnet it was not a real problem. "You just go back and get the radio worked on, and we'll get by here," he said.

We scrambled out of the ditch and ran along the road until we thought we were safe.

"You know the radio really is dead," I said. "I wasn't just making it up to get out of that ditch."

"You weren't?" Bonnet said. I gave him a poke on the shoulder. "Hey watch it," he said. "I'm fragile."

"Like a Mack truck," I said.

"No, I mean it. I got to go on sick call. I got the same illness your pal Howard seems to like getting."

"Gonorrhea? You got gonorrhea?"

"Yep. Must have been that gal Marie. Who'd expect that from *her?*"

Frank chipped in: "Doesn't it pain you?"

"You have no idea."

"How long have you known?"

"Since this morning."

For the next hour, we kept our eye on Andy. He sweated a lot, but so did we: the day was hot and the sky cloudless, and we were dressed for warmer weather.

We were expecting we might soon have to deal with a passed-out lieutenant, but then we saw a cloud of dust approaching us, and as it neared, we saw to our relief that it was a jeep. It drew up next to us with Rocky at the wheel. "The captain sent me for you," he said. "We're going on a task force."

Chapter 21

Now came the biggest surprise yet. We obviously couldn't go on the task force with a sick lieutenant and a dead radio, so Lieutenant Whidden and his crew were sent in our place. After Andy got his shot of penicillin and was not court-martialed, he showed how stormproof he was. "Guys!" he said, on his return from the aid station. "We're going to join General McAuliffe's headquarters as division artillery liaison."

Before I recall our experiences traveling with the commanding general's entourage, you need to know what happened to Lieutenant Whidden's section in the task force from which Bonnet's illness kept us. (I am positive that my radio's problems would not have had gotten us excused; another radio would have been loaned to us immediately.)

As it was told to me: The task force had two armored cars, followed by several jeeps—Whidden's among them—and four truckloads of riflemen. Their objective was to move forward until they met opposition, then disperse the riflemen and call for artillery, if necessary; in this way, they would get the division moving faster than the snail's pace at which it had been going.

Going around a bend in the road well up into the Swabian Jura Mountains, they were met by a sturdy roadblock of logs. When the scout cars stopped and opened fire, soldiers poured out of the woods all around them. These were SS fanatics intent on killing as many as they could before surrendering. The first jeep in the column behind the scout cars was lifted up by an explosion of a land mine set to allow the first vehicles to pass. The floor of the jeep exploded under the rear seat, and Len Harris, the radioman who replaced me, was wounded in both thighs by shrapnel. Lieutenant Whidden and Bob Wilmoth pulled him from the jeep and dragged him to a ditch, as enemy troops were rushing from the woods all around them. The radio remained in the jeep, so if the commander of the task force needed artillery, he was temporarily out of luck.

Whidden looked up to see a Kraut staring down at him, and he shot the man in the face with his .45. The enemy soldier was repelled backward, as expected. When hit with a .45, the victim is not just killed; the blunt bullet has many pounds of force and is meant to repel him. It was designed that way as the best defense against a bayonet for officers in World War I.

I don't know what happened after that, but I do know the enemy was quickly overcome. Harris was taken to a field hospital and did not return during the remaining days of the war.

I'm not sure of our exact route through Bavaria with McAuliffe's division headquarters company, but we spent our nights in the best, often plush communities, in such well-known cities as Oberammergau, Garmisch-Partenkirchen, and Landsberg. Here I saw things I might not have seen had I been with the battery during that time. Division headquarters jumped all over the place, not following the tide of combat or remaining inside the division's area of advance, and I can tell about the places we passed through only in the order in which I remember them.

We passed a concentration camp the first day, but I'm not sure which one. What I am sure of was the sight of those Jews who flooded the street in front of the prison. They wore vertically striped uniforms, and all of them looked more emaciated than any humans I had ever seen before.

These were only the lucky few—those who had escaped the gas chambers and the crematoriums. I was more than happy we were not going to enter that place to see the true horrors. One memory of that day was of a prisoner encountering a German civilian on the sidewalk to the right of our motor column. We were temporarily at a standstill, so we got to see the whole drama as it unfolded. The civilian was an old man who had passed many prisoners, all of whom were too busy experiencing the feeling of freedom to notice him. But I could see one prisoner eyeing the old man, and I was curious how this Jew would react to a civilian who lived near this awful place and seemed so unconcerned. The prisoner walked up to the civilian and said something, and the old man winced but did not speak. Then the prisoner walked behind the man and began methodically kicking him in the rear after every step they took, until the civilian ran. Of course the weak prisoner couldn't catch up to him, but I was surprised he was able to kick the man as many times as he did. When we applauded, the poor ex-prisoner was too weak to grin, but he did wave, with no show of enthusiasm.

Some GIs in the trucks threw C-ration candy to the prisoners, until officers walked along beside us and cautioned against it. We were told that these people had to be reintroduced to ordinary food slowly—that they could die from something as rich as the sugar in candy.

In Garmisch-Partenkirchen, our motor column was halted on the main street, and I heard the sound of breaking glass. Soon rioting groups of soldiers came down our side of the street, smashing plate-glass windows with their rifles. These were classy shops selling expensive cameras, radios, winter clothing, and ski equipment. I kept expecting to see officers interfere, but the GIs looted the stores freely. After that, we saw looting in every part of Germany in which we went. I was sure McAuliffe would not want this to happen, but while our section was traveling with McAuliffe's headquarters, I never saw him. I had seen him nearly every day during the last offensive in the Hardt Mountains, so I have to assume he was with active infantry units instead of with division headquarters during that time. I'm not sure whether such behavior was going on in other areas of the occupation. The Bavarian vacationland, with such apparent wealth—either garnered or retained while under the Nazis—may have disgusted our troops enough to precipitate the looting.

In Oberammergau, we moved into a house in a moderately wealthy neighborhood. Here, the ousted owners had stacked

fifty *National Geographic* magazines on the floor of a sunroom—
most certainly on display for the American soldiers they were
expecting. The magazines dated from the early 1930s to 1939,
the year the war began, so I knew they were a plant. Atop a
dresser in the dining room was further evidence that these evac-
uees were trying to impress us—a postcard showing the Gruen
Watch Company factory in Cincinnati, with a greeting on the
opposite side in English from Ohio friends, along with an appli-
cation for American citizenship, also dated in the 1930s.

I was not surprised by a knock on the door after we'd been
there an hour. At the door, I met a well-dressed middle-age
woman with a worried look. I knew before she spoke that her
English would be good. She was aware that we could not have
her in the same house with us, but she asked me in a midwestern accent if she could go to the cellar to get some preserves.
"The people where we are staying are not so well off as we are,
and I want to get them some peaches and pears."

When I complimented her on her English, she thanked
me and told me about living in Cincinnati and how her husband worked for Gruen. I asked why she chose to live in Nazi
Germany.

"We did not want to live here, but we came back for a family
wedding, and then my husband contracted tuberculosis, and we
thought the mountains here were good for him, so we stayed."

"Have you seen the concentration camps?"

"No, but we did hear rumors. You have seen this?"

"Yes, and not far from here. They are disgusting."

She began to cry. "Now I know why you Americans must
hate us. We did not want these things; they were forced on us."

A headquarters lieutenant, from whom I had to get permission for the lady to go to the cellar, heard similar apologies
a few moments later. "You aren't hurting much, lady, as I see
it," he said.

"Yes," she said between snuffles, "but we have worked hard
for these nice things."

"Take her to the cellar," the lieutenant said openly, "but keep a close eye on her. Make sure all she does is get cans of fruit." He did not try to hide his distrust of her.

She got the fruit and said one last thing to me before she left: "I hope you will be as we remember our Americans friends to be. You will not harm our things."

The sad thing about this encounter was that she did not once negatively mention Hitler or Nazis, and that left me suspicious. If the woman was telling the entire truth, and they were so innocent while staying there under a Nazi regime, their hands were smudged anyway. Looking the other way because you were comfortable was akin to aiding and abetting, as I saw it.

She may have gotten her wish to have her property remain safe, but other troops may not have been as kind as we were.

In Landsberg (the town, not the prison), I took part in some vandalism for which I have no regrets. We had seen the Kaufering concentration camp, where starvation-victim cadavers were stacked beside their intended mass graves, and we were made ill at the sight of the bloated bellies and the fly-and-maggot-covered remains of murdered human beings, people put to death by suffering. If ever we saw why we had needed to go to war against that criminal German government, we saw it in Kaufering, the camp near Landsberg.

Right after we witnessed such atrocity, division headquarters sent us into a large luxurious house, one in which we did not have to order the residents to leave. That they fled before we arrived said something was not right. People with such luxury could be expected to stay until shoved out; we did not automatically move into every house in every town, and at this time in our occupation, we did not search houses anymore.

The furniture in this house was expensive, as were the original oil paintings—though tastelessly sentimental or nationalistic. The owners had a Steinway grand piano and several glass china cabinets filled with Dresden figurines. In Nazi Germany, shows of wealth such as these made me automatically distrust the people displaying it, fair or unfair, but I tried to withhold judgment—that is, until I saw their library and the hobby room off the kitchen.

The library was huge, easily the largest room in the house, which had more square footage than most we had seen in either France or Germany, but instead of books, this library had only boxes of scientific papers, carefully cataloged and alphabetized. The owner of this house was obviously a scientist: a scientist who fled from his nation's invaders. Frank and I studied the printing on the boxes. The German words for nicotine and tobacco are similar to those in English, so we had a pretty good idea that these papers were about nicotine— especially cigarettes—and might well have been about diseases caused by smoking. That this scientist chose to live near a prison and a concentration camp added to Frank's and my distrust of his scientific integrity—could it be that prisoners were forced to smoke themselves to death?

The crowning blow was the room we entered from the kitchen. A table nearly filled the room—about twenty by twenty, as I remember it. On it was a battlefield in miniature, with tiny soldiers, a tank, an ambulance, and two army vehicles, all to scale The soldiers were about three inches high, and their painted features were perfect, even to facial expressions. Such tiny works of art had to be extremely expensive, rendered and cast in lead by professional dollmakers. There were about fifty soldiers, both Wehrmacht and SS among the Germans on one side of the table, with Russians on the other. Near the ambulance were a Red Cross nurse and two German medics with a tiny patient on a stretcher, and a doctor in a white blouse. The realism of the miniature war scene had the touch of Nazi sadism I should have expected: one of the gruesomely realistic Russian soldiers was bent over clutching his midsection, with red, yellow, and purple entrails bulging from between his tiny fingers. Another held his hands to a bloody face.

Lead is difficult to deface without a blowtorch, but Frank and I pushed over the table and systematically walked upon the soldiers, until all of them were simply lumps of painted metal. We wanted this scientist, whom we now were certain was a war criminal, to find half a million marks worth of trash (our guess at the value) on his hobby-room floor, should he ever return to his home.

Next we took over the dining room. We cooked C rations on our Coleman stove and ate off Dresden dishes. When finished eating, we threw them against the walls.

Frank and I later regretted not pulling down the boxes in the library and scattering the carefully cataloged papers.

As we approached the Austrian border, our motor column entered a small alpine village with a large and impressive public building on a gentle slope at its center. This could have been a school, post office, or town hall. Standing in front of this building—wearing bright-colored uniforms with broad red stripes on the trousers—was what looked like a convention of hotel doormen. They were a Hungarian regiment in three columns, a tall dapper officer wearing tasseled epaulets standing before them with his sword drawn. How long they had been standing at attention like that, I hesitate to guess, but most of the division headquarters vehicles had seen them and passed them by. We stopped there only because we were forced to by some delay up ahead.

A captain in the jeep in front of ours got out and walked up the slope, approaching the Hungarians. Bonnet, Frank, and I also got out to see what was going to happen.

"What can I do for you, my man?" asked the captain.

The Hungarian replied in a British accent: "I wish to surrender my regiment and my sword to an officer of equal rank."

"And what is that rank, may I ask?"

"I am a colonel."

"Okay, Colonel . . . I'll see what I can do for you." As he turned, he winked at Bonnet.

The captain then went back to his jeep and sent his sergeant on the errand of finding the man's equivalent to take the tendered sword—*or so we thought.* A few minutes later, the sergeant returned with a small PFC and told the captain, "Sorry, sir, I couldn't find a small buck private, but will this guy do?"

"Good man . . . You got me Sam! Perfect!" The captain and Sam then went up the slope to the tall colonel. We knew the captain was speaking loud for our benefit—he was now on stage and about deliver the speech he had been composing in his head these last few minutes. "Here, Colonel, is a man to take your sword. We don't have your equal in our army, so I found your superior. Sam, here, will take your sword." He turned to the PFC. "Now take his sword, Sam, and then kick his ass . . . if you can kick that high. Otherwise I'll have to do it for you."

Sam proved to be athletic, and when he had completed the physical humiliation of the colonel, the captain took over. He threw the sword to the ground and stepped on it. "This is not some war of officer gentlemen, you swine," he began. "This war was begun by a gangster for criminal purposes. When Hungary chose to get on the side of Adolf Hitler, they became scum like the rest of the Nazis. Now make the sign of the cross in gratitude that I don't immediately have you shot . . . My grandmother was Hungarian, by the way."

Later that day, we were sent back to our battery, never having found out just what it was we were sent to division headquarters for in the first place. Bonnet was given some papers to take back to General Wicks in division artillery headquarters, but he didn't think he did anything other than that of any importance. We didn't find out much else that happened while we were gone, except for one piece of news about our combat teammates, the 411th Infantry: they captured "Fatso" Hermann Goering, who was hiding out in a castle near the Swiss border.

The battery stopped for the night in a cluster of *gasthausen* in a scenic Alpine village beneath towering peaks. They had been traveling for two days with no need for setting up the howitzers, as the division was not encountering resistance. The 103rd was limiting the distances traveled, in order to not outrun other divisions from the Seventh Army or from the French First, who were still meeting sporadic resistance on either side of us.

The men from our battery, who stayed in the same building as Bonnet, Frank, and me, ignored the nonfraternization edict and allowed a frumpy woman to remain in a first-floor room, and the captain looked the other way. She had told them she was a psychic, and she agreed to read our palms for free, in order to remain. Of course, she also sneaked around to other parts of the small inn to sleep with men who paid her with cigarettes for services other than palm reading. Bonnet had learned his lesson, and he avoided her. She spoke halting English but understood it well. The thing I most remember about this woman, was that she was the only person in Germany I met who openly declared that she was a member of the Nazi party and loved Hitler. Ironically, it was while in this *gasthaus* that we learned of Hitler's suicide.

We had a conversation when she approached me and said, "You have an honest face. What is your name? I can tell you are a good man." I think this was probably her approach to most of us—along with her claim to having psychic powers. I fell for it enough to tell her my name and to let her read my palm. After she read my palm and told me I was far from where I wanted to be and that a woman far away longed for me (something she told all of us), she suddenly asked, "Why did America make war on Germany? We did nothing to you."

"Germany made war on all of Europe, and we would have been next. Hitler is evil."

"Ah, no, Bill. He was good for the world."

"Not if you were a Jew."

"He did nothing to hurt anyone. I like Jews."

"Then you are not a good Nazi. Have you seen any of the concentration camps? He starves Jews to death."

"That is Bolshevik lies. We do not do harm to them."

"Do you think I am a liar? A few minutes ago, you said I was an honorable man."

"If *you* say you saw this . . . then I believe you, but it was done by Bolsheviks in Nazi uniforms."

After that exchange, I gave her a kiss on the cheek and went outside for some fresh air. She was not an evil person; she was simply like too many European women of that time—a deliberate ignoramus, whose simpleness was easily used. This woman was like Eva Braun, the poor woman who became Hitler's mistress. I felt pity for such women who, by believing passive ignorance is admirable in females, let evil men use them. She *did* know how to survive, and I persistently admire that quality in people.

I lay awake that night, fretting. Even as the Krauts were surrendering, we'd been cheated. Hitler, with his suicide, deprived us of justice. I'm not a forgiving person, and remembering Ray York's death struggles, for which I blamed Hitler. I wanted some end for him worse than death at the end of a gun. I wanted Hitler to suffer. I imagined putting him in one of his death camps to await the gas chamber and the crematorium, where GIs could take turns lashing him with a bullwhip, then putting this on film to be shown at every theater from Berlin to Vienna, from Hamburg to Munich. I entertained myself with such ugly imaginings throughout the night, but in the end, I knew my frustration would never go away.

I usually dislike clichés, but to best describe what we began seeing from the day Hitler took the easy way out, I like this one: *the rats began leaving the sinking ship.*

While outside packing our trailers and trucks, preparing to leave these Alpine inns and admiring the tall, beautiful peaks surrounding us, we heard the sound of approaching planes and looked up to see—flying at a relatively low level—two twin-engine transport planes with no military markings. It was illegal during the war for such aircraft to fly anywhere near combat areas, and our antiaircraft guns quickly opened fire on them. They flew a straight line from north to south, several thousand feet below the mountaintops. I hoped they weren't Swiss transports that had wandered off course, but I sensed they were German, with a purpose other than combat. In seconds, they let me know what that was: they flew directly into the mountains to our south, crashing one into the other. I had no doubt they were suicides, and I wondered how many Nazis were aboard to require two planes for the mission. Ingraham, one of our .50-caliber gunners, took credit for shooting them down, but nobody believed him.

Later that same day, we were traveling down a road on mountainside, with a sheer drop of 1,000 feet to our right, when a Messerschmitt suddenly crossed our column, ten feet above us, and dived into the valley. I tried to get out of the jeep, thinking we were about to be strafed, but our column only slowed but did not stop. Our three machine guns immediately sent tracers flying toward the rapidly departing plane, which was now skimming the farmland several hundred feet below.

It happened so fast that even Rocky was calm. The enemy pilot flew toward a grove of trees ten or twelve miles away and disappeared behind it. I think every one of us expected we would see more Luftwaffe soon, but none appeared.

An hour later, we came to an intersection and saw a Messerschmitt, crashed and burning. Several truckloads of GIs walked nearby. I presume they were witnesses to the crash. That plane may have been the same one we saw earlier, and our machine-gun fire might have done him in, but I believed we were seeing another suicide.

We entered Austria before dark and saw signs that the Austrians were welcoming us as liberators: red and white flags flew from windows, and homemade signs proclaimed *Wilkommen*. I didn't feel more comfortable, just the same. We climbed back into the Alps and meandered over winding roads that took us up and back down constantly, and MP road markers had to signal us to slow down when the curves were dangerous and the drop-offs to our flanks were precipitous. Though the column moved slowly, Rocky was in his element: danger while at the wheel didn't frighten him.

Late in the afternoon, our column was stopped on a steep incline, and we kept expecting to move but remained suspended at a steep angle downward for an hour or more. A jeep passed, going the other way, with what we thought was a German soldier in the front passenger seat. Soon after, another jeep with several officers passed on the shoulder headed forward. Then we descended into a flat plain next to a river,

which Bonnet told us was the Inn River on his map. He said
that our next stop was going to be Innsbruck.

We passed some flat riverside terrain with a makeshift airport for scores of jet planes. There didn't appear to be any
landing strips, so we decided the planes might have used the
highway for takeoffs and landings. Because we thought we had
not seen any of them in combat, it's possible these jets never
did fly.

Now came the strange entry we made into Innsbruck. At a
fork in the road was an American soldier standing side by side
with a Wehrmacht soldier, both of them presenting arms to
vehicles with officers. They signaled us to go to the right—the
route to the Brenner Pass.

At some point back on that mountain road, Bonnet must
have gotten out and gone back to another vehicle where someone was well informed about what was going on, because in
our jeep, we knew why we waited on the mountain road and
why we were now going peaceably into Innsbruck. That knowledge later allowed me to research some of the things in this
book that contradict my division's history book. All we knew at
that time was that the enemy was allowed to remain armed in
this situation, because an OSS officer had preceded us there
by parachute and had prevailed on the *Gauleiter* of Innsbruck,
the Nazi regional leader, to let him intercept the approaching
Americans and get their commander's permission to allow the
Wehrmacht to remained armed, in order to prevent SS fanatics from resisting—as they had threatened—which would
surely bring about the destruction of this beautiful and historic
city. This was the man we thought was a German soldier in the
jeep that had passed us while we waited on the mountain road.

Snow began falling immediately after we left Innsbruck,
and the temperature dropped into the lower thirties. This was
May 4, and we had turned in all our winter clothing a month
before; we had not seen snow since January. On our first of
many stops along the way, we got out and brought blankets
and shelter halves from the trailer, something to huddle
under. We were beside a steep slope with a row of houses many

feet above us. A woman wearing a hooded parka came clambering down the steps from the house nearest us, and brought us the unexpected—a tray of mugs with steaming hot cocoa.

"I'm so happy to see you, my American friends," she said. "Here is some cocoa to warm you up. I have here also schnapps I can put in for those who might like that too."

She was an attractive middle-age woman and spoke English with the British accent required by educated Europeans. She told us how much she hated being under the Nazis for six years, and thanked us for getting rid of Hitler, whom she described as "that awful man, with his filthy friends," asking, "He is dead, no? You know he had our Chancellor Dolfuss murdered. And poor Chancellor Schuschnigg . . . he was put in one of those awful prison camps and starved—nearly to death—both he and his wife. I prayed for you to come, and now you are here."

Only Rockwell refused the schnapps additive in his cocoa, and I was surprised he even accepted the cocoa, considering it was from a stranger, but he hung his head when we said our thanks and handed back our mugs.

We were well back in the column and never entered Italy, but very early in the morning of May 5, we were told the front of our column had met the 88th Division of the Fifth Army in Colle Isarco, Italy, eight miles south of Brenner. Half frozen to death and sleepless, we tried to doze in the jeep with no success.

We withdrew to the area in the Brenner where the woman had served us cocoa and settled in one of the houses on the hill from which we'd seen her come. I hoped none of us pushed her out of her house or looted from that decent woman, but I despaired—my army was vengeful, like all armies.

The first day on that hillside, we slept until noon. Still dogtired, Frank and I went to a settlement across a bridge over a Brenner stream. We were hoping to find a lumberyard to get boards to replace some on our trailer. The weather had done an about-face: it was nearly 70 degrees, and snow was melting everywhere. On the narrow bridge with a crowd of soldiers, we were stopped by a lieutenant who wanted to know why we hadn't saluted him.

"I'm sorry, sir," I said, "but I didn't see you in this crowd."

"If you'd been paying attention, you'd have seen they were all saluting. I'm sorry, but I'll have to take your names, ranks, and serial numbers to put in my report. I'm on a division courtesy patrol."

"Would it make any difference if we told you we are combat soldiers, and saluting is dangerous up front?"

"Not a bit. Saluting is always proper, no matter where you are . . . or who you are . . . Your name, soldier?"

I sighed and gave him what he asked for, deliberately putting a superior smile on my face as he wrote. Frank did the same. The guy was obviously rear echelon, and I could see he was uncomfortable with this duty, so I refrained from being sassy. As the lieutenant was walking away, Frank said, "War's over, chickenshit's back." The lieutenant shot a quick look back but decided not to get into it with us. I knew we'd never hear about it again.

The next day, May 6, we moved up to a tiny settlement high in the mountains southwest of Innsbruck, having been assigned there by the military government, which was now in charge of the entire division. I saw no ski lifts, but because of the layout of the village, I knew it had to be a ski resort. On the south side of the road there were less than a dozen Alpine-style houses, and on the north side were four three-story hotels that we were told were empty of guests. The girls who moved between the houses and the hotels wore aprons and dirndls, so we knew the houses were for the employees of the hotels. While our comrades in Innsbruck proper were being kissed by pretty girls and pelted with flowers, the people here were cold and unfriendly—*or so I thought.* The first hotel in the row held all ninety men of our battery, with room to spare. To my knowledge, we did not search the other three hotels, and I wondered why we were sent up there in the first place, if not to search for arms and enemy soldiers.

An army can't tolerate inactivity, so even though the war was not officially over, athletic events were organized. The next day, we sent a three-quarter-ton truck with players and a two-and-a-half-ton truck with bystanders to a volleyball game somewhere in the Inn River Valley. A softball league was also in the works.

The following day, Bonnet had some sort of errand Battalion wanted us for, so we missed out on lots of excitement, which we heard all about when we got back. The guys in the battery were all stirred up because many of the attractive girls we'd seen going back and forth from the hotels to the row of houses had gone to a field east of the settlement and removed every stitch of clothing, and then brazenly sat on blankets in full view of the hotel where the battery was located.

Any group of men representing a cross section of humanity has a mishmash of personalities, some of whom would be too shy to openly look at naked women, and others as brassy as army coat buttons. I was told that there were enough of the latter to have all blankets on that hillside occupied by a twosome moments after they were spread, and that all of the former were at windows in the hotel.

I thought the whole thing was fishy. To our east, less than a mile distant, was a glacier that hadn't melted, and the ground upon which the girls sat in the nude had been frozen solid two days before. The nights since had not been warm, so even with the blankets spread out in bright sunshine, that day did not seem nearly warm enough to invite nude sunbathing. Furthermore, those girls, if they had to take their clothes off, could have gone where they would not be so easily seen by soldiers of their nation's enemy. Of course, I was disappointed not to have been there, and I hoped we'd stay another day so I could witness a repeat performance, but I never got the opportunity.

We moved to a town closer to Innsbruck, where Lieutenants Bonnet and Rebman were summoned to battalion headquarters. They were told to bring all their equipment—bedrolls, duffle bags, and so on—without bringing anyone from their sections, other than their drivers. By noontime, we learned why. Rebman was transferred to headquarters battery, a promotion of sorts, and Bonnet was sent to Delta Base Command in Marseilles, France—the military base our division had pioneered the previous October, now being used to process troops for return to America. Delta Base was notorious as an assignment for court-martialed officers and was considered equal to being put on garbage detail.

We never saw 1st Lt. Andrew D. Bonnet again. He wasn't even allowed to come say good-bye. Drunkard, renegade, roué—he was all of those things, yet I liked him, and so did Frank Lawrence. But then, he saw us as men—as brave and worthy men—and not just as soldiers holding ranks inferior to his own. In truth, the drunkenness and womanizing were not what did him in. There is room for all of those defects in the military, and if "fraternizing" with German women were used to send every officer caught doing it to Delta Base, it would have overloaded the base and the city of Marseilles enough to sink them into the Mediterranean. Bonnet was probably officially court-martialed for fraternizing, but we knew it was his sassiness with Major Thompson that drew his punishment. It had just taken longer than Frank and I expected.

The pretense in Austria—if it was that—of the U.S. Army as liberators instead of occupiers continued in this small town, which was across the Inn River adjacent to the airfield with the jet planes. Whether May 8 is a holiday in that part of the Tyrol, or whether the people were celebrating their May Day, delayed a week by our intrusion, I have no idea, but they began appearing on the street dressed in native costumes that morning. They held a parade and marched to a bridge they then crossed to the field with the jets. They had set up a platform and May poles there, and they began roasting sausages and chicken, and dancing the polka to the music of an accordion, clarinet, and tuba. Yodelers held contests, and children rode the backs of ponies led by adults.

While they were celebrating, our battery was installing a PA system outside a building in the center of the town, as ordered by headquarters. We were expecting Eisenhower to go on the air the following day and officially end the war in Europe.

The speech on May 9 brought most of the townspeople out on the street, where they listened intently and applauded frequently. Meanwhile, we soldiers were doing solo dancing and being hugged by our officers. The locals even brought us mugs of beer.

Our third and final move in Austria was to the small village of Pfaffenhofen, on the rapid-flowing Inn River, across from the still-operating rail line from Innsbruck to Switzerland. We were told this would be our semipermanent base for occupation duty. Here Frank, Rocky, and I were given our own apartment on the third floor of a Tyrolean-style apartment house—sort of payment for having been FOs. We had a two-room apartment with a kitchen and bathroom, and we had it all to ourselves. The other guys who operated as forward observers in the last offensive at the German border also had apartments on the floors below. The cannoneers were living indoors too in four other buildings in the block of houses and apartments. Across the street was a parade ground and sports field, and softball and volleyball were played there daily. In the courtyard at the rear of our apartment house was the dining area for the kitchen, which was on our first floor. Once a week, a truck was dispatched to Munich, sixty miles north of us, to get several kegs of beer. We had but to go downstairs to get fresh beer whenever we wanted it, and our refrigerator was filled with sausages we had obtained from a butcher in a nearby village, paid for with cigarettes.

To top it off, I was assigned to umpire a softball game daily in an area that covered fifty miles and took me into the northern tip of Italy. I was excused from all other duties, including being present at reveille and retreat, and Rockwell was my private chauffeur. If I got an average rating of B or better from the teams for which I umpired, at the end of the season I would be awarded an expensive Swiss watch.

I was excused from this duty only once: to go on a special trip to see Berchtesgaden, the site of Hitler's gorgeous aerie in the Alps. A stupid sergeant from service battery was put in charge of the expedition, and he took us there by way of

Munich, fifty miles (each way) out of the way. We took three hours to get there and had only an hour to see everything before it was time to go back. Meanwhile, a couple of us found out that if we had followed the Inn River for about thirty miles, we would have had another two hours to sight-see. We even got a sergeant from another group to show our dumbbell sergeant the correct route on a map—but do you think he would let us stay for a while? Not on your life. "I don't want us to get lost," he said. "I already know the way we came, so I want to go back that way."

In every event that goes sour, you always hope some good can come out of it. In this case, we *did* get to go on the autobahn from Munich, and by so doing, we saw the destruction that our air force had dealt the Luftwaffe bombers. Several hundred bombers that had been using the autobahn for runways lay in ruins among the trees beside it for miles. Apparently the trees did nothing to hide them effectively.

Munich itself was also something I'm glad I saw. The downtown area of that great city was bombed into trash, and the citizens were busy repairing the damage. They were sweeping the powdered mortar into perfect cones, and the streets were already dustless. Men and women were working in crews sorting broken bricks into neat stacks: three-inch, four-inch, five-inch sizes, all trimmed and squared off for future use. These were Germans, using the best part of what seemed to be an ethnic compulsion to clean. This time they were using it on their streets of ruins, instead of attempting to cleanse their nation of races they grew up being taught were impure. Germany was going to endure, if they could keep it that way.

I think I umpired ten games before the hatchet fell, as it always did in the army. I returned from that tenth game to find guys wandering around on the streets of Pfaffenhofen cursing—fifty of us were being transferred to the 5th Division to return to the United States. There we'd be trained for more combat, this time in Asia, very likely for the invasion of Japan. Because I was ten points short in the system used to determine who stayed and who left, I was one of those to leave. We were going immediately to join the 5th Division in Passau, Germany. The 5th was a regular army division, and the 103rd was a reserve division, so the 103rd would remain in Austria on occupation duty until the Japanese were defeated, then it would be disbanded.

Frank and I shook hands in our apartment and swore to remain brothers for life. He could look me up in Detroit and I would look him up in Santa Clara, whenever possible.

The forty of us who were going were already on trucks when Ruotolo and Rebman arrived from headquarters to see us off. Ruotolo had tears in his eyes and said, "Hanford, I'll never forget you." That brought tears to my eyes: I forgave him everything. I hugged Rebman and told him he was the best officer I ever met. Rocky actually began crying.

It only took two hours to get to Passau, which was at the confluence of the Danube and Inn Rivers, across the Danube from Austria and barely twenty miles from Czechoslovakia. Our new battery was still Battery B, and our new battalion was the 50th of the 5th Division, and we were billeted on a hill looking down on the beautiful Danube.

I was quick to discover I had lost little of the prestige I thought I was losing in this transfer.

My new battery commander, whose name I no longer remember, had me sit down with him and his executive officer an hour after we arrived. He told me I had a very good service record, and he implied I was up for better things as a result. The battery already had an FO radioman who had a Silver Star, he told me, and their FO lieutenant had a Distinguished Service Cross, a Silver Star, and two Bronze Stars. But the only member of their FO Section with enough points to get transferred to the 103rd was the sergeant.

The last day we were in Passau, I got a chance to explore and to see why the Danube was so special. I walked alone on a paved footpath along the river that day, and I was drawn to an excursion steamer docked there. It was a Mississippi River paddle wheeler look-alike, with a dozen swarthy Middle Europeans on board and on dockside, two of them playing an accordion and a balalaika. It was mournful Hungarian Gypsy music, and it moved me strangely. Something Germanic had touched me, and I disliked having the hate I still held for the German people. It is hard to hate something romantic.

We were only in Passau two days before we loaded up on the kind of freight cars called "forty and eights" in the American Legion parades I remembered from childhood. But instead of forty men or eight horses, as was their capacity in the First World War, we had fifteen men in each car. The ride was bumpy because the railroads had all taken a heavy bombing in Germany. We moved slowly and had frequent stops, and we were fed no warm meals. Our food was C rations and K rations, with coffee brought twice a day, and we were always hungry.

The greatest problem I had to confront was that we had no toilets. We were expected to relieve ourselves during stops, which were frequent, although for irregular periods of time. If I unbuttoned my fly to urinate and the train suddenly started up (there were no warning whistles), I had to rebutton quickly. It was worse for more intense needs, and furthermore, I had trouble squatting with my pants down in sight of my comrades. But there was no alternative—we had to stay close to the train or risk getting left behind—so consequently, I arrived at Camp Lucky Strike near Rouen, France, with a bad case of constipation.

The train stopped in Nuremberg long enough for all of us to get off and walk into the huge stadium where Hitler made all of his harangues that drew the "Sieg Heils!" I closed my eyes and could hear it from the ghosts. All that did for me was renew the frustration I felt knowing he outfoxed us with his suicide.

Camp Lucky Strike was only one of several "cigarette camps." I had to wonder whether the tobacco companies had something in their contracts with the army requiring these camps be so named in return for the free cigarettes they gave us. Lucky Strike had large perambular tents arranged in rows, and the entire 5th Division was being processed here at the same time. The 50th Artillery had one of the commanding officers who fit the military mold I spoke of earlier, sporting a waxed mustache, wearing a shiny helmet liner at all times, and carrying a riding crop, which he constantly slapped on his thighs as he walked. We called him "Lieutenant Colonel Haircut." After his first haircut inspection, I had three haircuts in one hour: he insisted on hair no longer than a quarter inch, and he carried a ruler to measure it. Most of the men in our battery spent one entire day having haircuts, and we had to pay the soldier doing it 50 cents each time.

One memory I have of Camp Lucky Strike was of the service battery guy who had mastered only "Lili Marleen" on his accordion; he played it continuously, only stopping for chow and the bugler playing taps, no matter how many guys from nearby tents yelled, "Shut the f—— up, yuh dumb jerk!" Needless to say, although this was the signature song of World War II, I can't stand hearing it played on an accordion to this day.

Our liberty ship was under the command of the Army Transportation Corps. Comparing it to the *Monticello*, our U.S. Navy transport in October, would have been like comparing life at Folsom Prison to life at Harvard. Coming over on the *Monticello*, a navy ship, we were stuffed into a small compartment and had only two awful meals a day at six in the morning and six at night, and our time on deck was limited to two hours a day. On this smaller Liberty ship, we had three meals a day prepared by men who *knew* how to cook. We had a latrine with regular porcelain plumbing, and our bunks were spaced far apart, with none atop another. We had all day to spend on deck if we wanted, and a USO troop was aboard and put on two shows in the six days we took to get to Boston. The weather was perfect, and the ocean was like a peaceful lake in central Wisconsin. We saw whales near Iceland.

The greeting we got coming into Boston Harbor made me feel guilty. Here we were, getting all this attention, while the soldiers who faced the worst part of the war were still in Europe and probably wouldn't get the sort of greeting they deserved. Just the same, I loved it.

In Boston Harbor, a tug-size craft came out to meet us and had a band aboard playing many states' songs: "On Wisconsin," the "Maine Stein Song," "Maryland, My Maryland," "Beautiful Ohio," "California, Here I Come," "My Old Kentucky Home," and others. Red Cross girls on the docks served us glasses of cold milk and doughnuts before we got aboard a train to Camp Miles Standish, near Taunton.

Most of us were in Miles Standish less than two days—two days of free telephone calls, steaks at two meals and pork chops at another, and pitchers of beer, as well as real milk. I called my parents to tell them where I was and talked only ten minutes because the phone booths all had lines of guys outside waiting. I also called West Brookfield, Massachusetts, to talk to my grandfather and other New England relatives.

My train was routed to Camp Sheridan, Illinois, with a load of midwesterners. From there, the army gave us round-trip tickets home and a thirty-day "recuperation leave," which wouldn't count on our accumulated furlough time. In the Chicago station, I got a shave and a mudpack to make my face rosy for when I got home. The train from Chicago went through places like Battle Creek, where my army career began at Fort Custer; Ann Arbor, where my band played for the last time at the Sigma Chi fraternity; and Ypsilanti, where I lived and went to school for three and a half years. The train seemed slow as a turtle, but I was met by Mom and Pop at Michigan Central eight hours after leaving Chicago.

A homecoming such as we had that day is a once-in-a-life-time-event—nothing can describe that kind of joy. There was no way for my parents to know how tenuous a thread held the life of their son, but they probably imagined it much worse than it actually was—and now it was over, as far as we all were concerned. *Forget about whether Sonny goes to Japan in two months.*

My parents held several parties with all the friends they had made in nearly thirty years in Detroit, and after that I had time on my hands. The nifty Ike jacket I was given in Austria was too warm for the summer weather, and I needed to look good for when I wore suntans and displayed my three ribbons: the Bronze Star, the European Theater Ribbon with two battle stars, and the Good Conduct Medal. (Later I was awarded four others.) I felt superior to most of the GIs I saw on the streets, and I wanted girls to know I was a veteran, and a neat guy, a distinctly rare man around Detroit those days. I had few companions, because all my girlfriends seemed to have gotten married. Jim Churchill, who was one of only two ASTP men who were made cannoneers, lived in Imlay City, up in the thumb, but he came down twice, and we pretended we had one-day passes and Detroit was the town in which we had to spend it. We went to the USO and got passes to parties and plays, and even picked up a couple of girls we saw ogling us from a streetcar stop and took them dancing that night at Eastwood Gardens to the music of Stan Kenton.

Chapter 22

The headline in that morning's *Detroit Free Press* screamed in banner headlines: "JAPS SURRENDER: WAR OVER." I called a girl I knew to see if she would like to go downtown to get in on the celebration. She had something to do but said she'd take a raincheck. So I went downtown alone on a DSR bus, expecting I'd be a big hero to the crowd, because few other veterans had come home yet.

Woodward Avenue is Detroit's main street, and it was already so crowded at six o'clock that the bus had to let me off about three blocks east, and I walked over.

What I was hoping to find was a chance to get comfortably drunk, though bars were closed, as were liquor stores, by a sensible decree from our mayor. What I needed was to be invited to one of the hotel parties going on in the Book Cadillac or the Statler.

I went along Woodward, pushed by the crowd, and I was in the middle of the street when my overseas cap was snatched from my head by someone following me. I half expected to see some buddy of mine trying to get my attention; instead, I saw a giggling girl throwing my hat back to some gleeful teenage boys, who immediately threw it farther back, all of them overcome with joy at what fun they were having. It was organized; collecting servicemen's hats was the fun for V-J night. I was so surprised I couldn't think of an appropriate action. "Thanks a lot, you young scum!" I said. Crowds in mob rioting like that are numb in the brains, and no one near me disapproved—in fact, most of them seemed to think it was terribly funny. A few minutes later, an ugly woman tried to kiss me, and I pushed her hand back into her face. I knew then it was time for me to go home.

Detroit, Michigan, on V-J Day was not a place to see truly joyous people. Unemployment had lasted too long in my city before the war came along and put everyone back to work, so the kind of celebration I expected turned out to be phony. I had to endure seeing the scorn of fellow passengers on the bus home, who surely thought I was a stupid GI, drunk and out of uniform.

Gov. "Happy" Chandler came to Camp Campbell, Kentucky, for a review of the troops and stood on a stand with General Brown, and the band, obviously drunk, played several marches at the same time and in several different tempos. In the cacophony, we marching soldiers were stumbling along, laughing and bumping into each other, our carbines clanking, and we looked like a mob marching to a strike.

When we returned to the battery we expected some kind of punishment would come down for this behavior. Instead, General Brown sent a telegram of congratulations, saying how proud he was of us and how pleased Governor Chandler was. We all knew we were being held only until the regular army divisions could be returned from Europe and the Pacific to be discharged ahead of us. We were an embarrassment for the government, and they did everything they could think of to mollify us.

In late September, I was called into the orderly room and told the army owed me furlough time. I was being furloughed home for forty-five days with pay and meal money. I knew this was special treatment reserved in the artillery for forward observers.

I had already spent most of my money on the thirty-day leave, so rather than remain broke in Detroit, I spent only a few days with my family before going to Ypsilanti, where I persuaded the registrar to let me enroll for two classes, though I was two weeks behind in instruction. I had no right to the GI Bill, but my army corporal's pay was about the same as the GI Bill subsistence. I promised I would be gone less than two weeks to get my discharge, and I would arrange with my instructor to take studies along with me in order to keep up. I signed up for a four-hour course, French, and a three-hour course, sculpture.

A big surprise awaited me at the men's dormitory. Ralph Gilden had been a quarter-miler on the track team with me, and he was now on the faculty as an instructor in industrial arts and had become head resident in Munson Hall. He greeted me at the desk as I signed in: "Wait'll you see who your roommate is, Bill." He told me there were so few male students on campus that only the first two floors of the dorm were filled. "You'll have the entire third floor to yourselves. I know you'll probably have alcohol in your room, but keep the door closed and don't ever tell anyone I said it was okay, because I didn't."

There at his desk studying when I walked into the room was Bob Archer—the surprise Ralph had promised. Archer and I had been teammates on the freshman track team and members of a two-mile relay team, both of us half-milers. En route from New Jersey to Texas, I had come home on a five-day delay and was told that Archer was missing in action. "My God, you're alive!" I said.

"Nearly," he said, "but not quite. You're back too? We're gonna be roommates!" He sprang to his feet, and we hugged and jumped around.

We had too much catching up to do to try to do it in this small room, so we adjourned downtown to the Avon Restaurant, where Georgie George, the owner, was delighted to see us. He brought us a pitcher of beer on the house and sat down in a booth with us to hear our stories.

The B-24 bomber on which Bob was the navigator was shot down over Austria. Bob told us how he had come out with the aid of partisans in Yugoslavia, then was returned to the United States immediately. He then went to fighter pilot training, from which he had barely earned his wings when the war ended. My own story was so pale beside his, that I merely told them I had been a radioman for a field artillery forward observer.

Bob and I were not the last men on the third floor after all; we got a new roommate the following day—Bill Coulman, who'd been a navy medical corpsman on a submarine. The three of us became a team, and later on, when Archer got around to resurrecting his fraternity, he talked the two of us into joining. Both of us had belonged to a prewar fraternity that disbanded, and we were now members of Phi Sigma Epsilon, a teacher's college national fraternity.

The three of us sometimes philosophized about the war and what it did to us. We agreed that we were presently in an elevated mood, which we called the "high of survival." We somehow forgot to bring in another mood that war induced: a "low of survival." Perhaps they didn't feel it.

I would usually be alone when one of the lows hit. Between classes, on a campus walk, I would occasionally stop stock-still and go stand against a wall, light a cigarette, and think of Ray York. I continue to blame the lieutenant for causing his death, but I was always aware that my changed status in the army and in life was a result of that death, and I hated that and felt guilty. I think that first year back from Europe was the only time in my life when I sometimes thought about suicide. On the other hand, when I was happy, it was the happiest time of my life. Later, I learned that highs and lows like that are part of clinical depression. I thank God I got over it.

But eventually, I had to return to Camp Campbell, and during those last ten days back in the army from college, I think I hated the army as badly as I ever did. It was November, and Kentucky was no longer warm after sunset. The battery was moved to a new barracks, and I kept getting up at night and throwing more coal in the potbellied stove. I pulled guard duty as corporal of the guard the night before I was to go for my discharge, and some silly major stopped me as I was posting my men. "Corporal, did you determine if all your men knew their general orders?"

I lied, said of course I did. Such a silly thing to know, when we were now in the army only until they let us out, when fighting another war was out of the question—and what the hell does knowing one's general orders have to do with anything at that stage? Fortunately, he didn't ask me what the sixth general order was, or the fifth, or the eighth, or any other frigging one; I wouldn't have known, and I probably would not have been discharged the following day. You need to know the general orders before you become a civilian. Right, Major?

After going through the discharge center—where they tried to keep some of my experience on hand for the future by claiming I would be able to keep the same rank if I signed up for the reserves, and they sold me GI insurance for life at much less than civilian rates—I got my medals and discharge papers and went out the gate to a train station, trying to understand just what I was feeling. Pride mixed with disgust, I thought. All of it for no reason other than I was now just a civilian like any other civilian, and I had to stop feeling like a hero. I thought then that I knew why prisoners didn't always welcome freedom, and why some guys couldn't pass up another chance to reenlist: freedom from a yoke you had to carry for nearly three years was mildly uncomfortable.

Twice before discharge, I was offered incentives to make the army a career. While on the ship, my new battery commander told me my previous battalion commander wanted me to be an officer and asked whether I would like to fill out papers for OCS? I only had to think it over for seconds: OCS was renowned for chickenshit, and the only reason I was less miserable in combat than in training camp, was there was less chickenshit. I knew I couldn't endure OCS just for a chance to be on the dishing end instead of the receiving end of that stuff.

In Camp Campbell, soon after we got there, I had another offer to entice me to stay in. If I would sign up for three more years, I would be promoted to master sergeant and would have a cushy job as a recruiter in Boston—specifically, in Sculley Square—where I would share a paid-for apartment with another sergeant. Meals, uniforms, laundry, and transportation (an army car) would also be taken care of. Attractive as that offer was with all its perks, and with so many of my relatives a mere ninety miles away in West Brookfield, Massachusetts, I had only to think how whenever something seemed great in the army, something else was hiding in there to make everything go wrong. I hated life in the army, and I was determined to get out as soon as possible.

I came home for Thanksgiving dinner in 1945 and was back on campus the following Monday.

Epilogue

Frank Lawrence got transferred to the 45th Division and didn't get discharged until March 1946, which gave him the same time in service as I had, minus some of the furloughs.

Ruotolo returned to Yale in the fall of 1946 and eventually reached the rank of lieutenant colonel in the reserves. I saw him in 2002 at a reunion in Chicago. He was easier to be around as a civilian, and he had a sweet wife.

I never was able to locate Andy Bonnet.

I wrote to Ken Rebman a couple times after he settled in Lake Charles, Louisiana. I always intended to look him up again but never did until it was too late. When I was trying to get some of my buddies together for a division reunion in 2000, I wrote to him through Cornell University and was informed that he had died the previous year.

My father was a loyal alumnus of Cornell, where each class has a reunion every five years. In 1948, my father's class had their thirty-fifth, but Pop had not completely recovered from a broken leg he sustained in a March fall on ice, so I went to the reunion with him. At his class's beer tent on the hill above Willard Straight Hall, I looked across the kegs and saw Len Harris. He was the guy who went on the task force in my place in the Alps that time, and I hadn't seen or heard anything about him since. I yelled out, "Harris! What are you doing here?"

Lenny squinted. "Do I know you?"

"You're joking?"

"No. Who are you?"

"Were you in Battery B of the 928th? Were you wounded in the Alps?"

"You knew me in the army? Who are you?"

"Whose place did you take on that task force?"

"Oh, for God's sake! Hap! You're Hap."

Harris had just graduated from Cornell and, with a member of his fraternity, was visiting that guy's dad, a classmate of my father's—what are the odds? Pop's class was so tickled by this chance encounter in their tent that they made me an honorary member of the class of 1913, and I was invited to their next reunion in five years.

Harris and I went to New York City three weeks later, when school was out in the Detroit system, where I was teaching. New York City was affordable for guys like us then. For many years after that, Harris and I looked each other up in either Rochester, New York, or Detroit. He received a small government pension because of the shrapnel wounds in both thighs.

Frank Lawrence, after graduating from Santa Clara, went to work for General Electric and was sent to Schenectady, New York, so I looked him up while traveling through there on one of my yearly visits to my New England relatives. Louis Pultz, our old CO, also worked for GE, so we telephoned him and got invited to come to his house. There we learned he had been in a hospital in France nearly a year after we last saw him. He'd had a chance to go to Brussels on pass shortly after the division began changing, and he was able to hitch a ride on an artillery Cub spotter plane going from Innsbruck to Brussels at the same time. Then the lucky break turned ugly: the small plane crashed in Luxembourg, the pilot was killed, and Pultz broke his back.

He told Frank and me that he regretted not getting to know us better during the war because of the separation caused by rank, and we all drank a few beers to make up for it.

Sally Ride, the first woman in space, was the daughter of Dale Ride ("Red Ryder"), the guy with whom I had all those political debates. I learned about that from Bob Wilmoth, one of the ASTP men who, along with Len Harris, was part of Lieutenant Whidden's FO team when he fired on G Company. Bob has made a point of connecting with as many of us as he can, and he has talked with Dale Ride's widow. Dale had retired as a professor in one of the University of California branches and died in the 1980s. I don't know if he ever got a chance to go to Haverford, Pennsylvania, as he told me he was determined to do, one time back in Texas.

Wilmoth got a degree in agriculture and farmed successfully in Arkansas. He put all his kids through college and has a daughter with a PhD. We met at the airport in Michigan when his flight from Europe came through and had a few hours' delay. With his son-in-law, an architect, he had revisited most of the ground covered by us in the war. It was his second such trip.

At the division's reunion in Flint, I sat down with Colonel Hawkins, who had been Major Hawkins as the officer who ran our Fire Direction Center. I didn't expect him to know me, but to my surprise, he told me he had recommended me for a battlefield commission. It was turned down by Colonel Caesar, who thought I could better serve our battalion by remaining a radioman. We talked about my first topkick, 1st Sgt. Ed Copeland, whom we both thought was the best NCO we knew in our battalion. Hawkins told me he'd read a sad story in the military news in Japan during the Korean War, telling how Copeland's wife had shot and killed him with his army .45 near Tokyo. Nearly everyone suspected he was a heavy drinker.

Another thing I learned at the Flint reunion was that Jim Churchill, my sidekick during my thirty-day leave when I returned home, became a federal judge in the Flint, Michigan, district. Capt. Tom Stagg, the George Company CO in that last offensive in March, is a federal judge in Shreveport, Louisiana. I met him at another reunion and found that he and Churchill have gone deer hunting in Upper Michigan, and each of them knows that the other was in the 103rd Division.

In doing research for this book, I wanted to find out about some of the mysteries I encountered in combat. High in priority on the list of things I needed to know, was why those girls in that mountain village east of Innsbruck were sunbathing in the nude on frosty ground, a quarter of a mile from an icecap, and within easy view of soldiers who were still their nation's enemy.

In the early years after the war, we learned that many war criminals went to South America through Italy. It seemed possible to me that the three hotels we didn't occupy in that mountain village might have held escaping war criminals, hoofing it over the mountains on their way to Italy. German-speaking Italy, where many Italian Nazis lived, was at the foot of the Brenner Pass, just a few miles east of there. Might the pretty girls have been wives, daughters, or lovers of Nazis on the lam, stripping bare to draw the attention of occupying troops from their men on the escape route over the mountains?

I went to the Holocaust Museum in Southfield, Michigan, and found nothing. The librarians there were of the opinion that the route to Italy taken by war criminals was through Trieste.

Now, in my quest for an answer, my attention moved to the OSS man who negotiated our peaceful entry into Innsbruck. I won't go into the barriers I encountered before finding the chairman of the OSS veterans' organization, except to say that at one time I found myself talking to a clerk in a Manhattan clothing store. When I finally reached the man I wanted, I had barely told him that I was in a division that came into Innsbruck and found both German and American road markers, when he interrupted: "You need to get in touch with Fred Mayer; here's his phone number."

Fred Mayer, I learned, has a thick German accent, is Jewish, and lives in West Virginia, where he is a jeweler. He became an OSS sergeant because he was born near Innsbruck and spoke with the local accent. His family immigrated to America when he was a teenager. As he explained it to me, he was parachuted onto a glacier near Innsbruck with ten other OSS men, and they were charged with finding out if the Nazis were going to build a redoubt in the Brenner Pass.

"One of us was a crook and got into the black market and got caught," he told me. "Then he turned us in. The Gestapo tortured me to find out what we were after, but I wouldn't talk. I have hideous scars behind both my ears where they twisted them, and I'm partially deaf because of it. I knew that even the

Gauleiter could tell the war was lost, so I said to him, 'Quit tor-
turing me and send me out to take the Americans your terms
of surrender, and they might go easy on you when the war
ends . . . and spare this beautiful city.' The SS wanted to fight
to the death, so we had to keep the Wehrmacht armed."

Mayer knew nothing about plans to stop war criminals from
using the mountains near Innsbuck to escape into Italy, however, so the mystery of the naked girls will not be solved by me.

A few years ago, I was watching the History Channel, and
the subject was OSS spies. Who should turn out to be the leading hero of them all? Fred Mayer. I learned more about him
than I did from my phone conversation. His photo, as he
looked back during the war, showed that he was a handsome
man, and apparently he used those good looks to his advantage. He found a pretty nurse who worked in a military hospital
and moved in with her. She, in turn, aided him by bringing him
the uniform of a German officer who died in her care.
Brazenly, he wore it to an officers' club where he got information to radio to the OSS. Through him, the Fifteenth Air Force
was told when a large trainload of supplies for Italy was due to
enter the Brenner Pass, and they bombed it to trash, preventing the supplies from reaching the Germans and blocking the
track for days. I purchased the tape of that broadcast and
showed it to my division at a reunion.

Stackpole Military History Series

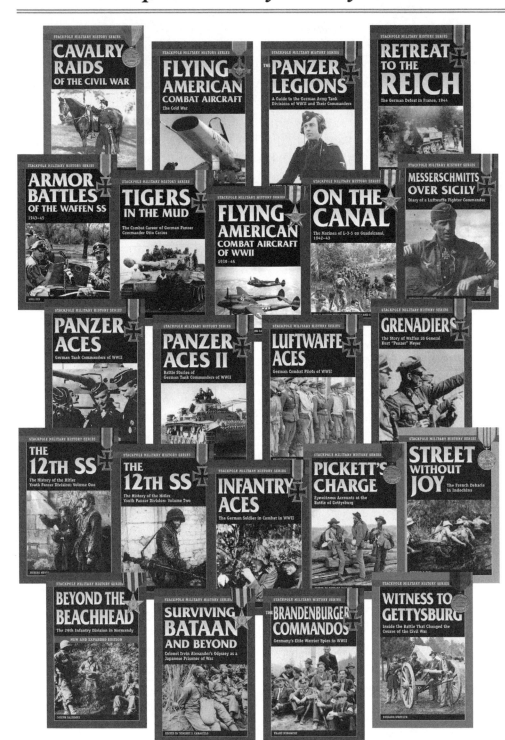

Real battles. Real soldiers. Real stories.

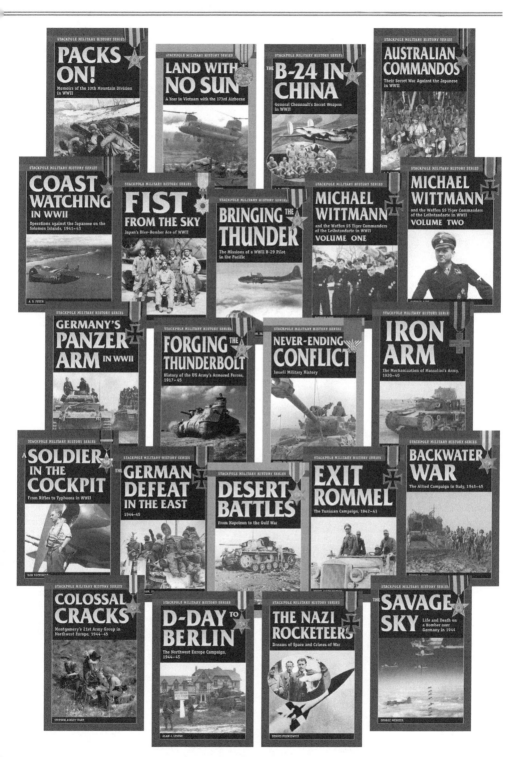

Stackpole Military History Series

Real battles. Real soldiers. Real stories.

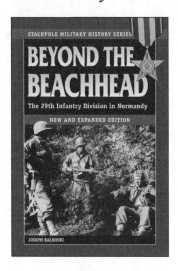

Stackpole Military History Series

D-DAY TO BERLIN

THE NORTHWEST EUROPE CAMPAIGN, 1944–45

Alan J. Levine

The liberation of Western Europe in World War II required eleven months of hard fighting, from the beaches of Normandy to Berlin and the Baltic Sea. In this crisp, comprehensive account, Alan J. Levine describes the Allied campaign to defeat Nazi Germany in the West: D-Day, the hedgerow battles in France during the summer of 1944, the combined airborne-ground assault of Operation Market-Garden in September, Hitler's winter offensive at the Battle of the Bulge, and the final drive across the Rhine that culminated in Germany's surrender in May 1945.

$16.95 • Paperback • 6 x 9 • 240 pages

WWW.STACKPOLEBOOKS.COM
1-800-732-3669

Stackpole Military History Series

TIGERS IN THE MUD
THE COMBAT CAREER OF GERMAN PANZER
COMMANDER OTTO CARIUS

Otto Carius,
translated by Robert J. Edwards

World War II began with a metallic roar as the
German Blitzkrieg raced across Europe, spearheaded
by the most dreadful weapon of the twentieth century:
the Panzer. Tank commander Otto Carius thrusts the
reader into the thick of battle, replete with the
blood, smoke, mud, and gunpowder so common
to the elite German fighting units.

$19.95 • Paperback • 6 x 9 • 368 pages
51 photos • 48 illustrations • 3 maps

WWW.STACKPOLEBOOKS.COM
1-800-732-3669

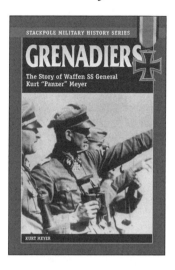

Stackpole Military History Series

ARMOR BATTLES
OF THE WAFFEN-SS
1943–45
Will Fey, translated by Henri Henschler

The Waffen-SS were considered the elite of the
German armed forces in the Second World War and
were involved in almost continuous combat. From
the sweeping tank battle of Kursk on the Russian
front to the bitter fighting among the hedgerows
of Normandy and the offensive in the Ardennes,
these men and their tanks made history.

$19.95 • Paperback • 6 x 9 • 384 pages
32 photos • 15 drawings • 4 maps

Stackpole Military History Series

RETREAT TO THE REICH

THE GERMAN DEFEAT IN FRANCE, 1944

Samuel W. Mitcham, Jr.

The Allied landings on D-Day, June 6, 1944, marked the beginning of the German defeat in the West in World War II. From the experiences of soldiers in the field to decision-making at high command, military historian Samuel Mitcham vividly recaptures the desperation of the Wehrmacht as it collapsed amidst the brutal hedgerow fighting in Normandy, losing its four-year grip on France as it was forced to retreat back to the German border. While German forces managed to temporarily halt the Allied juggernaut there, this brief success only delayed the fate that had been sealed with the defeat in France.

$17.95 • Paperback • 6 x 9 • 304 pages • 26 photos, 12 maps

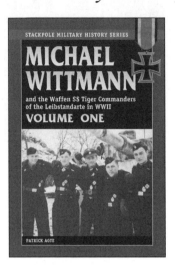

Stackpole Military History Series

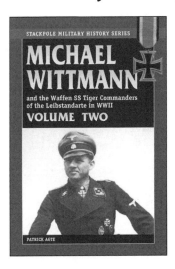

MICHAEL WITTMANN AND THE WAFFEN SS TIGER COMMANDERS OF THE LEIBSTANDARTE IN WORLD WAR II

VOLUME TWO

Patrick Agte

Barely two months after leaving the Eastern Front,
Michael Wittmann and the Leibstandarte found themselves in
Normandy facing the Allied invasion in June 1944. A week after D-Day,
Wittmann achieved his greatest success, single-handedly destroying
more than a dozen British tanks and preventing an enemy
breakthrough near Villers Bocage. He was killed several months later
while leading a Tiger battalion against an Allied assault. The
Leibstandarte went on to fight at the Battle of the Bulge and in
Hungary and Austria before surrendering in May 1945.

$19.95 • Paperback • 6 x 9 • 400 pages • 287 photos • 15 maps • 7 charts

Stackpole Military History Series

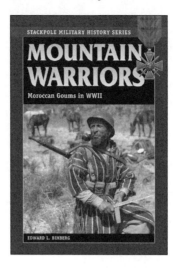

MOUNTAIN WARRIORS
MOROCCAN GOUMS IN WORLD WAR II
Edward L. Bimberg

Labeled "savage Africans" for their untamed ferocity, the Moroccan Goums served as irregular mountain troops for the Allies during World War II. Beginning with the Tunisia campaign in 1942, these tribal warriors frightened their opponents with their traditional garb, long knives, and merciless attacks. An impressed Gen. George Patton requested the Goums' service in Sicily, and they went on to fight in the final battle for Monte Cassino in May 1944 and later liberated Marseille in France. After helping to clear the Colmar Pocket, the Goums breached the Siegfried Line and ended the war in Germany, having secured their reputation as unorthodox but effective soldiers.

$16.95 • Paperback • 6 x 9 • 224 pages • 6 b/w photos

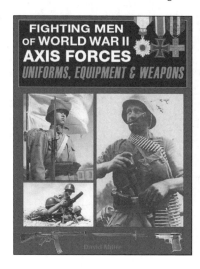 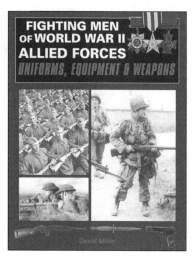